LARRY B. ATKINSON

Z8 6.75N

# OUR
# TROUBLED
# HEMISPHERE

# OUR TROUBLED HEMISPHERE

*Perspectives on
United States–Latin American
Relations*

ROBERT N. BURR

THE BROOKINGS INSTITUTION
*Washington, D.C.*

THE BROOKINGS INSTITUTION is an independent organization devoted to nonpartisan research, education, and publication in economics, government, foreign policy, and the social sciences generally. Its principal purposes are to aid in the development of sound public policies and to promote public understanding of issues of national importance.

The Institution was founded December 8, 1927, to merge the activities of the Institute for Government Research, founded in 1916, the Institute of Economics, founded in 1922, and the Robert Brookings Graduate School of Economics and Government, founded in 1924.

The general administration of the Institution is the responsibility of a self-perpetuating Board of Trustees. The trustees are likewise charged with maintaining the independence of the staff and fostering the most favorable conditions for creative research and education. The immediate direction of the policies, program, and staff of the Institution is vested in the President, assisted by the program directors and an advisory council, chosen from the professional staff of the Institution.

In publishing a study, the Institution presents it as a competent treatment of a subject worthy of public consideration. The interpretations and conclusions in such publications are those of the author or authors and do not purport to represent the views of the other staff members, officers, or trustees of the Brookings Institution.

# Foreword

After World War II the U.S. government lapsed into more than a decade of relative apathy toward Latin America. That apathy ceased, however, when Vice President Nixon was greeted with hostility during a South American tour and when it became evident that a Soviet foothold had been established in Cuba. Alertness changed to alarm when Cuba, seeking to widen its influence, exploited situations of discontent and unrest in certain major Latin American societies. The public of the United States now knew what specialists had long known—that the spirit of the "good neighbor" policy was threatened and that a major battle in the cold war was being waged.

Striving to prevent Cuban subversion and to shore up a shaken inter-American community, the United States resorted to some of its traditional policies and devised certain "new" policies. Among the latter was the Alliance for Progress—a prescription intended to alleviate the acute Latin American social and economic ills upon which the Western Hemisphere's international crisis was now being blamed. But those well-intended measures served also to emphasize contradictions in past United States policies and to create new tensions. Herculean labors are still needed to improve U.S. relations with the nations of Latin America.

Aware that the cooperative friendship of Latin America is not easily won, the United States has entered a new period in the history of its hemispheric relations—a period whose challenges demand a prompt and rigorous reevaluation of its Latin American policy. The purpose of this volume is to provide the concerned layman with a basis for such a reappraisal. The analysis concentrates on those main issues of public policy—political, economic, and social—that seem of greatest consequence to the United States.

The author of the volume is Robert N. Burr, Professor of Latin American History at the University of California, Los Angeles. He has travelled and studied extensively in Latin America and has served as chairman of the Committee on Latin American Studies of the Social Science Research Council and the American Council of Learned Societies. His publications include *The Stillborn Panama Congress: Power Politics and Chilean-Colombian Relations during the War of the Pacific* (1962) and *By Reason or Force: Chile and the Balancing of Power in South America, 1830-1905* (1965).

The Brookings Institution joins the author in thanking the many persons who advised him on the manuscript. These included the following members of the Advisory Committee that reviewed the manuscript in detail: Robert E. Asher, John Campbell, Howard F. Cline, John C. Dreier, Joseph Grunwald, George Marotta, Arturo Morales-Carrion, Harvey Perloff, David H. Pollock, Irving G. Tragen, Arthur P. Whitaker, and Bryce Wood. Two members of the Advisory Committee, John Dreier and Bryce Wood, and John Plank of the Brookings Senior Staff acted as a reading committee to advise on publication of the revised manuscript. The project was conducted under the general supervision of H. Field Haviland, Jr., Director of Foreign Policy Studies.

For research assistance as well as critical evaluation the author wishes to thank Hugh Campbell, Donald Castro, Jesus Chavarria, Norris Lyle, Robert Smith, Patricia Weiss, and Anthony White. He also wishes to express appreciation to Deluvina Hernandez for typing assistance and Elizabeth Burr for invaluable editorial and other assistance. The manuscript was edited by Alice M. Carroll; Helen B. Eisenhart prepared the index.

The Brookings Institution is grateful to the Ford Foundation for a special grant to support the study.

The interpretations and conclusions of the author do not necessarily represent the views of the persons consulted, nor of the trustees, the officers, or other staff members of the Brookings Institution or the Ford Foundation.

ROBERT D. CALKINS

*June 1967*                                                      *President*
*Washington, D.C.*

# Contents

# I

# Seeds of Discontent

After World War II, relations between the United States and Latin America were severely tested by the concurrent effects of two revolutions, one in United States foreign policy, the other in the aspirations of the peoples of the underdeveloped world. In the first of these revolutions the United States abandoned its long-standing policy of political isolation within the Western Hemisphere for a policy of active global engagement. It did not, however, change its traditional foreign policy goals—the security, the economic and political welfare, and the freedom of action of the nation and its people. In fact, its new policy was only a reluctant but inescapable response to the profoundly altered international milieu in which the United States found itself struggling to achieve its ends.

## New Demands

By the time the United States entered World War II it was clear that political isolationism was no longer a valid policy. In its place Washington attempted to substitute a program of participation in an effective world security organization. When the United Nations revealed its limitations, it was not possible for the United States simply to revert to

1

its earlier isolationism. Such a policy had appeared reasonable in a world where other great nations maintained among themselves a certain balance of power, and as long as the defensive value of the seas was undiminished. But when the protective power balance vanished with the simultaneous disintegration of British, French, German, and Japanese power and with the rise of an expansive Russian superstate, and when oceanic fortresses evaporated in the heat of atomic weaponry, the United States—for the first time in its history as an independent state—found itself face to face with a strong and inherently hostile power. Thus challenged, the United States, while continuing to support the United Nations, commenced feverishly to construct a new international power structure favorable to the attainment of its foreign policy goals. The armed forces were reorganized, strengthened, and modernized; economic assistance was given for the reconstitution of former power centers in Europe and the Orient; military alliances were sought. But no sooner had this program been started than it became evident that a new problem, caused by the unanticipated effects of a second major revolution, had arisen.

The second revolution, rushing into the vacuum created by the collapse of the pre-World War II political order, was engulfing the hitherto despised or underestimated, neglected or exploited peoples of the earth. The newly nationalistic leadership in the world's "underdeveloped" areas demanded on behalf of their fellowmen not only political independence but material advances and social justice and a status equal to that of other peoples of the earth. And those demands aroused aspirations that, in the face of frustrating obstacles, created mounting political conflict and individual discontent inviting to Soviet-inspired totalitarian solutions—solutions unacceptable to the government of the United States. At this juncture the seething have-not and would-be nations of the world assumed paramount strategic value to the earth's contending giants; it became obvious that their human and material resources were of incalculable weight in the scales of world power. The United States, believing that its security would be jeopardized if those nations were to gravitate into the Soviet orbit, began to provide military aid to underdeveloped nations and undertook programs of financial and technical assistance to help solve their economic and social problems.

## Traditional Policies

Among the adverse effects of these two revolutions on relations between the United States and Latin America was the United States' concentration of attention on Europe and the East at the expense of Latin America, and the consequent break with a tradition that dated from the time of Latin America's revolutions for independence. Under that tradition the Western Hemisphere was considered to be the center of paramount United States political interest: the nations of the new world formed, it was believed, a political system logically distinct from that of the old—a system from which, moreover, European political control must be rigidly banished. Such assumptions underlay a political policy toward Latin America that was in reality little more than a corollary of an isolationist European policy. The United States sought primarily to avoid involvement in European disputes and to prevent establishment of European military and naval bases in strategically important areas of "its" hemisphere. Without consulting the hemisphere's other nations, it proposed to contain and then to reduce to a minimum European political influence in the Americas.

### European Exclusion

Slowly, irregularly, but inexorably, the United States carried out its European exclusion policy. In 1823 President James Monroe, in a two-spheres dictum against European intervention and colonization in the new world, laid down the basic principles of his country's future Latin American policy—principles that were largely unimplemented until after the middle of the century. However, as its wealth and strength grew, the United States—in the later nineteenth century—moved more rapidly toward its goal. Not only was there greater disposition to enforce the Monroe Doctrine, but the United States took three other steps to contain and diminish European political leverage in the Western Hemisphere, while simultaneously augmenting its own. The Pan American movement was initiated with a major objective of maintaining hemispheric peace and thus removing a possible justification for intervention by Europeans in protection of their interests. At about the same time Washington, reversing a policy that from 1850 had provided for British participation in any interoceanic canal built through Central America, announced its desire for a waterway under the exclusive control of the United States. The concurrent commencement of a modern naval building program gave meaning and force to that desire.

As the nineteenth century gave way to the twentieth, the pressures grew for reduction of European sway in the hemisphere. Brandishing its new men-of-war, the United States stripped Spain of its remaining new world colonies—Cuba and Puerto Rico. London, troubled by its declining European position, took note of the new United States navy and not only relinquished its canal rights but commenced to withdraw its own naval power from the Caribbean. The Colombian government's resistance to Washington's canal proposals cost Bogotá the province of Panama, which declared independence and accepted both the canal proposition and the protection of the United States.

Then, when chaos and bankruptcy threatened to bring down upon several Caribbean lands the armed intervention of the governments of their European creditors, President Theodore Roosevelt announced, in 1905, a corollary to the Monroe Doctrine: henceforth the United States would police the Western Hemisphere in order to eliminate conditions that might encourage European intervention. By the time the United States entered World War I in 1917, it had implemented the corollary by landing marines upon the soil of Nicaragua, Haiti, and the Dominican Republic, converting all three into virtual protectorates.

World War I itself further enhanced the power position of the United States. The old world, too exhausted by more than four years of destructive warfare to challenge Washington's pretensions, in tacit recognition of a former European colony's hegemony in the new world agreed that ". . . nothing in this [League of Nations] covenant shall be deemed to affect the validity of international engagements, such as . . . regional understandings like the Monroe Doctrine, for securing the maintenance of peace."[1] Moreover, those same European powers accepted the United States' right to maintain the power necessary to secure its dominant new world position. Their acceptance was embodied in the creation of a "new order of sea power" at the Washington Naval Conference of 1921-22 where Great Britain reluctantly abandoned its

[1] As quoted in Dexter Perkins, *Hands Off: A History of the Monroe Doctrine* (Little, Brown, 1945), p. 294.

policy of naval preeminence and, by accepting naval parity with the United States, gave the latter undisputed naval hegemony in the Western Hemisphere.

In the century following the proclamation of Monroe's Doctrine, Europe's muscle in the new world had become flabby and the United States had largely achieved its objective of minimizing the old world's political influence in the new. But even during the process of the emasculation of European power, and directly related to it, a new threat to the interests of the United States was in formation. The foundations of that new danger lay in the fact that—unless purposely designed to destroy an enemy—no foreign policy can long succeed without comprehending the real, if unrecognized, interests of each and every involved nation.

## Latin American Reaction

The interests of the Latin American countries and of the United States had at first coincided in one important respect: both desired diminution of European power in the new world. Latin America, too, had sought to be free of the threat of old world intervention. Its nations, employing techniques appropriate to their relative weakness and instability, had (1) played upon rivalries among the greater powers, encouraging them to keep each other at bay; (2) sought, unsuccessfully, to institute multinational Latin American organizations that might constitute counterpoises to the stronger states of Europe; and (3) urged great power acceptance of "American" principles of international law, such as the Calvo (1868) and Drago (1903) doctrines, that would limit or outlaw intervention. But when success in the exclusion of Europe combined with a tremendous growth in the power of the United States to culminate in the latter's virtually unchallenged hemispheric predominance, the Latin American nations found that their interests no longer coincided with those of Washington. For they now found themselves confronting the new and potentially more dangerous threat of a far stronger, geographically closer, politically more unified and expansive people than any who now menaced them from across the Atlantic.

During the nineteenth century—before the United States had adopted an openly imperialistic and paternalistic posture toward the Latin American nations and assumed unasked the role of hemisphere police-

man—most Latin American leaders had placed the European danger
above that of the United States. But even then, following Mexico's vast
territorial losses to the United States, Francisco Bilbao of Chile
reflected the concern of politically sophisticated intellectuals when he
warned that ". . . The Disunited States of South America are beginning
to sight the smoke of the United States encampment. . . . That nation
which should have been our star, our example, our strength, each day is
converting itself into a menace to the AUTONOMY of South America."[2]
And toward the end of the century there were many who would have
echoed Cuban José Martí's characterization of the United States as a
land "which proclaims its right by self-coronation to govern, by geographic morality, on the continent, and announces, through the mouths
of its statesmen, in the press and in the pulpit, in the banquet hall and
in congress, at the same time that it puts its hand on one island and
tries to buy another, that all North America has to belong to it and that
its imperial right from the isthmus on down has to be recognized."[3]

By the early part of the twentieth century the United States had
definitively replaced Europe in the minds of many Latin Americans as
the primary threat to their interests. Following Great Britain's indication that it would not oppose Washington's pretensions in the Caribbean or elsewhere in the hemisphere, the United States moved decisively to establish its hegemony. Cuban and Panamanian protectorates
were followed by Dominican and Nicaraguan interventions, inspiring
the 1911 claim of Peruvian García Calderón that "to save themselves
from Yankee imperialism the Latin American democracies would almost accept a German Alliance, or the aid of Japanese arms. . . . Hostility against the Anglo-Saxon invaders assumes the character of a Latin
crusade."[4]

During the 1920's fear and suspicion of the United States rose to ever
greater pitch. Not only was Latin America faced with the political and
military might of Washington; it was now experiencing the suddenly
accelerated impact of United States economic power. New York had

[2] As quoted in Robert N. Burr and Roland D. Hussey (eds.), *Documents on
Inter-American Cooperation* (2 vols.; University of Pennsylvania, 1955), I, 130-
31. Hereafter cited as Burr and Hussey, *Documents.*

[3] As quoted in *ibid.,* II, 40.

[4] As quoted in John A. Crow, *The Epic of Latin America* (Doubleday, 1946),
p. 691.

replaced London as the center of the financial world, and United States trade and investments were spreading far beyond their pre-World War I Mexican and Caribbean boundaries, penetrating vast portions of South America. Moreover, the Latin American nations found themselves forced to depend upon the United States for critically needed new capital, for their traditional banker, Europe, was economically exhausted by the war and unable to provide sufficient financing for important economic development projects.

But even as Latin American countries felt forced to seek augmented United States investment, they were disturbed by fear that, as in the Caribbean, the Yankee dollar might be followed into South America by Washington's political influence. In the Caribbean, where United States economic interests had become entrenched prior to World War I, marines were stationed in Nicaragua; and Haiti, Cuba, Panama, and the Dominican Republic were being governed by directives from Washington. In the middle and late 1920's, as allegedly "temporary" police action taken under the Roosevelt corollary appeared to be assuming the character of permanent intervention, anti-United States sentiment in Latin America became intense.

Washington's continued paternalistic policies, in spite of several nations' significant progress toward political stability and economic development, contributed to the volume and violence of hatred of the United States. Even before World War I such advanced countries as Argentina, Brazil, Chile, and Mexico had resolved both to reject any United States attempts to infringe their sovereignty and independence and to renounce any inferior position in hemispheric affairs. As their progress continued in the postwar decade, these nations became increasingly determined to fulfill those intentions.

In the decade following World War I the Latin American states tried, together and separately, four different methods of securing political parity with the United States and freedom from Washington's political interference. First, they continued to seek acceptance of nonintervention doctrines, with a shift in emphasis to United States rather than European commitments. Second, they pressed for stronger economic bonds with Europe because, as Bogotá's *El Espectador* expressed it, ". . . the expedience of creating a counterweight to the influence of yankee money is hidden from no one. We have the unforgettable misfortune of knowing the methods of penetration of our unwanted protector. . . ."[5] Third, they attempted to promote some form of Latin American union that would enable the cooperating states, in the words of a 1919 Colombian senate resolution, ". . . to carry out a joint international action with regard to the maintenance of their integrity and sovereignty. . . ."[6] Such respectable intellectuals as Manuel Ugarte and José Ingenieros of Argentina added their voices to political pleas for Latin American collective action, but all for naught. No league of Latin America's states, although based upon a theme hallowed in their political mythology, could hope to surmount the bitter national rivalries that—in the twentieth century as in the nineteenth—far outweighed the cultural bonds among the Latin American nations.

Finally, in their quest for freedom from United States political interference Latin American leaders sought to encourage and utilize international peacekeeping bodies. Such groups were, after all, based upon the notion that law rather than force should decide issues between countries and they might thus be supposed to work for the protection of the weak against the strong. Two such organizations were in being during the decade following World War I—the League of Nations and the Pan American system. The former, because of its provisions for sanctions against aggressors and its members' solemn treaty obligation ". . . to respect and preserve as against external aggression the territorial integrity and existing political independence of all members of the League,"[7] seemed to offer the Latin American states their best hope of protection and they supported the League strongly until United States abstention and the primary interest of the European powers in their own special problems made it evident that the League of Nations would be virtually useless in solving the Western Hemisphere questions of the nations of Latin America.

## Pan American System

No solemn treaty, nor any formal peacekeeping machinery, underlay the Pan American "system," the only other institutional organism that

---

[5] *El Espectador*, Nov. 23, 1923.

[6] As quoted in Luis María Murcia, *La armonía boliviana; exposición y desarrollo de la "doctrina Suárez"* (Bogotá: Editorial Minerva, 1925), p. 36.

[7] For the text of the Covenant of the League of Nations, see League of Nations, *Ten Years of World Cooperation* (Geneva: Secretariat of the League of Nations, 1930), pp. 417-30.

the Latin American countries might use in the effort to hold their own against the larger, more powerful, and expanding United States. The system was represented on paper in a series of resolutions approved by the American republics at four successive international conferences, the first of which took place in 1889. Moreover, its stated functions were primarily technical and commercial rather than political. The two major operative elements of the system were the International Conference of American States (popularly dubbed the Pan American Conference) and the Pan American Union. The Conference, in which diplomatic agents of all Western Hemisphere nations except Canada participated with one vote each, set the system's policies. The Washington-based Union, on the other hand, constituted a permanent secretariat under the control of a Governing Board composed of envoys residing in Washington. Because the board both prepared the agenda of Conference meetings and implemented their mandates, it was the predominant influence in determining the future course of the Pan American movement.

The Pan American system, as it was constituted in the decade following World War I, was manifestly unsuited to the task of protecting the interests of Latin American states. It was dominated by the United States, partly because of that country's wealth, power, and prestige and partly because of its privileged position within the Governing Board. The United States Secretary of State was permanent chairman of the board, whose other members were diplomatic agents accredited to Washington; thus, countries unrecognized by the United States possessed no voice on the board, while the diplomatic envoys of recognized but usually weak nations were in a poor position to oppose the wishes in regard to board policy of a powerful state the courting of whose favor was generally their primary purpose for being in Washington.

The foregoing situation reflected Washington's success in designing a Pan American system to fit its policy needs: prevention of wars among the Latin American countries; stimulation of trade and commerce between them and the United States; prevention of public airing of controversial and possibly embarrassing political questions. The system's conformity to United States requirements was based, however, not alone on the power and prestige of the United States but also upon the fact that Washington's aims happened to coincide with those of several larger Latin American nations that were eager to avoid public discussion at Pan American conferences of their pending controversies with weaker neighbors.

When Latin American leaders, reacting against the power without counterpoise of the United States, began to reappraise the Pan American system, few of them sought to transform it into an American counterpart of the League of Nations. Most hoped rather to bring the system under genuinely international control in order to prevent its possible use by the United States to extend Washington's political influence over Latin America. Meanwhile, through the existing Pan American system, Latin American leaders attempted to secure from the United States a self-denying nonintervention commitment. They argued for a distinctive American international law whose principles included nonintervention for any purpose whatsoever; acceptance of that doctrine would force the United States to liquidate its Caribbean interventions and, in effect, to renounce the use of its superior military power in relations with Latin American nations. Throughout the 1920's the United States only mildly resisted Latin American attempts to internationalize the operation of the Pan American system; but to the dismay of Latin Americans, Washington flatly refused to relinquish the right of intervention. It began to appear that the United States was bent upon political domination of the entire Western Hemisphere.

At what appears in retrospect to have been the darkest hour in that epoch's Latin American-United States relations, Washington softened its posture. European intervention in the new world was now so unlikely that the United States could no longer pretend even to itself that continued interventions under the Roosevelt corollary were justifiable. Moreover, there was widespread dissatisfaction in the United States with the results of past and existing interventions that had not only failed to create stable representative institutions but had also entrapped both Washington and important business interests in increasingly unsavory complications. Furthermore, certain religious and political sectors in the United States now devised a moral issue in the question of intervention and had commenced to denounce the practice of imperialism. All the while Latin American resentment grew more bitter, so that by the time the Sixth Pan American Conference met in Havana in 1928 it was no longer possible to prevent an open clash. The events of that meeting shocked Washington into the realization that the hemispheric system tottered on the brink of an angry disruption that might endanger not only United States political interests but considerable commercial interests as well. Such were the considerations that, on the eve of the Great Depression, forced Washington to reappraise its policy toward Latin America.

## Good Neighbor Policy

Central to that reappraisal was the need to reconcile the interests of a single tremendously powerful nation with those of a group of weaker free and independent states that, seeing their own interests damaged through systematic subordination to those of the United States, threatened to become seriously disaffected. And from the reconsideration of United States-Latin American relations there eventually emerged the policy of the "good neighbor," one of whose important distinguishing characteristics was its conscious effort to harmonize the interests of the United States with those of the nations of Latin America. Not only did the United States commence to liquidate its interventions and protectorates, but it also both signed and ratified a solemn treaty stating that ". . . the High Contracting Parties declare inadmissible the intervention of any one of them, directly or indirectly, and for whatever reason in the internal and external affairs of any other of the parties."[8] Moreover, Washington—while not specifically renouncing the unilateral Monroe Doctrine—promised to consult with Latin American nations on matters of hemispheric concern and thus appeared to be adopting a multilateral approach to new world security.

## Organization of American States

By agreeing to nonintervention and consultation the United States clearly implied its acceptance of the Latin American nations as juridically equal free and independent states; and they responded to the "good neighbor" policy warmly and positively. The resultant aura of good feeling provided an appropriate atmosphere for the establishment of a formal American international system through which the United States might achieve its traditional objectives with regard to Europe and might at the same time maintain friendly relations with the Latin nations of America. The new system took form before and during

[8] Burr and Hussey, *Documents*, II, 114.

World War II in a series of conferences and foreign ministers' meetings that first discussed defense against extra-hemispheric threats and intra-hemispheric peacekeeping, and later dealt with the actual war challenge and Axis activities in the Americas. The system-in-formation was recognized in the Charter of the United Nations (1945) and attained the status of an international organization with political, military, economic, and social functions with the signing of the Inter-American Treaty of Reciprocal Assistance (1947) and the Charter of the Organization of American States (1948). Thus, as the midpoint of the twentieth century approached, the Western Hemisphere at last possessed the meaningful international organization for which so many of its statesmen had so long labored.

It was a cruel twist of fate that upon the eve of the birth of the Organization of American States (OAS) the ideas that nourished its conception and gestation had begun to lose validity. The OAS was the end product of the "western hemisphere idea" that "the peoples of this hemisphere stand in a special relationship to one another which sets them apart from the rest of the world."[9] That view justified the existence of a special regional peacekeeping and defensive body. But the very facts that the United States had become a belligerent in a *world* war and had experienced a revolution in its foreign policy in response to changed *world* conditions constituted incontrovertible evidence that the "western hemisphere idea" had become anachronistic. Nevertheless, an inter-American organization had come into being which, together with the historical experiences of its creation, was greatly to influence postwar United States-Latin American relations.

There were now stored in the attic of the United States' Latin American policy the disparate and contradictory programs that had accumulated during fifteen decades. The Monroe Doctrine against outside interference and the concept of Western Hemisphere solidarity, for example, had been devised as instruments for isolating the hemisphere from the mainstream of European politics and keeping old world influence at a safe distance. But now that the United States considered Western Europe—rather than the Atlantic Ocean—its first line of defense, programs based upon the assumption that Europe and America constituted mutually exclusive political spheres did not appear

---

[9] Arthur P. Whitaker, *The Western Hemisphere Idea: Its Rise and Decline* (Cornell University, 1954), p. 1.

to make sense. Yet in both the United States and Latin America the sentiments associated with those traditional policies made the open abandonment of the policies very difficult.

Moreover, Latin America's view of the United States had markedly changed as a result of the manner in which the inter-American system had developed. Implementation of the good neighbor policy, improved communications, more intense and less exploitative economic relations, and shared international political experiences had combined to convince Latin Americans that their political independence was no longer menaced by a northern colossus. In fact, Latin America had begun to see certain positive advantages in the "special relationship" which, although long advocated by Washington, was now being grossly neglected by the United States because of the press of global business.

Meanwhile, the conspicuous success of the good neighbor policy and the cooperation of Latin American nations in Allied efforts during World War II had convinced the United States that all was well with its Latin American relations. And in fact, except for a perennial Argentine crisis in the immediate postwar years, no major government-to-government tensions then existed to disturb that comfortable fantasy whose error lay in the assumption that the sociopolitical structure of the nations of Latin America was relatively static and that their future international behavior would be much the same as their past. There were, of course, individuals both in and out of government who knew very well that, on the contrary, rapid social, economic, and political changes were coursing through Latin America and would inevitably affect the international posture of its states. But it was generally felt in the United States that Latin America was "safe." That complacency, combined with the need to deal with far more urgent problems in other areas of the world, resulted in failure to assess correctly the subsequent significance of the changes then taking place in Latin America and to prepare long-range policies that would enable the United States to cope effectively with those changes.

## Postwar Unrest

The stirrings in Latin America were part and parcel of the revolutions sweeping the world that sought to modernize the societies of the underdeveloped world in order to eliminate their dependence upon the great powers and to provide decent nutrition, adequate housing, basic health care, and even certain cultural amenities for long-deprived peoples. But while such general goals were common to the preindustrial, colonial, and underdeveloped areas of Africa, the Middle and Far East, and Latin America, each separate people and region demonstrated peculiarities rooted in its own historical experience. Latin America differed from the others in two vital respects. First, most of its nations had long enjoyed political independence, in contrast to other aspirants to dignity which had only recently, if at all, escaped their political bondage to the great powers. Second, save for the considerable nonintegrated indigenous populations in Peru, Bolivia, Guatemala, and Ecuador, the nations of Latin America constituted an integral part of Western civilization, in contrast to the Eastern and African orientations of the world's other less developed peoples.

Early political independence set the stage in Latin America for a long series of intra-Latin American political and military conflicts, as well as for continued resistance against great power influence and intervention. As a result, in Latin America the concept of the nation-state was early developed, along with a spirit of nationalism that arose first among the elite and later spread to the masses of many countries. The Western culture of Latin America gave it contact with the developing technology of Europe and the United States, so that by mid-twentieth century a number of Latin American countries had travelled further along the road to modernization than most of the nations of other contemporary underdeveloped areas. The sum of these factors accounted for early initiation by certain Latin American states of fundamental social and economic changes, before the peoples of the Middle East and Africa were independent and could embark upon programs designed to alleviate the social and economic distress of their masses.

A major reform goal of Latin America's nationalistic leadership had been the eradication of colonial-type, dependent economic systems and their replacement by more self-sufficient structures. Latin American economic systems tended to revolve about the exploitation of a limited variety of foodstuffs, raw materials, and minerals; moreover, since the mid-nineteenth century much of Latin American economic development had been largely the result of foreign capital and technology. Public utilities, mineral and petroleum production, the meat packing industry, and the production and sale of tropical fruits had been organized and were largely controlled by foreign interests. Thus, the essence of the Latin American economy was dependence—dependence upon the outside world for markets, capital, and techniques. Because a nation's economy was intimately related to the success in the world market of a severely limited group of products, it was at the mercy of price fluctuations over which it had no control.

Eradication of economic dependence would, it was thought, eliminate four evils at one blow: chronically unfavorable trade balances; economic crisis resulting from the instability of the world market; reliance upon a few primary resources or crops whose depletion or failure could mean disaster; and the influence of foreign business interests in the political life of nations whose economic dependence vitiated effective resistance. Acting especially against foreign political influence, several Latin American countries took steps early in the twentieth century toward regulation of foreign interests; but it was the calamitous world depression of the 1930's that set in motion the widespread programs of xenophobic nationalism designed to abolish economic colonialism in Latin America promptly and definitively.

Even as substantial areas of Latin America wrestled with problems of balance of trade, diversification, market instability, and foreign political influence, it became obvious that colonial-type dependence would continue to exist until the condition of the masses of people was substantially improved. Only then would there come into being domestic buying power for diversified national manufactures, a trained labor source for projected factories, and a broad and educated electorate presumably less corruptible and reactionary than the traditional ruling cliques. The prerequisites to socioeconomic reform, not to speak of reform itself, were thus so enormous as to be almost beyond the imaginative grasp of those who sought to remake their nations. Nevertheless, in the 1930's and 1940's several Latin American nations sought desperately to achieve such reform. The weapons of nationalism were rushed to the economic front; tariff walls were thrown up against foreign goods; consumers were admonished to "buy national"; and in the good name of patriotism there of course arose demagogues who everywhere devised "foreign interference" which was sometimes real and sometimes imagined, but which, when denounced, could be counted upon to produce applause and a political following.

The movement of certain nations toward economic reorientation re-inforced existing pressures to end the social and political grip of elites composed (according to the country) of various proportions of the large landowners, mining and commercial interests, the higher clergy, and the top-ranking military. Industrialists, professional people, increasing-ly organized elements in labor and the peasantry, and a growing and politically skillful class of white collar employees commenced to de-mand the abolition of barriers that had traditionally prevented their participation in the fruits of production and the determination of na-tional policy. Where an entrenched elite resisted those aspirations, as it usually did, there arose tensions conducive to the advocacy of radical solutions. To some such situations elite groups responded with in-creased determination to retain control. In other cases minimum palli-ative reforms were granted while at the same time attempts were made to increase national production through industrialization and diver-sification. In this way, it was hoped, greater economic well-being would become available to nonelite groups. But industrialization was often disappointing. As agricultural workers were lured into cities hopeful of improving their status by securing industrial employment, foodstuffs became both scarce and expensive for the urban masses, whose number was constantly growing. Moreover, both because of need for foreign exchange with which to pay for capital goods imports and because of controls designed to protect incipient national indus-tries, the importation of consumer products was curtailed just as de-mand for them was rising. And not only did rapid industrialization create economic imbalances as painful as those it was supposed to cure, but it contributed to unbridled inflation that inflicted hardship upon classes whose trials already seemed beyond human endurance. To make matters worse, as the 1950's matured, the aspirations of Latin America's burgeoning populations were expanding far more rapidly than its severely dislocated production.

After 1948 the concurrent effects of the political and social revolu-tions commenced, as was inevitable, to place a strain upon United States relations with Latin America. While the blame for tension was not exclusively Washington's, its existing policy did bear a heavy re-sponsibility. Operating on the assumption that relations with Latin America were proceeding smoothly (i.e., that Latin America was "not a critical area in the cold war") and that other regions were of greater strategic importance in countering Soviet expansion, the United States, just as in the first quarter of the twentieth century, failed to take into account the interests of the Latin American nations and to reconcile United States interests, where necessary and/or desirable, with them.

## United States Cold War Policy

The major goal of the United States after 1948 was to secure the Western Hemisphere against Soviet penetration. To this end primary emphasis was placed on military and political measures. In the early 1950's mutual security pacts were negotiated with twelve Latin American nations. Military aid was provided to governments which, whatever their dictatorial or representative nature, proclaimed themselves to be anticommunistic. A resolution providing for inter-American solidarity against "international communist control" of any Western Hemisphere government was pushed through the Caracas Inter-American Conference of 1954. That resolution's purpose was to include resistance to "international communism" within the framework of collective defense measures established in the 1947 Inter-American Treaty of Reciprocal Assistance and it did so by providing that ". . . the domination or control of the political institutions of any American states by the international communist movement . . . would constitute a threat to the sovereignty and political independence of the American States, endangering the peace of America, and would call for a Meeting of Consultation to consider the adoption of appropriate action in accordance with existing treaties."[10] Following the Caracas conference, the United States also acted against "international communism" unilaterally and without reference to the above pacts and resolution by supporting, at first clandestinely and then openly, a revolution that toppled a freely elected Guatemalan regime that had become infiltrated by communists.

While most Latin American statesmen shared the interest of the United States in preventing Soviet penetration, they disagreed sharply with Washington's choice of means toward that end. Some felt that military aid absorbed funds badly needed for economic development and social betterment and that, in raising the status and strength of an

[10] As quoted in John C. Dreier, *The Organization of American States and the Hemisphere Crisis* (Harper & Row, 1962), p. 51.

army, navy, or air force, military aid encouraged inherently antidemocratic elements, thus both failing to eradicate with all possible haste
conditions that made Soviet-type solutions attractive and perpetuating
dictatorial regimes by nature hostile to the presumably basic common
democratic aspirations and interests of the United States and Latin
America. The security of the hemisphere, critics insisted, could be guaranteed only by rapid acceleration of Latin America's political, economic, and social modernization.

Of course the United States did not deny the need for such modernization. In fact, in 1948 Washington had supported the creation of a
special OAS agency—the Inter-American Economic and Social Council
—for ". . . the promotion of the economic and social welfare of the
American nations through effective cooperation for the better utilization of the national resources, the development of agriculture and industry and the raising of the standard of living of their people. . . ."[11]
Again, as in the case of the Soviet threat, it was a matter of emphasis
and method and degree of urgency that divided the United States and
the nations of Latin America concerning development needs. Latin
Americans tended to envision sufficiently rapid development as possible only under conditions of economic nationalism, government-
planned and government-directed, but financed by both private and
public, domestic and foreign capital. They emphasized the need for extremely large amounts of public investment in such areas as education,
road building, and low-cost housing—areas that could not provide the
return expected by private investors. As the only free world nation in
the immediate postwar years with sufficient resources to provide such
vast amounts of public capital, the United States was called upon for
such assistance. In addition to requests for direct loans, Latin Americans advocated the establishment of a special regional inter-American
development bank as a source of capital for long-range development.

United States support was also sought for agreements to stabilize the
prices of exports—agreements that, it was argued, would assure the
high levels of government revenue necessary for development. Moreover, Latin Americans wished Washington's approval of the integration
of their economies into a kind of Latin American common market that,
it was believed, might stimulate industrialization and diversification.

[11] Burr and Hussey, *Documents,* II, 190.

## Latin American Development

Underpinning the position of the Latin Americans was the work of the United Nations Economic Commission for Latin America (ECLA). The commission, established in 1948, became especially prestigious in Latin American circles under the leadership of Argentine economist Raúl Prebisch. ECLA provided data documenting Latin America's economic plight and sponsored a body of theory that appealed to Latin Americans not only because it blamed their economic difficulties on the international trading system rather than the policies and practices of the Latin American nations but also because it emphasized the role of the state in the development process. ECLA contended that nations dependent upon exports of primary commodities had always suffered and would continue to suffer deteriorating terms of trade, causing the progressive enrichment of the more developed manufacturing nations and the corresponding impoverishment of the less developed ones—all of this because of the very nature of a world system utterly beyond the control of its victims. However, ECLA seemed to argue, such inequities might be corrected if the state applied all available means to bring about economic development, obtaining from developed nations the assistance that they should grant in compensation for the profits they enjoyed under the unjust international trading system.

The world's developing nations had already received some assistance from the United States which had pioneered technical aid programs as early as the 1930's and, with the passage in 1949 of the Act for International Development, had stated that its policy was ". . . to aid the efforts of the peoples of economically undeveloped areas to develop their resources and to improve their living and working conditions. . . ."[12] Moreover, through its Export-Import Bank, established in 1934 to finance the sale of United States products abroad, Washington had by 1961 authorized $12.5 billion in hard, repayable loans of which about 36 percent went to Latin America for development of transportation, steel production (including Brazil's Volta Redonda and Chile's

[12] As quoted in Herbert Feis, *Foreign Aid and Foreign Policy* (St. Martin's Press, 1964), p. 52.

Huachipato plants), and electrical power among other things, and for correcting balance-of-payments deficits. Washington also contributed heavily to the policy formulation and capitalization of two post-World War II international lending agencies which, unlike the Export-Import Bank, it did not solely control: the International Bank for Reconstruction and Development (commonly known as the World Bank) and the International Monetary Fund (IMF). The World Bank, a commercial-type institution that included the Latin American nations among its members, was created ". . . to assist in the reconstruction and development of its members by facilitating the investment of capital for productive purposes,"[13] and was supposed to encourage *private* investment through both guarantees to and participation with private investors. In practice, however, the World Bank found itself largely using its own funds, which it devoted primarily to the augmentation of infrastructures and the encouragement of private investment. By 1958 it had invested some $900 million in Latin America, of which about 52 percent was in electric power production and 34 percent in transportation, and all of which it was understood would be repaid on schedule and with interest. The IMF, which also included the Latin American nations as members, was established to deal with balance-of-payments problems. In the 1950's, because of fluctuations in the prices of major export commodities and because of heavy capital goods imports for development, the Latin American nations required considerable assistance from the IMF, owing a balance of $333 million at the end of 1958.

In the ECLA-influenced Latin American view, however, even the combined activities of the IMF and the Export-Import and World banks fell short of the need, and their nature did not serve the most urgent requirements of the developing countries. Some members of the United States government tended to agree, but in general, and especially between 1953 and 1958, Washington supported "orthodox" economic policies for development, pointing to the undeniable economic advances achieved by the Latin American nations as a whole in the first post-World War II decade. Maintaining that most national developmental goals could be met by private investors, Washington insisted that Latin American countries would get all the private money they needed if they would simply put their fiscal houses in order and prom-

[13] As quoted in *ibid.*, p. 224.

ise to protect private capital against loss and expropriation. Moreover, claimed the United States, much private capital was already at hand in the very countries that needed it and they could get it by instituting certain obvious tax and fiscal reforms that would discourage speculation in foreign securities, prevent the establishment of inflation-hedging foreign bank accounts, and hinder unproductive status-oriented domestic investment. The United States believed, moreover, that the Latin American countries could increase their gross national products and accelerate their domestic investment by removing various complex and allegedly unnecessary restrictions that were the result of what Washington considered to be ill-advised efforts at government planning, regulation, and direct participation in economic activities.

## United States Attitude

The United States, distressed by the apparent blindness of the Latin American nations to the fact that it was a "free" economy that had made the United States the great and successful land from which they now sought assistance, refused to aid Latin American government agencies that were operating in areas considered more appropriate for either domestic or foreign private investment activities. Thus, vast and vital industrial complexes upon which might depend the stability or success of governments and nations, such as Mexico's Pemex, Brazil's Petrobras, and Argentina's YPF (Yacimientos Petrolíferos Fiscales)—all of which acted as sole developers, refiners, and distributors of petroleum resources—were refused public loans by the United States. Both as a matter of principle and because of heavy commitments in other parts of the world, Washington also rejected any appreciable increase in direct loans for other purposes; and it opposed, as unnecessary, the special inter-American bank advocated by the Latin American countries. Insisting that price stabilization agreements would hinder the free and desirable operation of the law of supply and demand, and would also in practice be extremely difficult to negotiate, the United States opposed them too. And toward the idea of a Latin American common market Washington was equally cold, arguing that the Latin American nations were insufficiently advanced to emulate the exciting example of their European colleagues.

Latin American displeasure with such United States positions mount-

ed in inverse proportion to the steady post-1953 decline in the prices on
the world market of primary raw materials. Latin American governments were then more hard pressed than ever to fulfill both the persistently rising expectations and the genuine needs of their rapidly expanding populations. To those governments the attitude of Washington
seemed neither obvious nor sensible but rather one more reflection of
arrogance, indifference, and an unrealistic appraisal of the Latin American reality. They believed that nothing else could account for the fact,
for instance, that from the end of World War II through 1958 communist Yugoslavia, with only 20 million inhabitants, received more aid in
United States public funds than did all of the nations of Latin America,
whose populations totalled some 175 million.[14] The nature, as well as
the quantity, of United States loans came under severe Latin American
criticism. It was charged, for example, that Export-Import funds were
excessively costly because in addition to their high interest rates, they
often forced borrowing nations to purchase United States products at
prices higher than those of competing manufactures of other nations.
Latin Americans further complained of the preponderant influence of
Washington upon the policies of the World Bank and the IMF—an
influence that forced those supposedly international and independent
lending agencies to press "orthodox" economic policies upon the Latin
American countries, including the granting of preferences to private
capital and enterprise and a "hands off" attitude by government except
in respect to protecting and guaranteeing private capital against loss or
expropriation. Washington's advocacy of unfettered free enterprise for
Latin America merely proved, in the eyes of critics, that the United
States was abysmally ignorant of Latin American economic problems.
What was good for the United States in the nineteenth century was
not, they insisted, good for Latin America in the twentieth.

But above all Latin Americans believed that—whatever the pro-
nouncements or actions of the United States—Washington was simply
uninterested in their problems. And to that charge there was a good
deal of truth, for in the decade after 1948 the Latin American policy of
the United States was essentially one of postponement or, where un-
avoidable, placation—never of positive policies, promptly implemented.
Washington, regarding Latin America as peripheral to the cold war in

[14] Donald M. Dozer, *Are We Good Neighbors* (University of Florida, 1959),
p. 371.

comparison with other areas of the world, and believing that Latin America was already committed irrevocably to the Western cause, assigned it a low priority for attention. Those complaints that filtered through the diplomatic maze to reach Washington's reluctant ear were largely disregarded. Warnings of the political urgency of economic and social problems were frequently viewed as blackmail or as the mouthings of communists or "radicals" who would, it was felt, complain about the United States whatever its policies. There was some basis in experience for such cynicism, and it was true that entrenched elites balked at self-denying reforms; but the overriding facts were, first, that the Latin American reality had markedly altered, and second, that notwithstanding the efforts of knowledgeable individuals to respond appropriately, the United States government not only had failed to adopt long-range, imaginative policies to deal with that change before 1958, but even seemed to be unaware of any major policy implications in the rapidly emerging new situation in Latin America. When, at times, the United States' failure to deal with this change threatened to cause serious difficulties, the United States government, like Canute, attempted to turn back the tide with a barrage of slogans. But it did nothing.

## National Planning

Meanwhile, in Latin America, the established ranks of nationalism had encountered and joined forces with the newer legions of socioeconomic revolution and together they were now doing battle in the political arena. Accentuating the traditionally important role that the state—under both the Spanish and Portuguese empires and the independent national systems—had played in all social and economic matters, Latin America's new nationalism, in a period of crises, demanded that the state assume a greater part than ever in planning and directing the solution to social and economic problems. Washington was apparently unfamiliar and essentially unsympathetic with that unique and vital fact of Latin American history and life, and it remained convinced that the limiting of public financial aid to developing nations would automatically force private investors and free enterprise to do the development job. United States insistence upon an approach that ran so sharply against the growing nationalist, state interventionist trend not only frustrated the financial needs of Latin American nations but convinced them that the United States was resolved to impose upon them its own way of life—a way of life Latin Americans professed to find repugnant.

United States reluctance to expand its financial assistance to Latin America was due also to the conviction that those nations somehow shared its belief that it was of paramount importance to contain Soviet expansion. Such an assumption made acceptable, it was imagined, the allocation of available United States financial resources to those nations believed at the time to have the greatest strategic importance in stemming Soviet aggrandizement. But Latin American leaders were incapable of political empathy with Washington: not only were they physically distant from that capital; not only did their stakes in the cold war seem comparatively lower than those of the United States; but they also felt that their own severe and inescapable problems were of paramount importance and simply not subject—even at the request of Washington—to subordination to the demands of the struggle between Russia and the United States.

Further alienating the democratically oriented sector of Latin America's leadership was Washington's adamant refusal to adopt a strong policy of opposition to dictatorship in Latin America. Claiming that such a position would violate nonintervention agreements, the United States government aided, along with democratic regimes, such dictatorial governments as those of Batista of Cuba, Trujillo of the Dominican Republic, and Gustavos Rojas Pinilla of Colombia. When Washington crowned its aid with bestowal of special awards of merit upon dictators Manuel Odría of Peru and Marcos Pérez Jiménez of Venezuela, democratic elements commenced seriously to fear that the United States positively favored military dictatorships because they might manage strictly to preserve law and order while keeping the country on a steadily anticommunistic course, whatever the cost in personal freedoms to its citizens and in life and property to its victims.

That the situation in Latin America required urgent attention began to be taken seriously in 1958 when Vice President Nixon's goodwill tour to South America produced hostile and violent reactions in several countries. The President of the United States, seeking to find out what was the matter, sent his brother, Milton Eisenhower, to Latin America, asking that he return with specific recommendations for improvement in Latin American-United States relations. Moreover, the 1958 proposal of the president of Brazil—a plan called Operation Pan America—whose major new idea was that an inter-American, government-sponsored crash program was essential for the achievement of Latin American development, met with sympathetic reaction in Washington and became the basis for discussions with several Latin American leaders. By November of that year Washington had responded to the deteriorating Latin American situation with official assurances that ". . . no matter what our commitments in other areas of the world the United States will never forget the needs of its sister republics. . . ."[15] Several weeks later the President's brother reported that ". . . Latin America is a continent in a ferment. The people generally, including the most humble of them, now know that low living standards are neither universal nor inevitable, and they are therefore impatiently insistent that remedial action be taken. . . ."[16]

## United States Cooperation

Washington now began to retreat from certain policies most sharply censured by Latin Americans. Withdrawing its opposition to a special inter-American financial agency for development, the United States joined in creating the Inter-American Development Bank (1960) and accepted a relaxation in the policy of the World Bank, with the result that in 1960 the Bank established a new affiliated lending institution, the International Development Association, empowered to make loans for essential but possibly non-revenue-producing development projects. Washington also dropped its objections to a common market, following which seven nations accounting for 70 percent of Latin America's population established the Latin American Free Trade Association (LAFTA). Moreover, relaxing its uncompromisingly negative attitude toward an international commodity price stabilization mechanism, the United States began to cooperate with Latin American governments in a study of the matter.

It was in 1959 and 1960, while Washington was taking the first steps in recognition of Latin America's importance to its interests, that the sound of cannonfire in the Caribbean called the hemisphere's attention to the Cuban revolutionary whose bearded visage was to loom so large in the future nightmares of American statesmen. As relations between

[15] U. S. Department of State, *Bulletin*, Jan. 12, 1959, p. 49.
[16] *Ibid.*, Jan. 19, 1959, p. 90.

Washington and Havana went from bad to worse, new tensions, products of various Fidelista and Fidelista-related activities, built up in
Latin America. The charismatic Castro was threatening to become the
personification of the aspirations of Latin America's hungry and angry
millions and to attract as well the loyalty or tacit approval of broad sectors of wage laborers, salaried white collar employees, and university
students. Fidelismo, alluring not only those who saw in Cuba the answer to their own socioeconomic predicament but also those who constitutionally opposed the United States, became a serious threat to the
domestic order in individual Latin American nations and provided a
highly visible international rallying point for anti-United States sentiment. In 1960, when Castro requested and received help from Peking
and Moscow in order to keep his revolution alive, the Western Hemisphere was confronted with the existence in its bosom of a Soviet satellite assiduously seeking to spearhead communist penetration of Latin
America. Washington's lingering doubt concerning the importance of
Latin America promptly vanished.

## Alliance for Progress

During the final months of the outgoing Republican Administration
and the first of its Democratic successor, the United States sought both
to protect itself and to bar the spread of Fidelismo. Vigorous support
was given to the attempted solution of Latin America's multiple serious
problems, on the basis that such problems made the Latin American
nations easy targets for Cuban, Chinese, or Russian subversion. Washington, acting upon an intention officially expressed in the 1960 Act of
Bogotá, commenced to cooperate with Latin American governments in
the formulation of a comprehensive program designed to achieve social
and economic advances. In March 1961 President Kennedy announced
that the United States was proposing an "Alliance for Progress" with
the nations of Latin America. Together the Act and the Alliance recognized the need for broad institutional reforms in Latin America and
committed the participants to a ten-year cooperative program peacefully to achieve social and economic modernization.

At the same time Washington asked the Organization of American
States to act regarding the emerging Cuban threat to the security of the
Western Hemisphere. The member nations' foreign ministers, meeting in

Costa Rica in August 1960, did ". . . condemn. . . emphatically intervention from an extra-continental power in the affairs of the American republics" and declared that ". . . the existence of such a threat jeopardized American solidarity and security."[17] But that statement's lack of specificity—due to the reluctance of several important member nations, including Mexico and Brazil, to risk any appearance of having condemned the domestic aspects of the Cuban revolution—greatly disappointed the United States.

Washington then moved actively to topple the Castro regime with an intervention of the type that had in 1954 succeeded in Guatemala. United States government agencies, in cooperation with official Guatemalan and Nicaraguan elements and with exiled anti-Castroites, assisted in the preparation of an invasion of the latters' homeland. In April 1961 about fifteen hundred Cubans went ashore at the Bay of Pigs, hoping to ignite a triumphant island-wide uprising. But Fidel, who had for months been preparing for precisely such an invasion, crushed it easily and must surely have relished the subsequent bitter condemnation hurled against Washington by both friends and foes of the United States. In the wake of the Bay of Pigs incident, Castro declared that Cuba was, officially, a "socialist" state and moved even closer to those communist nations most hostile to the United States. At the same time, the bitterness aroused throughout Latin America by Washington's intervention in Cuban affairs had made more remote than ever the possibility for joint action against Cuba by the Organization of American States.

Temporarily abandoning the campaign for joint OAS political action, the United States turned toward social and economic reform. At Punta del Este, Uruguay, in August 1961 the Charter of the Alliance for Progress was adopted; it stated that the Alliance would labor for ". . . accelerated economic progress and broader social justice within the framework of personal dignity and political liberty."[18] The goals of the Alliance would be implemented, according to the charter, through preparation of detailed individual national development plans that would include provisions for tax and land reform and for the encouragement of both foreign and domestic investment.

United States support of the Alliance for Progress Charter repre-

[17] *Ibid.*, Sept. 12, 1960, pp. 407-08.
[18] For the text of the Charter of Punta del Este, see Karl M. Schmitt and David D. Burks, *Evolution or Chaos* (Praeger, 1963), pp. 265-75.

sented a major policy shift. Events in Cuba had apparently supported Latin American warnings about the need for social and economic modernization; Washington had concluded that only by a peaceful revolution—and one supported by the United States—could Latin America escape a bloody revolution that would deliver it, via Fidelismo, to the enemy camp. At Punta del Este the United States not only accepted the validity of admonitions previously dismissed as blackmail, but it also assented to Latin America's proposed solution—cooperative economic and social development, utilizing, where necessary, extremely large amounts of public funds. In exchange for its dramatic reversal of policy Washington managed to secure Latin American commitments to allocate far greater sums from their own resources than previously contemplated, together with agreement to formulate detailed plans for development including basic social, fiscal, land, and other reforms; that agreement, secured in free and open debate, was crucial, for it placed squarely upon the nations of Latin America the ultimate responsibility for the success or failure of the Alliance for Progress.

### The Cuban Problem

The Alliance in motion, Washington again sought Latin American political cooperation and early in 1962 asked a consultative meeting of foreign ministers to affirm the incompatibility of communism with the American system and to recommend the expulsion from the OAS of the Castro regime. While no serious resistance was encountered to the first matter, the second was rejected by almost one-third of the voting nations, which represented 70 percent of Latin America's population and included the prestigious nations of Brazil, Mexico, Chile, and Argentina. That important opposition was due not merely to fear of domestic repercussions from groups sympathetic to Fidelismo but also to lack of conviction that Cuba genuinely threatened Western Hemisphere security and to reluctance to establish the precedent of ejecting a member at the behest of the United States. But since a two-thirds vote sufficed, Washington gained a "victory" and the way was paved for exclusion of the Castro government from the Organization of American States.

But Fidelista Cuba still lived and was creating serious problems for the American countries. Not only were its agents providing money, weapons, and propaganda to subvert various Latin American governments, but on the island itself Soviet military personnel were secretly installing sophisticated missile-delivery systems. By September 1962 President Kennedy was moved to warn:

. . . if at any time the Communist build-up in Cuba were to endanger or interfere with our security in any way, including our base at Guantanamo, our passage to the Panama Canal, our missile and space activities at Cape Canaveral, or the lives of American citizens in this country, or if Cuba should ever attempt to export its aggressive purposes by force or the threat of force against any nation in this hemisphere, or become an offensive military base of significant capacity for the Soviet Union, then this country will do whatever must be done to protect its own security and that of its allies.[19]

The President's warning was promptly seconded by a joint congressional resolution:

. . . the United States is determined (a) to prevent by whatever means may be necessary, including the use of arms, the Marxist-Leninist regime in Cuba from extending, by force or the threat of force, its aggressive or subversive activities to any part of the hemisphere; (b) to prevent in Cuba the creation or use of an externally supported military capability endangering the security of the United States; and (c) to work with the Organization of American States and with freedom-loving Cubans to support the aspiration of the Cuban people for self-determination.[20]

At the same time the United States Secretary of State convoked an informal meeting of the OAS foreign ministers, whose communique included the declaration that ". . . at the present juncture the most urgent [problem] . . . is the Sino-Soviet intervention in Cuba in an attempt to convert the island into an armed base for communist penetration of the Americas and subversion of the democratic institutions of the hemisphere. . . ."[21]

A few weeks later the world shook with fear of global nuclear conflict as President Kennedy announced confirmation of secret construction by the Soviet Union of Cuban missile bases and issued an ultimatum demanding their removal, pending which the United States would maintain a naval "quarantine" to prevent delivery of further offensive weapons. In that crisis the nations of Latin America—whose OAS representatives had been informally consulted prior to issuance of the ultimatum

[19] U. S. Department of State, *Bulletin*, Oct. 22, 1962, pp. 481-82.
[20] *Ibid.*, Oct. 22, 1962, p. 597.
[21] *Ibid.*, Oct. 22, 1962, pp. 598-600.

—met in an emergency Council session and unanimously supported the United States, committing themselves to use all means including force not only to prevent the delivery to Cuba of offensive war material but also ". . . to prevent the missiles in Cuba . . . from ever becoming an active threat to the peace and security of the continent."[22]

As a benumbed world waited, the United States and Russian heads of state reached an informal agreement leading to solution of the immediate crisis. But the problem of Castro did not thereby vanish; not only did there remain the possibility of Cuba's becoming a Soviet military base, but Fidelismo continued to seek adherents throughout the hemisphere and to menace the internal order of Latin American nations. While this was obvious to an OAS committee charged with making appropriate recommendations, it was equally obvious that several influential Latin American governments, although strongly opposed to Castro, would refuse to submit to a call for collective anti-Fidelista action because of alleged sovereignty-affecting aspects of the committee's recommendations. And now not only was Washington experiencing frustration in its effort to wrest strong and unanimous political support from the nations of Latin America, but it was also becoming evident that the Alliance for Progress was failing to achieve the degree of social and economic progress believed necessary to prevent the violent implementation of antipathetic revolutionary doctrines.

## The Alliance's Advances

But while the Alliance's progress had been disappointing, it had not been nonexistent. In fact, an evaluation of the first year's operations under the charter indicated advances in some respect or other in almost all participating countries. Nevertheless, it was increasingly clear that certain reforms stipulated as necessary in the charter were meeting with strong resistance from both elite and leftist groups—resistance that both slowed desired advances and heightened political and social tensions. Moreover, the charter's demand for carefully formulated development plans was encountering both theoretical opposition and practical difficulties and was being frequently circumvented with the reluctant acquiescence of the United States. Above all, a series of crises in Brazil and Argentina, together with continued guerrilla strife in Colombia, peasant seizures of land in Peru, terrorism and sabotage in

[22] *Ibid.*, Nov. 12, 1962, p. 723.

Venezuela, and continuing barbaric violence in Haiti, seemed to indicate that the Alliance might be impotent to alleviate hardship and reduce tensions in time to avert disaster.

Finally, certain basic principles of the Charter of Punta del Este came to be compromised, among them the principle that the charter's envisaged peaceful revolution was to occur within the framework of representative institutions. The Kennedy Administration, supporting that principle, had attempted to implement it by denying recognition and military and economic aid to several military regimes that seized power by force and by giving special support to democratic governments that were encountering difficulties in their efforts to survive. While that policy had not been applied with absolute rigor—i.e., in connection with the 1962 fall of Frondizi in Argentina—and while it had not been conspicuously successful, it was still in effect in 1963 at the time of President Kennedy's assassination, for at that moment a two-month-old revolutionary military regime in the Dominican Republic and another in Honduras remained unrecognized and unaided by the United States.

## Johnson's Hardening Policy

The active promotion of democratic government in Latin America was, however, de-emphasized as part of a general hardening of policy that developed under the following Administration. The Johnson Administration did not altogether cease to support the Alliance for Progress, continuing to press energetically for the now more promising strictly developmental aspects of the charter. But in the political sphere the range of United States objectives was palpably contracted and the rigorous achievement of those narrowed goals was sought in an atmosphere of inelastic insistence. For example, justifying abandonment of the principle of active encouragement of representative regimes upon the grounds that Washington could not impose democracy on the Latin American states, the Johnson Administration placed greater emphasis upon military and political measures for preventing subversion by external forces. Toward that end it smiled upon political groups in proportion to their actual or alleged opposition to communism. Such groups included not only the democratically oriented Christian Democratic Party of Chile, whose candidate Frei triumphed over communist-supported Allende in a heated presidential election in 1964, but also the force-born Dominican and Honduran military regimes previously refused recognition by the Kennedy Administration, but which convinced the Johnson government that continued denial of military and economic aid might lead to the triumph of "subversive" elements. In 1964, when the Brazilian military overturned a legally elected representative government, the United States did not suspend relations even momentarily. In fact, Washington's view of the ousted democratic regime as "soft on communism" and economically and politically inadequate was widely known, so that it was not totally surprising that Secretary of State Rusk managed to commend the military usurpers for saving constitutional government in Brazil and to find large sums of money to assist the new military government's economic stabilization programs.

In regard to the Organization of American States, the Administration of President Johnson seemed at first to follow the policy of its predecessor, supporting a Venezuelan proposal—approved in 1964 by a consultative meeting of foreign ministers, with four votes in opposition—for sanctions against Cuba for the latter's effort to foment revolution in Venezuela. But the response of the United States to an April 1965 Dominican revolution made it clear that in fact the Johnson Administration was determined not to rely upon collective action altogether and considered itself bound neither by previous OAS commitments related to communist subversion in the Western Hemisphere nor by Washington's past promises to abstain from unilateral intervention. The April revolt sought to reestablish the presidency of legally elected Juan Bosch who had been overthrown by certain military officers who charged him with being "soft on communism." Those officers, threatened by revolt, managed to convince the Johnson Administration that communists and/or their sympathizers were directing the uprising and might ultimately gain control of the Dominican government. Haunted by the success of Castro's guerrilla action, confronted with grave insurgency problems in Southeast Asia, and convinced that domestic United States political disaster would be the inevitable result of the Dominican Republic's following in Cuba's footsteps, Washington responded affirmatively to a plea for assistance from the anti-Bosch faction. Landing over twenty thousand men on the soil of the Dominican Republic, the United States produced a further and still unresolved crisis in its Latin American relations.

*Mutual Interests*

The consequences of the United States' Dominican intervention are discussed in Chapter III, but it may here be noted that this crisis like those before it was the result of failure to base policy upon interests *shared* by Latin America and the United States. The serious estrangement of the early twentieth century found the United States insisting that it must intervene unilaterally in the Caribbean in order to remove conditions conducive to European intervention; Latin Americans, on the other hand, were equally determined to uphold their rights as independent nations and demanded that the United States desist from actions that injured the freedom of action of weaker countries and betrayed an attitude of arrogant paternalism denigrating to the Latin American states. The alienation of the 1950's revolved about the threat of Soviet penetration of the Western Hemisphere—a threat the United States sought to counter by political and military means while the Latin American nations advocated solution of serious economic and social problems in order to remove conditions that might facilitate Soviet subversion. Both major periods of friction were ended only by the conscientious search for mutual interests and the initiation of efforts to forward those mutual interests in a spirit of cooperation. The Administration of President Johnson, in its basic reliance upon Washington-managed politico-military security measures for the entire Western Hemisphere and its recourse to unilateral intervention in the affairs of a nation of the new world, stirred up the sleeping shades of Latin America's past deep fears for its independence and integrity. But it does not necessarily thereby follow that the United States, in order to extricate itself from the present crisis and regain the good graces of its Latin American neighbors, must or should return to a strict nonintervention policy, or shift its exclusive attention to the solution of economic and social problems as a means for guaranteeing the security of the Western Hemisphere. A future policy for the United States can be suggested only upon the basis of an analysis of the interests of both the United States and the Latin American nations and of the problems that have been encountered in the efforts to advance those interests.

# II

# United States Interests, Problems, and Policies

The complex problem of the United States' relations with Latin America becomes conceptually more manageable when broken into four parts that may be expressed as the following questions: What are the general global objectives of United States foreign policy? What type of "world order" would most favor realization of United States purposes? What roles do the Latin American nations play in the fulfillment of United States goals? To what extent do those roles coincide with the national interests of the Latin American countries?

## United States Foreign Policy Objectives

The United States government must adhere to two major general objectives: assurance of the nation's physical safety and protection and development of the "way of life" of the people of the United States. The former must include not only conventionally conceived territorial defense but also prevention of nuclear war, since such a war's annihilation of existing civilizations would make impossible the achievement of the second objective. This second goal, it should be emphasized, does not envision creation of a cordon sanitaire but encompasses rather the protection of the lives and property of United States citizens abroad, the facilitation of international exchanges and activities in the fields of trade,

34

investment, culture, ideas, personal relationships, and travel, and the establishment, eventually, of a world order conducive to an environment harmonious with the "way of life" of the people of the United States.

### World Order

The model for that world order most hospitable to United States aspirations must be selected from among theoretical possibilities that range along a spectrum with a unified quasi-utopian world state at one end and total anarchy at the other. Few people are untouched by the appeal of the former, as long, at least, as it in no way interferes with what they consider, rightly or wrongly, to be their interests. At the same time few regard such an order as an immediately realizable goal. As for the United States government, it must strive for a viable world order within the existing reality of intense nationalism, cultural and ideological pluralism, and the general acceptance of force as an instrument of policy. Such a viable world order would be composed of stable prosperous states—each governed in accord with the traditions and aspirations of its peoples—that would resolve both domestic and international conflicts of interests by law rather than by force. In such a world order there would, presumably, arise fewer of those tensions and hostilities that cause the people of the United States to concentrate a large proportion of their energy and national resources on self-defense.

The late President Kennedy outlined an eminently reasonable goal when he announced that his Administration desired ". . . a peaceful world community of free and independent states, free to choose their own future and their own system so long as it does not threaten the freedom of others."[1] Such principles harmonize with foreign policy traditions of self-determination of peoples and good-neighborliness that originated in the early history of the United States and were given expression in the twentieth century by Presidents Woodrow Wilson and Franklin Roosevelt. They are also in accord with existing conditions. "Freedom" and "independence" would be compatible with nationalistic sentiment both in the United States and in other nations of the world. Ideological and cultural pluralism would be accommodated

[1] As quoted by Dean Rusk, U.S. Department of State, *Bulletin,* Nov. 6, 1962, pp. 683-89.

by recognition of the right of each nation to choose its own system. United States interest would be protected by agreement that the desired world order was to be a peaceful community of nations and that no nation would have the right to threaten the freedom of others.

The problems of establishing such a world order are obviously manifold and include above all that of defining the point at which the "freedom of action" of one nation begins to threaten the legitimate interests of another. With respect to the Western Hemisphere President Kennedy made it clear that he would not hesitate to use force against an American nation that, by *becoming* or *acting like* a Soviet satellite, threatened the security of the United States. The succeeding Johnson Administration went further, developing a *preventative* policy in which military force was wielded (in the Dominican Republic) to remove what was considered to be a threat that communist elements *might* take over the government of an American nation. Moreover, the Johnson Administration not only declared that ". . . the American nations can not, must not and will not permit the establishment of another communist government in the western hemisphere . . . ,"[2] but it also made it clear that if the American nations would not take collective action to prevent any future communist "take-over," the United States would intervene unilaterally. Although such a policy, by proscribing even popularly elected communist governments from the Western Hemisphere, clearly subordinates to the interests of the United States the freedom of other nations "to choose their own future and their own system," the Johnson Administration, in adopting it, did not seem to believe that it was abandoning the Kennedy goal of "a peaceful world community of free and independent states." Rather, the Johnson Administration assumed a "communist dictatorship" that would prevent or inhibit the Dominican people's freedom of choice, and believed that the United States must remove that threat. As President Johnson states it, "our goal in the Dominican Republic . . . is that the people . . . must be permitted to freely choose the path of political democracy, social justice and economic progress."[3]

The establishment of "a peaceful world community of free and independent states" both can and should be a major goal of the United States. The outstanding problem facing United States policy is to make

[2] U.S. Department of State, *Bulletin,* May 17, 1965, p. 746.
[3] *Ibid.*

that goal operational, and this involves both defining more precisely the nature of such a community and developing methods for encouraging its growth. In reality the United States government has for many years been concerned with the solution to this problem, for it is the essence of the foreign policy of a peaceful democratic nation. But now it should be given the top priority it has seldom had.

### Importance of Latin America

As a basis for considering Latin American policy, and thus in effect suggesting the degree of commitment of United States energy and resources to that area, it is necessary to evaluate the importance of the Latin American countries to the United States. Such an evaluation must include a review of the role of those nations in world affairs—a role that in turn depends upon the shape of a world whose political possibilities range from nuclear  ruin to total global harmony. Neither extreme need be considered, for conditions following a nuclear holocaust would be qualitatively so different from any hitherto known as to preclude the formulation of any remotely meaningful policy, whereas current policy issues would have been resolved by definition if absolute harmony were to prevail. World politics of the foreseeable future will probably continue to be characterized by one form or another of the cold war between the United States and its allies on one hand and the Soviet Union and/or Communist China and their allies on the other. This conflict will continue to be highly fluid and will be increasingly affected by China's growing influence upon world affairs. Both the Soviet Union and the United States will seek to maintain their freedom of action in the face of China's mounting challenge and will thus tend to soften their relations with each other. The rise of Chinese power and the easing of relations between the Soviet Union and the West will accelerate the existing trend away from a bipolar and toward a polycentric international system. This in turn will lead to a heightening of tensions between the developed and the less developed nations and push the latter into increasingly effective international political cooperation. Consequently, the international importance of the nations of Latin America must be calculated not only in terms of their contribution to "winning the cold war" but also with respect to their present and future role in the international politics of the world's developing nations.

MILITARY ASPECTS. In an age of nuclear capability it is clear that the nations of Latin America cannot brandish significant military influence; nor are they now any more capable of a decisive conventional role on the world scene than in the past. Although there are a million men in all Latin American armed forces (roughly 33 percent of the number in the United States armed forces), they form no effective fighting body. Those million men are of twenty different nations and not under joint command. Brazil, the largest and most populous Latin American nation, maintains an army about one-tenth the size of that of the United States. None of the nations has now or will soon have the economic and technological basis upon which to support an effective military establishment except for local purposes and defense against other Latin American states. Rivalries and conflicts among the countries of Latin America, whetted by mounting nationalism, will long prevent the creation of a coordinated Latin American military force of any significance.

But while in a world war Latin America can neither substantially threaten nor aid the United States militarily, and even though long-range ballistic missiles may have minimized the strategic importance of the Caribbean region and northern South America which guard the approaches to both the continental United States and the Panama Canal, nevertheless the existence there of bases of any kind controlled by a hostile power would affect adversely both the offensive and defensive military position of the United States. And in an age when the nuclear stalemate has encouraged use of insurgency and guerrilla warfare rather than direct attack, the individual military forces of Latin America can help to prevent powers hostile to the United States from obtaining bases in Latin America. The armed forces of Latin America might also contribute to a joint peacekeeping force of the type the United States advocates under the Organization of American States to prevent the subversion of any Latin American nation by a hostile extra-continental power. Moreover, the Latin American nations have military value in terms of strategic materials whose availability to the United States or to its potential enemies might affect the outcome of a conflict or recovery in its aftermath. These materials include petroleum, copper, antimony, bauxite, quartz crystals, tungsten, iron ore, tin, zinc, sulfur, and a limited amount of fissionable matter.

ECONOMIC ASPECTS. The chief material value of the Latin American nations to the United States is neither military nor strategic but economic.

In order to win the cold war, or merely to preserve a stalemate, the United States must not only keep its own internal economy operating at its present high level but must expand its production. In this respect Latin America is important, for although it contains less than 7 percent of the world's population, it buys more than 25 percent of the United States' exports, provides nearly 25 percent of its imports, and is the locus of one-fourth of all direct United States foreign investments. It is true that foreign trade is less economically important to the United States than to most countries. It may be, as Adolf A. Berle has claimed, that "the United States does not need Latin America as a field for investment for her capital . . . nor are Latin American products essential to the United States economy"[4] and that the United States, more easily than most Latin American nations, could pursue an independent policy without "any unmanageable strain"[5] upon its economic life. But that is quite beside the point. The United States must not merely eke out an economic existence without "any unmanageable strain"; rather, it must actively expand economic activity, in which sphere Latin America is already significant and should become more significant in the future.

Not only have the resources of Latin America been scarcely exploited, but many of its nations seem to have reached or are fast approaching a "take-off" point in their economic life. Finally, Latin America's population is the world's fastest growing and may well have doubled that of the United States by the end of this century. The potential in Latin America for larger markets (the result of an expanding population plus increased purchasing power), for a greater supply of useful raw materials such as copper and oil, and for heightened investment opportunities cannot be neglected by those concerned with the economic vitality of the United States.

POLITICAL ASPECTS. It is in the sphere of international politics, however, that the nations of Latin America most deeply affect the interests of the United States. Their twenty votes in the United Nations, for example, give them a voice in proceedings that may either strengthen or weaken the position of the United States with respect to both its adversaries and its allies. Because of their traditional close ties with the United States, the role of the Latin American nations, as a group, is entirely

[4] Adolf A. Berle, *Latin America, Diplomacy and Reality* (Harper & Row, for Council on Foreign Relations, 1962), p. 6.
[5] *Ibid.*, p. 10.

distinct from that of the African and Asian states. Other nations are well aware of those special links—links that were given formal recognition and an institutional basis in the Rio Treaty of Inter-American Reciprocal Assistance of 1947 and the Charter of the Organization of American States in 1948. If the United States, from such an advantageous position, proves unable to convince its Western Hemisphere allies of the justice and wisdom of its policies, it may not be able to exercise effective leadership in other underdeveloped areas of the world—areas that might, disenchanted, shift sharply toward the Soviet Union or Communist China and thus seriously impair the existing precarious world balance of power. Latin America in fact has a unique role to play as a gauge of United States ability to cope effectively with the issues of the cold war; it thus merits an expenditure of United States energy and resources as great as or greater than any other underdeveloped region of the world.

As the extirpatory attributes of nuclear warfare become increasingly recognized, the great powers, in order to survive, must agree to assign an exclusively deterrent role to nuclear devices. While conventional weapons in the hands of guerrillas will doubtless assume increasing importance, it is with ideological, economic, and political artillery that the world's great nations will win or lose the battles of the future. The United States, as it deploys these instruments in the Western Hemisphere, will show other underdeveloped lands what it really means by a "peaceful world community of free and independent states." If the United States, in relations with the Latin American nations, comprehends their interests as well as its own and consistently demonstrates a reasoning and conciliatory but firm attitude, rather than a blustering and intimidating one, it will indicate to the world its genuine support of a world order based upon a mutuality of interests rather than upon the purposes of the United States alone. Such comportment will appeal strongly to the numerous weaker nations of the world and encourage their cooperation with the United States.

## World Policy and Military Strength

While the importance of Latin America to both the national security and the international success of the United States makes imperative the formulation and implementation of effective Latin American policies, such policies cannot be developed in isolation. There is an intimate interrelationship between the global and Latin American policies of the United States. For example, in an epoch of potential nuclear warfare the physical survival of the United States cannot be assured simply by creation of a solid Western Hemisphere anticommunist bloc. However important such a grouping may be to the general cold war situation, it would be meaningless if United States military strength were insufficient to deter potential enemies from direct assaults upon it or its allies. Moreover, serious deterioration in the military posture of the United States, or disintegration of the North Atlantic Treaty Organization, might enlarge the existing crack in the Western Hemisphere bloc. An effective Latin American policy must be based upon military power sufficient to inspire Latin American confidence in the ability of the United States to defend both itself and, with their collaboration, the nations of the Western Hemisphere.

## Two Policy Objectives

If the United States insures such military capability, it may proceed toward achievement of two major objectives: (1) prevention of hostile-power control, either military or political, of any part of Latin America, and simultaneous assurance of maximum Latin American moral and material support for the United States and its allies in any contest with communist or other hostile non-Western Hemisphere forces; (2) development of "a peaceful . . . [Latin American] community of free and independent states, free to choose their own future and their own system so long as it does not threaten the freedom of others"—a community that will comprise an integral part of the desirable world order.

If the United States wishes to reconcile its policy with the values of a majority of its own citizens as well as with the nationalistic aspirations of the world's peoples, it will seek these two objectives by means compatible with a world order of "free and independent states."

## Threats to United States Policies

During the next decade the achievement of these two major objectives may be frustrated by several existing and potential threats. Identification of those threats can be useful both in evaluating present policies and in anticipating future policy problems. Such dangers are of two general kinds: those that directly or indirectly menace the security of the United States by depriving it of elements of support from the Latin American nations or by making this aid available to hostile powers, and those that impede development of a group of free and independent Western Hemisphere nations.

## United States Security

Among the dangers to United States security are several possibilities that will exist as long as the cold war follows its current course. One is the direct threat that would be posed by the establishment of offensive hostile-power bases in Latin America. Soviet bases in areas nearer to the United States than existing bases in Europe would facilitate attack upon the United States; bases farther removed—in southernmost South America, for example—would be less strategically dangerous but would have inestimable political repercussions. United States policy in this respect was defined during the Cuban crisis when the United States government expressed its willingness to use force, including nuclear weapons, preventively. The substantial retreat of the Soviet government has reduced but not eliminated that problem, for as long as Havana clings to its virulent hate-United States policy, offensive bases may be reestablished either by the Soviet Union or by another power hostile to the United States.

Another order of threat to United States security is represented by a regime that, while not permitting establishment of offensive bases, is both sympathetic to the Sino-Soviet systems and antagonistic to Washington. Cuba, again, has provided an excellent example of how such a government might act were it to gain power in another Latin American nation. It has consistently voted with the Soviet Union and against the United States in the United Nations and has repudiated its obligations as a member of the Organization of American States. Although Cuba has received more from Russia than it has given in return, it has expressed every willingness to assist the Soviet Union and its allies. Cuba has demonstrated hostility to United States interests on its territory and has assiduously disseminated anti-United States propaganda throughout Latin America. The Castro regime has schemed persistently to bring about other Latin American regimes like itself and has gained sympathizers in many countries, especially for domestic Cuban developments. Should those Fidelista groups wrest power, legally or by subversion, they might shift their nations into the category of those sympathetic to the communist powers and antagonistic to the United States. The Cuban pattern might then be repeated, with vastly more menacing implications in such key lands as Brazil or Venezuela. Since 1965 the probability of Fidelista-inspired revolutions has declined as a result of inescapably evident domestic difficulties and a growing awareness of Cuba's satellite relationship to the Soviet Union. Nevertheless, Colombia's endemic guerrilla warfare, Indian land seizures in Peru, continuing violence in Guatemala, and mounting social and economic tensions all over Latin America make it important to consider the possibility of future Cuban-type revolutions. Moreover, the United States government cannot avoid regarding as a potential threat to its security any revolution whatsoever in Latin America, for fratricidal chaos obviously provides an excellent milieu for seizure of power by an extremist minority that abominates the United States.

The possible establishment of nonaligned Latin American states represents another potential danger to United States security. By definition such a state would support no particular "side," but would vacillate opportunistically in response to momentary individual problems as they presented themselves. Nonaligned Latin American governments would be inimical to United States interests, for they not only could not be relied upon for support but might also at any juncture adopt policies hostile to the United States; moreover, while in a phase of cooperating with the Russians or Communist China, such a nonaligned state might slip beyond the point of no return.

Following World War II there appeared a pronounced tendency toward nonalignment in some Latin American countries, an outstanding example of which was the "third position" vigorously promoted by Juan Perón both inside and outside Argentina. Some Brazilian opinion favors an "independent policy" whose logical consequences would be nonalignment. Some Mexicans and others who favor "Pan Latin-Americanism" are thinking in similar terms, for while that doctrine is an old one with roots in a common peninsular culture, such an international bloc would, in the contemporary world political environment, have the practical effect of subtracting support from the United States without openly supporting the adversaries of the United States—a result similar to nonalignment. Nasserism—a kind of nonalignment with exotic overtones—has recently interested certain military elements in Latin America, especially in Peru, but it seems doubtful that this plant from the banks of the Nile can thrive in the shade of the Andes.

Repressive dictatorships and wars between and among the nations of Latin American are two further potential threats to United States security. The former may be exemplified by that of Batista in Cuba which maintained friendly relations with United States business and government interests and vehemently professed its detestation of communism and love of free enterprise, only to be toppled with violent reactions against its policies. Intraregional wars are dangerous not alone from the humanitarian standpoint but also because such conflict weakens established order and paves the way for power seizure by extremist elements hostile to the United States.

### Community of Free and Independent States

More difficult to identify are menaces to the achievement of ". . . a peaceful community of free and independent states, free to choose their own future and their own system so long as it does not threaten the freedom of others." In the first place, such a community has never been unequivocally defined in universally acceptable terms. Is a "free and independent" state merely one subject to no other authority than the law of nations which forbids it to threaten others, or must it possess other attributes, such as guarantees of individual rights, representative institutions, etc., etc? Is the goal of the United States a *mixed* community including peacefully coexisting totalitarian repressive and representative democratic systems? Or does the United States seek a group of states whose institutions uniformly resemble its own?

Since World War II United States policy with respect to these questions has been highly ambiguous. The desire for the development of democracy in Latin America has frequently been expressed and the United States government has entered into several international agreements pledging the goal of a democratic Western Hemisphere. The preamble of the Charter of the Organization of American States (1948) proclaims that ". . . the true significance of American solidarity and good neighborliness can only mean the consolidation on this continent, within the framework of democratic institutions, of a system of individual liberty and social justice based upon respect for the essential rights of man."[6] In the Charter of Punta del Este (1961) it was agreed ". . . to unite in a common effort to bring our peoples accelerated economic progress and broader social justice within a framework of personal dignity and political liberty" and to implement "national programs of economic and social development . . . in accordance with democratic principles."[7] But in fact such statements of intention have not legally bound the United States to any specific course of action, and in practice Washington has since 1961 backed and filled, leaving much room for doubt concerning the nature and degree of its commitment to the promotion of democracy in Latin America.

On one hand the United States has five times sought to use the tools of diplomatic recognition and foreign aid to secure greater democracy. When a Peruvian military junta annulled a free election in June 1962 and seized power, Washington suspended aid and withheld recognition until civil liberties had been restored, a date set for new elections, and all parties promised full political rights. In the case of the Dominican Republic, in December 1962 the newly elected government of Juan Bosch, an enemy of former dictator Trujillo, was granted a loan that the State Department declared to be not only for economic and social development but also ". . . in recognition of the valiant efforts of the Dominican government and people to establish a viable, democratic state. . . ."[8] When military elements shortly ousted Bosch, Washington reacted at first as in the case of Peru. In the case of El Salvador, recognition and foreign aid were temporarily withheld from a government that came into power through military intervention. Regarding Haiti, an unsuccessful and unconcealed effort was made to bring about the downfall of President Duvalier. And in November 1964 the Bolivian government of General Rene Barrientos, who had gained power in a complex revolt against President Paz, was denied United States aid and recognition pending an ideological clarification.

On the other hand the United States not only failed to halt aid but

[6] Robert N. Burr and Roland D. Hussey (eds.), *Documents on Inter-American Cooperation* (2 vols.; University of Pennsylvania, 1955), II, 180.

[7] Karl M. Schmitt and David D. Burks, *Evolution or Chaos* (Praeger, 1963), p. 265.

[8] U.S. Department of State, *Bulletin*, Dec. 24, 1962, pp. 958-59.

granted rapid recognition to governments established through military coups d'etat in Argentina, Guatemala, Ecuador, and Brazil. Moreover, in the latter two instances Washington appeared to welcome the replacement of governments considered unacceptable to the United States.

One may ask if the United States *should* promote democracy in Latin America or anywhere else. Does not every nation have the right to decide upon its own political system? In 1792 Thomas Jefferson affirmed that "we certainly cannot deny to other nations that principle whereon our own government is founded that every nation has a right to govern itself internally, under what form it pleases, and to change these forms at its own will."[9] United States attempts to impose its own system may be interpreted as intervention and may consequently alienate its objects from the United States. As a practical matter, it may be virtually impossible to "sell" democracy to nations that lack the economic and social bases, the tradition, and the values fundamental to United States style democracy. This was certainly the case in such unsuccessful efforts as those of Presidents Woodrow Wilson and John Kennedy.

## Promotion of Democracy

But while such arguments should be given weight, founded as they are in the democratic ethos of the United States and in a realistic evaluation of the historical record, closer analysis reveals they are based on faulty assumptions the correction of which can lead to the conclusion that the promotion of democracy is a legitimate purpose of the United States government. One faulty assumption is that the United States can avoid affecting the political philosophies of other peoples. A great power, with programs of military, economic, and technical assistance and influence in the councils of the world's more developed nations, cannot help but influence smaller, weaker countries, whether by action or inaction. That being so, its influence might with both wisdom and profit be consciously directed in favor of democracy.

It is also erroneous to assume that inherent in a policy of promoting democracy is the use of coercion sufficient to violate the democratic

[9] C. Neale Ronning, *Law and Politics in Inter-American Diplomacy* (Wiley, 1963), p. 8.

principles of the American people and to alienate the peoples toward whom the policy is directed. In fact, democracy can be advanced most effectively, if slowly, through programs of example, persuasion, and political education, all of which are in the best democratic tradition.

Finally, the argument that economic and social conditions, attitudes, and political traditions in a number of Latin American countries preclude democracy is invalid. In the first place it reflects the unrealistic and extreme position that the United States must either produce a carbon copy of its own or another Western democracy or be considered a failure. This view overemphasizes one form of democracy as the absolute goal and overlooks the fact that democracy embraces not only the mechanics of government but also a special way of regarding individual and governmental relationships. Rather the position should be more flexible, emphasizing a gradual approach toward the ultimate goal of advanced democracy. A policy of forwarding democracy that increased acceptance for democratic values could certainly not be regarded as having failed. Moreover, the argument that conditions in Latin America make encouragement of democracy hopeless is weak also because such a policy could obviously include efforts to ameliorate those conditions. A policy, to be regarded as successful, need not quickly produce constitutional, representative regimes throughout Latin America. In many countries such a policy might be reasonably viewed with satisfaction were it simply to have paved the way for, or to have encouraged even the first steps toward, democratic institutions.

Not only are arguments against a policy of promoting democracy in Latin America lacking in substance, but there are compelling positive reasons for supporting the adoption of such a program. The acts and outlook of a generally democratic rather than authoritarian Western Hemisphere community would be clearly more compatible with the style of the United States and its people. Moreover, Latin American culture, being essentially Western, provides a far more hopeful milieu for the development of democracy than do the world's primarily non-Western cultures. Promotion of free representative institutions in Latin America is therefore an entirely realistic goal for United States policy, above all if that policy is sufficiently flexible to seek preservation of existing constitutional regimes in some cases and merely to encourage gradual steps toward democracy in others. But however flexible, such a program would require genuine and sustained efforts not only to convince Latin Americans of the virtues and advantages of the democratic orientation but also to demonstrate that the United States government is firmly committed to the policy of forwarding democracy in Latin America. Such firm commitment would earn the added dividends, first, of bringing Washington's policy into greater accord with the ideals of the people of the United States and, second, of providing government policy with the ideological basis it now lacks. The United States, therefore, should seek to establish not merely "a peaceful community of free and independent states" but a system of free and independent *democratic* states.

However desirable and feasible may be a policy of encouraging the proliferation of democratic institutions throughout the Western Hemisphere, many obstacles will have to be surmounted in the course of its implementation. Some will imperil existing democratic regimes and others will impede the establishment of a democratic community as a whole. Some, of primarily Latin American etiology, are described in succeeding chapters. Of those originating in the United States, three major obstacles are considered here, United States attitudes toward the Latin American nations and their people, United States zeal for absolute and total "security"; and the domestic politics of the United States.

## Attitudes Toward Latin America

It is widely assumed in the United States that the nations of Latin America are an inferior species of states that belong rightfully in the sphere of influence of the United States, existing primarily for the purpose of implementing its foreign policy, contributing to its defense, and servicing its economy. That arrogant attitude springs from the double conviction that in their ability to govern themselves and to exist in the modern world Latin Americans are inherently inferior to the people of the United States and that Latin America as a region consists of countries that are comic opera states or unstable satrapies. The historical origins of this bias lie in the sixteenth and seventeenth centuries when England, arguing its cause in a long-lived and bitter international rivalry with Spain, denounced Spaniards as naturally cruel, bigoted, and retarded socially, intellectually, and morally. The British, ultimately convinced by their own propaganda, bequeathed their attitudes to the forefathers of the United States; those attitudes were strengthened by the ideas of the eighteenth century "Enlightenment," which was highly influential in molding the modern Western view and which pointed to Spain, its institutions, and its people as the *exemple horrible* of degradation due to intolerance. Spanish Americans inherited the bad reputation of their peninsular forefathers, and the widespread political instability and lack of social and economic progress that characterized large areas of Latin America in the nineteenth century seemed to confirm the reputation.

Of special importance in forming the United States' attitudes of superiority was its growing acceptance, during the late nineteenth and early twentieth centuries, of the idea of Anglo-Saxon superiority over non-Anglo-Saxons in general. The fact that many Latin American peoples were Indian and Negro in origin placed them in a clearly inferior position in the minds of a growing number of United States citizens. Such racist views were so widely accepted that as late as 1925, when many of today's politically articulate and influential individuals were in their formative and impressionable youth, the United States Department of Labor felt it entirely appropriate to publish an official pamphlet, *The Racial Problem Involved in Immigration from Latin America and the West Indies to the United States,* whose theme was that the large Negro and Indian elements in those areas' populations made immigration undesirable because ". . . the immigrants from these countries tend to lower the average race value of the white population of the United States."[10] While overt expressions of feelings of racial superiority have virtually disappeared, there is reason to believe that the underlying bias is far from extinguished. Even where racial intolerance plays no conscious role in attitude formation, the continued political, economic, and social difficulties of many Latin American nations serve, where necessary, to rationalize the generally accepted view of Latin Americans as inherently inferior people.

Contributing to the paternalistic and contemptuous view of the Latin American states as falling rightly within the sphere of influence of the United States is the wide conviction that they are not "real" nations. This is partly a matter of ignorance. The individual national goals of

[10] U.S. Department of Labor, *The Racial Problems Involved in Immigration from Latin America and the West Indies to the United States* (1925), p. 57.

the Latin American nations, their special foreign policy objectives, their
unique social conflicts and economic problems, their individual history,
culture, and leadership are completely unknown to most United States
citizens, whose mental image of Latin America tends to be a blurred
collage of stereotypic caricatures—tequila-drinking peons dozing under
cacti at noon; Argentine gauchos galloping wildly from one place to another; shiny, brown Cubans holding a bottle of rum in one hand and a
monstrously large cigar in the other. They are not viewed as peoples
who, like the people of the United States, have jobs, raise families, go
to school, and grapple with social, political, and economic problems day
after day in the effort to leave their country a better place than they
found it.

Most United States citizens have lacked both the desire and the opportunity to develop a more realistic image of the Latin American nations. The cultural and educational orientation of the United States has
long been directed toward Western Europe, while the intellectual and
artistic work of Latin Americans has failed to arouse excitement in the
United States. Above all, the nations of Latin America have generally
been too weak to compel the respectful attention of a people who attach considerable importance to visible material power. In times of crisis the people of the United States seek simple and rapid solutions that
will permit them quickly to return their attention to "more important"
areas and avoid the continued involvement that would be required by
the effort to reach a deeper understanding of the origin of the crisis and
a more durable solution. As James Reston has written, ". . . somehow
the people of the United States would do anything for Latin America
except read about it."[11] Reston might have added that those who
wished to read about Latin America would be confronted with a most
abbreviated bibliography, itself a reflection of the fact that scholars
have shared with the general public a general disinterest in Latin
America.

The distorted view of the peoples and nations of Latin America held
by the people of the United States constitutes a serious obstacle to the
development of a peaceful community of free and independent democratic states in the Western Hemisphere. Latin America's deep resentment over any suggestion that it belongs rightfully within the United
States sphere of influence tends to produce a chronically unpeaceful

[11] *New York Times*, Feb. 13, 1966.

and disruptive centrifugal atmosphere in the Western Hemisphere community. Moreover, the failure of the people of the United States to attach any genuine value to most Latin American countries as nation-states tends ipso facto to nullify the concept of *community*. Present United States attitudes thus serve to encourage an *un*peaceful or at least highly restless *non*community toward whose blurred and un-differentiated components the United States cannot possibly develop an effective and realistic policy.

*United States Zeal for Physical Security*

Not only attitudes of superiority but also zeal for physical security, however understandable, may prevent the development of a peaceful community of free and independent democratic states in the Western Hemisphere. Such zeal may impel the United States to seek to crush those forces in Latin America that are working toward the economic, social, and political reforms conducive to stable democracy. Implicit in reform is disturbance of the present status quo which may appear to threaten certain United States interests. Such disturbance may at times lead to periods of instability and violence which—while not necessarily more serious than those that would occur if reform failed to take place —might provide opportunities for enemies of the United States to advance their influence or seize power. The temptation to maintain the status quo in Latin America, for "security" reasons, must be resisted by any United States government genuinely interested in promoting the cause of democratic government in the nations of Latin America.

*United States Domestic Politics*

United States domestic politics combine with the zeal for security to place potential barriers in the way of Latin American social and economic reforms. The constituency of most national legislators is satisfied with the status quo in domestic affairs. Any reform seeking more than the mere improvement of the existing system tends to be labelled "socialist" or "communist" and to be regarded as a threat to the "American way of life." Most legislators, projecting that viewpoint upon a highly superficial knowledge of Latin America, respond to suggestions for decisive reform in Latin America with a suspicion at times almost paranoid, and after supporting the maintenance of the status quo in Latin America by every channel open to them in Washington, return to the hustings to accept the applause of their constituents for having fought the good fight to keep communism out of the Western Hemisphere. The 1965 Dominican intervention clearly reflected the role of domestic politics in Latin American policy, for although there was much controversy among very knowledgeable people concerning the wisdom of intervention, the Johnson Administration appears to have been decisively influenced by the idea that it "could not afford another Cuba," because of possible electoral repercussions at home.

It is clear that unless policy-making and policy-influencing sectors in the United States manage to overcome their doubts about the worth and validity of the Latin American peoples and nations, no policy, however cleverly devised, can succeed in welding a peaceful Western Hemisphere community of free and independent democratic states. This is particularly true because, as will be discussed later, the people of Latin America attach overriding importance to personal ties which can only be developed upon the basis of mutual respect.

# III

# Instruments of United States Policy

The existing apparatus for implementation of any United States policy designed simultaneously to assure a genuinely secure nation and a desirable Western Hemisphere community is complex. That apparatus consists of three major parts, each in turn composed of innumerable separate and overlapping entities. These are (1) policy tools under the direct control of the United States government, (2) international organizations of which the United States is but one of many members, and (3) private agencies and institutions presumably free of government direction and control.

## Nongovernmental Instruments

The private agencies and institutions that serve as United States policy instruments include many elements acting to implement, or at times to obstruct, the Latin American policy of the United States. The nation's press, for example, both places editorial pressure upon government policy and, by necessarily selective news reporting, influences public opinion. The press allots to Latin America a minimum of space and personnel, so that the private citizen is virtually unable to keep well informed about Latin America through his daily newspaper. The same applies in an even more exaggerated sense to television, which now surpasses the

53

newspapers as a source of information for the United States public. Along with the press, various churches have in the past, and increasingly at present, sought to mold public opinion and to influence government policy. Their activity has ranged from placing God squarely on the side of the "American way of life" to sponsoring thoughtful studies of social and economic problems in the various underdeveloped nations and transmitting the results of the studies to lay congregations for discussion and action. Organized labor too has involved itself in questions of Latin American policy, most dramatically in connection with the exclusion of the Mexican *bracero* and less obtrusively in efforts to cooperate with certain Latin American labor leaders in the promotion of democratic unionism in their countries.

## Research and Educational Agencies

Of particular importance in the nongovernmental category are educational, research, and philanthropic institutions, and businesses operating abroad. The nation's universities, such establishments as the Brookings Institution, the Council on Foreign Relations, the Social Science Research Council, the American Council of Learned Societies, and a group of Latin American and United States university administrators known as the Council on Higher Education in the American Republics (CHEAR) in their totality exert a meaningful influence upon the Latin American policy of the United States. As reference groups for the academic profession, they tend to set the tone for educational policies that concretely affect the image of Latin America that prevails among the leadership of the United States as well as the general public. Through research activities they are in a position both to make that image conform more closely to reality and to deal directly with concrete problems. From those institutions emerge the technical and managerial personnel to carry out government programs of technical assistance and development, as well as individuals who will enter government service to make and implement policies. Such establishments therefore play a crucial role in the realm of foreign policy. In respect to Latin America that role has not been played with distinction. Not only in the humanities, but in such disciplines of practical importance to contemporary Latin American problems as economics, political science, and sociology, the body of knowledge so far developed has tended to be limited in both quantity and quality.

Philanthropic bodies, including the highly visible Ford, Carnegie, and Rockefeller foundations, have performed the dual functions of financing activities that may lead to an increased understanding of Latin America, and of supporting concrete programs intended, directly and indirectly, to lead to the development of independent democratic states in Latin America. For example, in 1959 the Carnegie Foundation granted funds to the American Council of Learned Societies and the Social Science Research Council to establish a Joint Committee on Latin American Studies which has both supported scholarly study of Latin America and considered ways to expand research on the area. The Rockefeller Foundation, while supporting United States scholarship, has been increasingly concerned with the improvement of Latin American education, health, and agriculture. The Ford Foundation, having become seriously interested in Latin America in the late 1950's, has followed a double program of developing institutions and training personnel in Latin America, and strengthening research and graduate studies at selected United States institutions.

## Business Enterprises

The role of United States business in Latin America is significant both because it is frequently able to influence policy decisions in Washington and because certain of its activities in Latin America create tensions in relations between the United States and Latin American countries. Business interests, for example, have consistently pressed for government promotion of unfettered free enterprise in Latin America and for government protection of both specific products and investments in general. Problems in United States-Latin American relations are based on the residue of ill will acquired earlier in the twentieth century when aggressive and unenlightened United States business enterprise not only made no attempt to accommodate itself to the sentiments and traditions of Latin America but also was felt to have despoiled certain areas without adequate compensation and to have intervened ruthlessly in the domestic political affairs of certain nations. Superimposed upon that unfortunate heritage is the vital part that United States industrial interests continue to play in the economic life of some countries. For example, United States corporations control most of the copper and oil production that provides the bulk of foreign exchange for Chile and Venezuela, respectively, leading those nations to feel themselves at the mercy of foreign interests. Finally, by the mere fact of its foreignness, United States business creates tensions in relations with areas where an already strong spirit of nationalism is still growing.

Since the end of World War II United States business enterprise in Latin America has made efforts to improve its position. Greater managerial responsibility has been delegated to nationals of countries in which operations are carried on. Demands that larger shares of profits be made available for use within host countries have not been resisted. Attempts have even been made to contribute to national economic development, outstanding among which have been the activities of such large corporations as Standard Oil of New Jersey's Venezuelan subsidiary, Creole Petroleum, and the Grace Company, which operates in several west coast South American countries. But the problems raised by United States business in Latin America remain far from solved, aggravated as they are by increasing nationalistic fervor and the fact that many United States businessmen continue to share their fellow countrymen's unfortunate illusions concerning Latin America and thus find it difficult to deal with that fervor.

## Government-Controlled Policy Instruments

Those policy instruments directly controlled by the United States government are of two general kinds: those related to education and information services and those traditionally associated with formation and execution of foreign policy. In the former group are several agencies, such as the Departments of State, Commerce, and Labor, that include among their duties the dissemination of information about Latin America. But especially important in this sphere are the Library of Congress, the National Defense Education Act, and two government-supported foundations. The Library is one of the world's greatest repositories of publications on Latin America; its Hispanic Foundation, among many other activities, both publishes the *Handbook of Latin American Studies*, a unique annual bibliography of current material in a wide range of scholarly fields, and promotes the study of Latin America in the United States. The National Defense Education Act, passed and repassed since 1960, supports both university and field studies in the languages and cultures of certain presumably "critical" world areas, including Latin America. Finally, both the National Science Foundation and the National Endowment for the Humanities constitute sources of financial backing for research on Latin America.

## The Foreign Service

Important among those government-controlled instruments traditionally associated with United States foreign policy is the Foreign Service. The effectiveness of this well-known service in its Latin American operations seems to suffer because of the low esteem in which Latin American posts are held by many Foreign Service officers. This attitude reflects not only the more important role of the larger European nations in world affairs but also the bias of United States culture and acts to impair the quality of official United States relations with the various nations of Latin America. Serving further to vitiate the competence of the Foreign Service is its practice of rotating officers to new posts after relatively short tours of duty, usually about three years. The practice of rotation responds to the service's desires to distribute equitably the more and the less desirable posts, to provide its personnel with a broad view of the foreign policy problems of the United States, and to prevent excessive personal involvement and identification of its officers with the interests of any single nation. The last of those three purposes should be seriously reevaluated. Not only does the United States' lack of intimate and fundamental understanding of the interests of the various Latin American countries constitute one of the more serious obstacles to mutually satisfactory relations, but its extreme shortage of high-ranking officers with a broad knowledge and experience in Latin America is detrimental to the guidance of junior officers on short tours of duty and to the defense of the interests of Latin American countries in Washington where hundreds of officials who know absolutely nothing about Latin America are superbly well equipped to defend the powerful United States against the possibly excessive pretensions of the weak Latin American nations.

## The Public Information and Cultural Relations Program

The official propaganda arm of the government seeks to create a favorable image of the United States abroad and to inspire foreign countries to emulate the United States in domestic affairs and support it in world affairs. Development of a favorable image is a long-term matter and will ultimately depend upon how the United States *acts* rather than upon what it *says*. But the information program plays a continuing and vital role in the current international political struggle by working for support of specific United States policies and by combatting the public information programs of countries hostile to the United States with either direct replies to charges or direct attacks upon adversaries' programs and policies.

The administrative apparatus of the public information and cultural relations program includes the United States Information Agency in Washington and a staff assigned abroad, including cultural affairs officers in United States embassies. Many different media are utilized in the program's mission of persuasion: radio, television, the press, motion pictures, and translations of books about the United States and by United States writers. In Latin America more than one hundred "cultural centers" are given some support for programs of teaching English and sponsoring cultural events such as concerts, poetry readings, art exhibits, and lectures. In Latin America also, key groups such as potentially hostile student and labor elements are paid special attention; labor information officers and student affairs officials are attached to United States Information Agency posts and selected individuals are sent on trips to the United States to see for themselves what it is like.

That the public information and cultural relations program has in the past seemed to accomplish little has been due at least in part to its false assumptions, first, that all Latin Americans see the world in the same way, which is exactly as the people of the United States view the world, and second, that all Latin American nations have national interests similar to each other and to those of the United States. Responding to both criticism and experience, the program has been and is being modified so that it will be more meaningful in Latin American terms. If a reorientation toward reality is vigorously pursued, the public information and cultural relations program can be of great importance as a weapon in the international political struggles of the United States and can be an instrument of persuasion in the effort to develop a Western Hemisphere community of free and independent democratic states.

### Economic Aid

Another major tool in the implementation of United States Latin American policy is economic aid, including both technical and financial assistance. Aid may be used both to establish conditions conducive to democratic processes and to advance United States political and economic interests. In recent years funds have been granted to Brazil, Argentina, and Venezuela either to stave off threatening political situations or to prove that social and economic change can occur within the framework of democratic government. In 1962 the promise of a special loan to Haiti secured its favorable and decisive vote at the Punta del Este Conference for the expulsion of the Castro regime from the Organization of American States; but the following year all aid to Haiti was suspended in a vain effort to bring down the dictatorial government of Dr. Duvalier. Whether, and to what extent, economic aid should be used as a political instrument is discussed in Chapter VIII.

## The Peace Corps

A foreign policy instrument closely related to the aid program in purpose, but operating as a distinct agency with different methods and approaches, is the Peace Corps. It seeks to impart the technical skill and knowledge of the United States directly through the medium of dedicated United States citizen volunteers and to do so without the expectation of concrete political favors in return. Their useful work and their adaptable and positive attitudes have made the Corps increasingly welcome in many underdeveloped countries and have served to improve the image of the United States. The volunteers' more realistic and sophisticated view of the people and life of areas where they have worked is especially significant, for they will play an increasingly important part in establishing a milieu, within the United States, for realistic and fruitful discussion of foreign policy questions.

## Diplomatic Recognition Policy

The question of recognition, as an instrument of foreign policy, does not ordinarily arise when a foreign government experiences a constitutionally anticipated change. It is the use of force, or extra-legal devices, that raises the matter. The tremendous economic and political power of the United States makes it desirable although not essential to any revolutionary Latin American regime to obtain Washington's recognition as soon as possible. Failure to do so would be interpreted as disapproval by the United States of the new regime, or as doubt of its capacity for survival, and might encourage the revolt of opposition elements.

Controversy over the use of recognition as a political tool has revolved around the question of whether the United States should grant automatic acceptance of any de facto controlling regime that assumes the previous government's international obligations, or whether it should exact other conditions as the price of de jure recognition. This is a delicate and complicated matter, for the possible preconditions of de jure recognition may cover a broad range of economic and political concessions. Major recognition quarrels have sprung from United States attempts to secure a government favorable to its political and economic interests. An outstanding example of this was President Wilson's insistence upon a constitutional regime in Mexico following the 1913 overthrow of Madero—a demand that delayed reestablishment of Mexican-United States relations for three bitter years. More recently, since 1961 nonrecognition has been used to promote a desired form of government in Peru, the Dominican Republic, El Salvador, and Bolivia.

Supporters of recognition as a tool of diplomacy believe that the United States should use the threat of nonrecognition to discourage military coups d'etat against legally constituted regimes and to encourage the development of democracy in Latin America. While this position seems superficially reasonable, it is open to question upon two bases. The first is doubt as to whether such a practice would be consonant with the United States' goal of a community of nations ". . . free to choose their own future and their own system. . . ." Does the United States have the prerogative to sit in judgment upon another nation's type of government, so long as that nation does not seriously threaten the interests of the United States? Might it not be argued that the use of recognition as a tool is tantamount to intervention in the internal affairs of a supposedly independent people and thus betrays the principles for which the United States stands and undermines its position of moral leadership in the Western Hemisphere and the world?

The second question concerns whether recognition as a political instrument works. In most cases the answer is no. Unilateral nonrecognition, unaccompanied by other pressures, is not ordinarily sufficient to cause a radical change in a revolutionary regime. Wilson brought about the downfall of the post-Madero government only after depriving it of munitions while arming its foes. A Peruvian junta that seized power in 1962 did finally agree to free elections, but aid had been withheld along with recognition. It would appear that instruments other than recognition policy were more successful in gaining United States objectives in Latin America.

## The Monroe Doctrine

As an instrument of United States policy the Monroe Doctrine is today little more than sentimental fiction, however glorious its past history. Its basic assumption that the old world and the new should be mutually isolated has been repeatedly and firmly invalidated by both the revolution in United States foreign policy and the development of an Atlantic community of political interests. Moreover, various Western Hemisphere multilateral pacts clearly affirm official United States recognition that hemispheric matters are and should be of concern not to it alone but to all the American nations. Long before completion of those pacts the unilateral Doctrine had become anathema to Latin Americans. They resented both its condescending paternalism and its implication that Latin America was within the exclusive sphere of United States influence. Reactivation of the detested Doctrine would be interpreted by Latin Americans as a move away from inter-American cooperation and would deal a serious blow to the creation of a peaceful and democratic Western Hemisphere community. Finally, the Monroe Doctrine's objective of securing the peace and safety of the United States through unilateral preventive action can obviously be achieved with no reference whatever to that anachronistic formula; it can be achieved merely by defining clearly, as did President Kennedy in the Cuban missile crisis, what types of penetration in the Western Hemisphere would elicit unilateral, self-defensive United States action. While such a policy might in certain aspects resemble the Doctrine, the mere erasure of that hated name from the vocabulary of United States foreign policy would remove a continuing source of irritation from its relations with Latin American countries. At the same time the United States government would be freed to base policies upon a realistic appraisal of contemporary world politics rather than to react with a conditioned reflex inherited from a period of political isolationism.

*Military Assistance*

Another political instrument available to the United States for implementing its Latin American policy is the military assistance program. Although naval missions had been assigned to a few Latin American nations as early as World War I, the current program has its roots in the late 1930's when potential fascist penetration led Washington to undertake, in its own interests, the main burden for the defense of the Western Hemisphere. In cooperation with several Latin American governments, military assistance was increased during the war, and after a brief postwar decline was given a permanent basis in the Mutual Security Act of 1951.

In the early 1950's the United States justified such assistance on a purely military basis, claiming that the training and equipping of Latin American armed forces would enable those countries to defend their part of the hemisphere against aggression and free United States forces for service in other areas. Thus rationalized, Mutual Defense Assistance agreements were negotiated with twelve nations including Cuba; those agreements reserved to the United States and denied to its adversaries any part in training or equipping the armed forces of the Latin American signatory.

By 1961, however, the United States was forced to admit the obvious facts not only that in an age of nuclear warfare Latin America's contribution to the defense of the Western Hemisphere would be negligible but that the global nuclear stalemate virtually precluded direct attack upon any part of the hemisphere except the United States itself. At the same time the overthrow of Batista in Cuba and events in the Far East were vividly demonstrating the potentialities of guerrilla warfare and convincing Washington that the major threat to Latin America came not from outside the Western Hemisphere but from within, in the form of subversion. The military assistance program was therefore revised with the aim of strengthening the internal security of the Latin American nations. Under the new approach, which continues in effect, the United States commenced to provide equipment and financial and technical support for the establishment of counterinsurgency forces. Washington moreover undertook to ascertain the nature of the social, economic, and political conditions in each Latin American nation that produce internal warfare, sending to Latin America various scholars as well as utilizing the more "orthodox" techniques of intelligence gathering and interpreting. To complement the counterinsurgency program, Latin American armed forces were encouraged to undertake so-called civic action programs, such as road-building, school-construction, irrigation, and sanitation projects, all of which would not only contribute to national development but would more importantly improve civilian-military relations.

Whatever its official justification at any given moment, the principal basis of military assistance is political. In most Latin American nations the military possesses overwhelming influence—influence that the United States wishes to attach to itself and to its policies. Through military assistance the United States hopes to prevent Latin American armed forces from turning to hostile countries for supplies and training. Above all the United States hopes to appeal emotionally to the pride and self-interest of Latin American armed forces officers whose power and prestige are dependent upon the size and efficiency of the forces over which they preside.

Military assistance has aroused opposition in both the United States and Latin America. It has been charged that while receiving military support, dictators such as Batista and Trujillo—themselves army officers —cooperated with communists for domestic political advantages. It has been pointed out that even when Latin American nations have collaborated politically with the United States and provided it with strategic resources, their action has been based primarily upon national interest rather than upon the military aid program. Another objection to military aid has been that the program encourages military dictatorship by strengthening antidemocratic elements and that this danger extends even to the counterinsurgency program. In Peru, for example, democratically elected President Prado was forced from office as a result of a movement headed by antiguerrilla elements of the Peruvian army. After President Bosch had been toppled by the Dominican army, it was charged that ". . . both the police and the anti-guerrilla units, trained during 1963 by a forty-four man United States Army Mission, were used to hunt down Bosch's non-communist partisans in the name of anti-communism."[1] It has further been maintained that military assis-

[1] Edwin Lieuwen, *Generals vs. Presidents: Neo-Militarism in Latin America* (Praeger, 1964), p. 127.

tance, fostering a kind of arms race in Latin America, exacerbates existing rivalries among the Latin American nations and strengthens the military at the expense of desperately needed economic and social development, since a strong military often manages to wrest an excessive proportion of the national budget.

Finally, it has been argued that the military assistance program may actually advance rather than hinder the cause of communism in Latin America. Former President Eduardo Santos of Colombia, a conservative and anticommunist, has charged:

> . . . what we are doing is building up armies which weigh nothing in the international scale but which are Juggernauts for the internal life of each country. Each country is being occupied by its own army. . . . If in Latin America, the dictators prevail, if they continue to discredit freedom and law, a fertile field for Communist harvest will be provided. Why? Because our resistance will be gone. We are poor nations who have no investments or great fortunes to defend. What we would defend against Communism would be our freedoms; but if we have already been stripped of them, we have nothing left to defend. It is thus that the gateway for the communist invasion is thrown open by the anti-Communists.[2]

Proponents of military assistance, while admitting that there is some truth to such charges, reply that militarism is a fundamental fact of Latin American life; that United States aid is only a small fraction of most nations' budgets; that whatever the policy of the United States, a large part of the budgets of most Latin American nations will be devoted to the armed forces. Therefore, the United States should be realistic and cultivate the military who are so highly influential. This is an "if you can't beat 'em, join 'em" policy somewhat softened by the hope that "they" can be encouraged and trained to play constructive roles in their nation's development. It is a tempting policy, for at first blush it seems to reconcile the aims of United States security with the goal of developing a free and independent Western Hemisphere community of democratic states. The military will keep order and keep out communists at the same time that it assumes leadership in the promotion of national social and economic welfare, with some help from the United States. This is a simple formula, easily understandable and sure to win

[2] Edwin Lieuwen, *Arms and Politics in Latin America* (rev. ed.; Praeger, 1961), pp. 237-38.

the approval of the unsophisticated United States voter or his congress-man when the time for appropriations comes around in Washington. However, it is also simplistic, failing to take into account the complex and often bewildering realities of the individual Latin American na-tions, and above all failing to recognize that there are in Latin America groups of presently and potentially crucial importance that strongly op-pose military intervention in politics—groups that may, if such a policy is implemented, become deeply alienated not only from the United States but from even the idea of democratic government.

## Intervention

Intervention by military force is another instrument of foreign policy available to the United States. From a purely military point of view, it will be remembered that the United States, after freely employing in-tervention in Central America and the Caribbean in the early twentieth century, agreed to outlaw the practice in the Western Hemisphere in a series of pacts the first of which was signed in 1933. Subsequently, not-withstanding accusations of intervention in Guatemala in 1954 and Cuba in 1961, there was no United States armed intervention in Latin America until April 1965, when uniformed troops were landed upon the soil of the Dominican Republic. At that time the United States govern-ment indicated that it would not hesitate to intervene in other areas should circumstances require. That use of intervention as a policy in-strument is intimately related to the United States' use of international organizations to further its purposes.

## International Organizations

The two international organizations through which the United States may pursue its objectives in relations with the Latin American nations are the United Nations (U.N.) and the Organization of American States (OAS). They have in common two attributes: their charters pro-vide guidelines (one global, the other regional) for peaceful communi-ties of free and independent states; and both have failed to live up to the expectations and hopes of the United States.

## The United Nations

The cold war has not only made realization of the ideal of the United Nations difficult but has also aroused fear in the United States that the United Nations might become a vehicle for the extension of Soviet political influence in Latin America. This fear derives from a combination of three conditions: the U.N. Security Council's primacy over regional organizations in the maintenance of international peace; the Soviet Union's position as a permanent and veto-armed council member; and the intensification of communist party activity in Latin America, manifested particularly in the Guatemalan and Cuban crises. The United States has been concerned lest the Soviet Union, by exploiting its position on the Security Council, both extend its own political power in the Western Hemisphere and dilute the anticommunist activities of the United States. A Latin American nation, communist-dominated or otherwise, might be encouraged to take its differences with the United States to the United Nations, where Soviet influence would presumably assure it a more favorable hearing than it might receive in the OAS, where Washington's influence is strong. Moreover, the Soviet Union might use its veto to prevent U.N. imposition of sanctions against a communist-dominated Latin American state that had engaged in aggressive acts against noncommunist neighbors.

In adjusting its U.N. policy to meet such potential threats to its Western Hemisphere interests, the United States has exploited certain ambiguities in the Charter of the United Nations. In attempting to resolve a conflict between "universalist" and "regionalist" concepts of world organization, the charter clearly assigns an important role to regional peacekeeping and security bodies, such as the inter-American system, in stating that ". . . the Members of the United Nations entering into such arrangements or constituting such agencies shall make every effort to achieve pacific settlement of local disputes through such regional arrangements or by such regional agencies before referring them to the Security Council." Yet in another place that same article (52) states that articles 34 and 35, which give the Security Council the right to investigate all disputes and permit member nations to bring such disputes to the Security Council or the General Assembly, are not thereby invalidated.[3] The United States has thus been able to change its position from universalist to regionalist, subordinating its wish for a world community of free and independent nations to the exigencies of the cold war. In 1947 and 1948, when the threat of Soviet aggression became clear, the Western Hemisphere nations agreed to submit controversies among themselves to the OAS *before* resorting to the U.N. That agreement was strictly observed until 1954; since then Guatemala, Cuba, Panama, and the Dominican Republic have attempted to circumvent it. In dealing with those cases the United States, with the support of most Latin American governments, developed the principle that the U.N. *should not consider disputes simultaneously* with their review by the OAS. That principle collapsed in the 1965 Dominican crisis when, with the concurrence of the United States, the Security Council voted to request the Secretary-General to report on the Dominican situation even as the OAS was actively engaged in seeking a solution to the conflict. In regard to enforcement action, as distinct from the resolution of conflicts, the U.N. Charter states that ". . . no enforcement action shall be taken under regional arrangements . . . without the authorization of the Security Council." But because the United States sought political sanctions by the OAS against the Dominican Republic and Cuba, in the face of a certain Russian veto, it and other members of the OAS took the position that the term "enforcement action" referred to only military force and obtained implicit U.N. acceptance of that interpretation by the failure of the Security Council to take any position opposing it. In short, the United States has acted to restrict United Nations political activity and authority in Latin America and to establish the Organization of American States, in which its voice is powerful, as an instrument for attaining its objectives in the Western Hemisphere. And the Organization of American States would appear at first sight to be an effective political instrument.

## The Organization of American States

In theory the OAS constitutes a ". . . peaceful community of free and independent states," originally composed of all the independent nations

[3] Inis L. Claude, Jr., "The OAS, the UN and the United States," *International Conciliation*, No. 547 (March 1964), p. 10.

of the Western Hemisphere except Canada, and since 1962 excluding Cuba as well. The charter of the OAS requires its members to
maintain peace among themselves, to refrain from intervening in each
other's affairs, and to cooperate for their common defense and for the
promotion of their economic, social, and cultural development. Those
commitments have been amplified and defined in supplementary agreements. The Inter-American Treaty of Reciprocal Assistance brings the
United States and all the Latin American nations except Cuba into a
defensive alliance in which ". . . an armed attack by any state against
an American State shall be considered as an attack against all the
American States."[4] Its signatories promise to assist one another in meeting such aggression. Moreover, the signatories agree that "if the in-
violability or the integrity of the territory or the sovereignty or political
independence of any American State should be affected by an aggression which is not an armed attack or by an extra-continental or intra-
continental conflict, or by any other fact or situation that might endanger the peace of America. . ."[5] they will hold a consultative meeting to
agree upon measures to deal with that menace.

Complementing the Reciprocal Assistance Treaty is the Declaration
of Solidarity for the Preservation of the Political Integrity of the American States against the Intervention of International Communism which
was embodied in a resolution approved by all but three members
(Mexico, Guatemala, and Argentina) in 1954. "The domination or control," it states, "of the political institutions of any American state by the
international communist movement, extending to this hemisphere the
political system of an extra-continental power, could constitute a threat
to the sovereignty and political independence of the American states,
and would call for a meeting of consultation to consider the adoption
of appropriate action in accordance with existing treaties."[6]

The OAS should thus be a useful instrument to the United States,
and in several respects it has been. Since 1948 it has contributed to the
maintenance of a peaceful community of states in the Americas by

[4] Robert N. Burr and Roland D. Hussey (eds.), *Documents on Inter-American
Cooperation* (2 vols.; University of Pennsylvania, 1955), II, 172-73. Hereafter cited
as Burr and Hussey, *Documents.*

[5] *Ibid.*

[6] John C. Dreier, *The Organization of American States and the Hemisphere
Crisis* (Harper & Row, 1962), p. 51.

stopping armed conflicts and successfully mediating other disputes that might have led to open warfare. In the heated dispute of 1963-64 between the United States and Panama, the OAS contributed to the restoration of normal relations. It has given the United States a convenient place in which to hear Latin American opinion and a proving ground for ideas on how to deal with small nations in general. In recent years it has also played an increasingly important role in facilitating the economic and social development of the Latin American nations.

THE OAS AND THE CUBAN QUESTION. Nevertheless, the OAS has in certain respects disappointed the United States, for since the early 1950's its members have been seriously divided on the matter of how best to deal with communist penetration in the Western Hemisphere. That division was emphasized in its actions toward Castro Cuba. Many Latin American governments were at first unwilling officially to recognize that a security problem had been created by the Cuban–Sino-Soviet rapprochement. When in January 1962 Washington finally secured Cuba's exclusion from the OAS, it was barely by the minimum two-thirds vote necessary, and in spite of the open opposition of governments representing 70 percent of Latin America's population. In October of that year, the United States did receive unanimous OAS support in the missile crisis, for Soviet missile installations in Cuba unequivocally constituted an aggressive act under the terms of the Inter-American Treaty of Reciprocal Assistance. In fact, however, the issue was settled not by OAS intervention but by a direct confrontation between Moscow and Washington.

As the missile crisis subsided, the major Cuban security problem became, in Washington's view, Fidelista activities carried on in other Latin American nations. Here too the OAS failed to satisfy the United States. A committee established to investigate those activities reported that they were indeed a threat to the internal security of some nations, but the OAS failed to authorize effective multilateral steps for their elimination. At the same time several Latin American nations, including Brazil, Mexico, Chile, Uruguay, and Bolivia, continued to maintain normal diplomatic relations with Havana. Over a year and a half after the missile crisis, at the initiative of Venezuela, which had suffered severely from Fidelista-inspired subversion, the OAS called upon its members to break relations with Cuba and to adopt economic sanctions against it.

However, the governments of four of the nineteen nations represented did not approve the action, although three of the four eventually severed relations; Mexico continued to recognize the Castro regime.

Not only did the OAS react weakly and unenthusiastically to problems raised by the Castro regime, but its principles acted as a brake against unilateral action by the United States, which was forced, by the nonintervention doctrine and the rule that cooperative action has priority over unilateral moves except in the case of clear and present danger, to move with great caution in the use of coercion against Cuba. Thus the feeling developed in Washington that the United States had relinquished the use of its own overwhelming force in hemispheric relations in exchange for a system of collective security that could not deal effectively with the new problems created by insurgency and subversion within individual Latin American countries.

Moreover, the OAS had not been particularly effective in facilitating progress toward a community of free and independent democratic states in the hemisphere. Although, with the possible exception of Cuba, those states were free and independent, many were not democratic. Varying degrees of repression still existed in Haiti, Guatemala, Paraguay, and Nicaragua. Argentina, Brazil, Peru, Ecuador, the Dominican Republic, and El Salvador were to some extent dominated by the military. Following the 1962 military coup in Peru, most Latin American nations indicated little taste for cooperative political action against antidemocratic governments. And only slow progress, if any, had been made in most Latin American nations toward removal of social and economic inequalities that both inhibit the establishment of representative regimes and encourage totalitarian subversion.

THE OAS AND THE DOMINICAN INTERVENTION. The failure of the members of the OAS to behave as the United States would like raised serious doubts in the United States concerning the maintenance of the OAS in its existing form. The strongest of those doubts related less to the lack of progress toward democracy and social and economic modernization than to the inadequacy of the OAS in security matters. The question was thrown open for discussion when the Administration of President Johnson intervened in the Dominican Republic in April 1965 in clear contravention of Article 17 of the Charter of the OAS which states that "the territory of a State is inviolable; it may not be the object, even temporarily, of military occupation or of other measures of force taken by another State, directly or indirectly, on any grounds whatever. . . ."[7] Moreover, the Dominican occupation was carried out with neither prior consultation nor advance notice to fellow members of the OAS.

The landing of United States troops upon the soil of the Dominican Republic pushed into the limelight two long-festering questions: Should the United States use armed intervention as an instrument of policy? What future, if any, was there for the OAS? The confused and contradictory justifications advanced by the Johnson Administration and those who supported its action did little to answer the question of whether or not intervention should be a permanent tool in United States policy implementation. While at first the Administration justified its intervention as necessary for the protection of numerous United States citizens living on the island, it shortly confessed that the motive had been to prevent communist leaders and their sympathizers from taking control of the forces fighting to restore deposed President Juan Bosch. At first the Johnson Administration insisted that it possessed incontrovertible evidence that such a "takeover" was imminent. Later it admitted that this was a mere possibility and shifted its justification to somewhat more defensible ground. This was that existing OAS agreements obligated members, of which the United States was one, to defend the Western Hemisphere against the incursion of the influence of international communism; and since the OAS could not have been expected to deal effectively with the Dominican situation in time to prevent the island from falling into communist hands, the United States had been forced to intervene unilaterally in order to compensate for the defective OAS security system. That the United States sought not to evade but rather to fulfill the substance of its OAS commitments—in a manner unanticipated by the OAS Charter, to be sure—was clearly evidenced, according to those who justified the intervention, by the fact that the OAS was promptly asked to step into the situation and find a solution, as well as by the fact that once the island had been secured against control by international communism, United States troops were integrated into an OAS peacekeeping force designed to maintain order until the holding of free elections. Nevertheless, and notwithstanding its efforts to involve the OAS in the Dominican intervention after the

[7] Burr and Hussey, *Documents*, II, 183.

fact, the United States government made it clear that unless some means were found for future collective action against communist subversion, it would again employ unilateral armed intervention if it saw the need to do so.

The question still remained of whether the United States, in view of its OAS commitment on nonintervention, should use armed force in relations with other American nations, and if so, under what circumstances. In the United States a few specialists have favored rigid adherence to the doctrine of nonintervention, but more have accepted a certain, if small, degree of flexibility in the interests of United States security. This second group has in turn been split between unreserved supporters of the Dominican intervention and its critics. Supporters claim that armed intervention, as disturbing as it may be to Latin Americans, is preferable to taking chances on communism. Critics believe that the Administration acted precipitately, without adequate information, and with no regard for the interests and sensibilities of the members of the OAS. They have presented evidence indicating that United States officials in the Dominican Republic, fearful lest the revolution restore Juan Bosch and his program of reform, encouraged conservative Dominican military elements to request United States intervention.[8] According to them the Administration, badly informed and under the impression that it must choose between another Cuba and armed intervention, chose the latter and afterwards discovered that it was supporting a rightist movement and opposing a reform movement with popular support—a position from which it was able to extricate itself only through strenuous efforts to establish an unsatisfactory compromise interim government. Such critics charge that the Dominican matter was neither so serious nor so urgent as to have precluded prior consultation with other members of the OAS or, at least, advance notice of United States intentions and the reasons behind them.

The varying degrees of support and criticism of the Dominican occupation betray underlying philosophies ranging from total rejection of intervention as a tool of diplomacy, through conditional acceptance of its limited use, to complete approval of its regular employment as an instrument of United States policy. Somewhere along that range of options the United States will have to take a policy stand, for excessive,

[8] Theodore Draper, "Dominican Crisis," *Commentary*, Vol. 40 (December 1965), pp. 33-68.

impetuous, and unpredictable use of force in its international behavior ill becomes a powerful nation seeking a peaceful world community.

Reaction to the Dominican intervention within Latin America was as unfavorable as might have been expected. Nevertheless, when faced with the fait accompli, most Latin American governments accepted the establishment of an OAS peacekeeping force into which United States troops on the island would be incorporated. That acceptance was due less to enthusiasm for the concept than to the desire to have a voice in the ultimate resolution of the Dominican crisis. Latin American lack of enthusiasm was clearly demonstrated by the fact that only the military government of Brazil attached a substantial number of men to the peacekeeping force, while the large majority of Latin American nations did not even make a token contribution. Moreover, since the intervention most Latin American governments have resisted the United States suggestion that a permanent OAS peacekeeping force be established. Significantly, even the recently installed military government of Argentina headed by General Juan Carlos Ongania, which was expected to support the idea of a peacekeeping force, announced in November 1966 that it did not favor it. Nevertheless, the involvement of the OAS in the settlement is not without potential importance, for its stated purpose of restoring order and protecting democracy may have set a precedent for future collective intervention in the internal affairs of a member nation.

THE FUTURE OF THE OAS. As it had with the question of the use of intervention as a tool of diplomacy, the Dominican matter brought into the open long-smouldering questions concerning the basic structure of the OAS. The occupation's immediate repercussions caused a delay in a planned foreign ministers' meeting at which ways for increasing the effectiveness of the OAS were to have been discussed. However, it is important to note that, in spite of the United States' failure in the Dominican intervention both to abide by the principle of nonintervention so important to Latin Americans and to repent its actions, the inter-American system has not been destroyed. This is partly because of the importance that Latin Americans attach to the economic and social functions of the OAS and partly because discussions on ways to revitalize and modernize it were commenced.

Those deliberations began in November 1965, when the postponed foreign ministers' conference convened in Rio de Janeiro. It was there agreed to call annual rather than less frequent meetings of foreign ministers, to incorporate the principles of the Alliance for Progress into a revised OAS charter, and to make economic cooperation equally as important as the organization's security functions. A United States proposal for a permanent OAS peacekeeping force was not, however, acted upon at Rio; it was evident that the Latin American nations continued to resist, as they had since the early 1950's, the desire of the United States to mold the OAS into a more effective collective security agency, and at the same time that they sought to transform the OAS into a more efficient instrument for advancing their own economic and social progress. In spite of such apparently basic differences, disagreements on security matters have been largely over means rather than ends. Every Latin American government represented in the Organization of American States is just as anxious to prevent communist penetration of its nation as is the United States and each is therefore as concerned as the United States over the security of the Western Hemisphere. Moreover, it is significant that those governments that have most sharply and openly disagreed with Washington represent nations that most closely approximate the United States ideal of free and independent states—Mexico, Brazil, Argentina, Chile, Venezuela, and Uruguay.

Lack of agreement between such nations and the United States concerning OAS policies reflects basic differences in interests and attitudes. Hope of achieving agreement lies in a thorough understanding of the concerns of the Latin American nations in international affairs.

# IV

# International Interests
# of Latin American Nations

Those who seek to resolve the problems in United States relations with Latin America generally overlook the fact that the countries of that area quite properly cling to certain overriding objectives common to all sovereign nations: the assurance of their physical safety, and the safeguarding of the free development of their citizens' way of life. While it may at times be to their interests to contribute to the security of the United States, it is *their own* needs that are of primary interest to them. The erroneous assumption of the people of the United States that Latin American nations are primarily or exclusively cogs in the machinery of United States security is inimical to United States interests because it is both unrealistic and repugnant to the Latin American nations.

## Common Weaknesses

In pursuing their objectives the nations of Latin America have since their inception been forced to act from a position of weakness all the more acute in comparison with the mounting power of the United States. Today each of the Latin American countries is, by comparison with the world's greater powers, "underdeveloped." Moreover, except in Brazil, Mexico, and Argentina, questions of limited area and/or population appear to place a stringent limit upon their power potential in the immediate future. In addition, the abject poverty of a great proportion of those countries' populations both subtracts from the effective manpower pool available for productive economic, political, and cultural activities and adds to the strength of those divisive internal and external forces that feed upon human misery and discontent.

Augmenting the generally weak position of the Latin American nations in their international relations is a specific weakness in the industrial sector, reflected both in per capita productive capacity and in total industrial capability. Combined with and closely related to that weakness is their dependence upon the export of a few primary commodities to the more highly industrialized nations of the world upon whom they must rely not only for sophisticated manufactures but for technical skills and investment capital as well.

Finally, most of the Latin American nations function with administrative, political, social, economic, and educational institutions that appear inadequate to cope with existing critical situations, much less to provide the impulse for any meaningfully expeditious modernization.

Thus, in terms of practical international politics, the Latin American nations must rely upon other than physical power to maintain their independence and sovereignty. At the same time they must press urgently to improve their power position, something they can achieve in today's world only through the modernization of their societies. In the effort to modernize, however, they must have foreign assistance of one kind or another; this in turn raises entirely new problems such as prevention of undue foreign political influence as an accompaniment of foreign skills and investment, safeguarding of national resources against excessive exploitation for the benefit of non-national interests, and avoidance of cultural imperialism.

The fact that the Latin American nations share these common problems and interests as well as their historical and cultural roots establishes in a limited way the basis for their cooperative action in world affairs vis-à-vis the non-Latin American world. Among the Latin American nations themselves, however, there exist not only divisions that sharply differentiate the interests of each country from the others but unique national characteristics that strongly affect each state's international behavior.

## Nationalism

Nationalism in Latin America is not the parvenu that it is in some of the world's other underdeveloped regions. It is the sum of long-felt distinctions among the countries of the region and of an historical process in which the people of each country have shared experiences in triumph and disaster and in severe conflict with other nations, both inside and outside Latin America. The sentiment of nationality in Latin America was at first the attribute of the small elite groups that assumed power upon independence and was often superficial and imitative of European nationalism. In some countries—for example, Nicaragua and Haiti—the nature of nationalism has changed little; in others nationalism is now deeply rooted and widely diffused.

After the middle of the nineteenth century in certain countries the process of technological modernization and the sense of nationalism tended strongly to encourage each other, one often providing an emotional stimulus for the other. Improved communications enhanced the sense of national geographic identity, helping to counteract the strong regional sentiments of some countries. As modernization progressed, societies became more complex; new groups emerged—professional, industrial, and labor—that turned to the national government for aid in fulfilling their aspirations, justifying their demands on the ground of the "national good." In many countries these developments imparted to nationalism a populistic character whereby the welfare of the less privileged elements of society became equated with the welfare of the nation. Latin American nationalism furthermore tended to become xenophobic, at times seeing foreign threats to national autonomy where none existed. Independence in foreign policy became a highly cherished desideratum. Things foreign became suspect per se. In particular foreign investment and enterprise—an integral part of the modernization process—became the target of hostile nationalistic sentiment, their denunciation becoming an especially useful political instrument.

The interacting phenomena of nationalism and modernization have contributed to the creation in Latin America of twenty very distinct peoples, each with an individualized sense of national destiny, a more or less sharply defined concept of its own national interests, and a desire to assert its distinctive international personality. Any Latin American political candidate or officeholder who wishes popular support cannot ignore the nationalistic ethos of his country.

## Intra-Latin American Rivalries

Above all, the Latin American nations are concerned with rivalries among themselves. Argentina and Brazil vie for influence especially in Paraguay and Uruguay. Chile is often involved in disputes with Peru and Bolivia, nations it deprived of valuable territories in the late nineteenth century War of the Pacific. Peru and Ecuador have been almost constantly on the verge of conflict in recent years over a boundary dispute that supposedly was settled in 1942. Guatemala, which is viewed with suspicion by the other Central American nations because of its larger population and past attempts to dominate them, in turn views its larger neighbor Mexico with mistrust, referring to it as the "colossus of the north." Argentina and Chile have barely escaped recent military confrontation over an uncertain boundary and at the end of 1966 appeared to be involved in a rivalry for jet-fighter supremacy—a rivalry into which Peru was reported ready to enter in order to maintain its position vis-à-vis Chile.[1]

Such rivalries have always poisoned inter-American relations, and they still do. The Eleventh Inter-American Conference, scheduled to meet in Quito in 1959, has not yet convened, in part because the Ecuadoran government refuses to proceed with its arrangements until its dispute with Peru is settled in Quito's favor. In 1962 the endemic hostility between Haiti and the Dominican Republic threatened to break out once again and thus facilitate extension in the Caribbean of elements inimical to United States interests. In the same year Bolivia weakened the effectiveness of the Organization of American States (OAS) by suspending its membership because of a dispute with Chile. The indefinite postponement in 1966 of a summit meeting of American presidents suggested by Lyndon Johnson was attributed in part to conflicts and rivalries among the Latin American nations.[2] The United

[1] *New York Times*, Oct. 24, 1966.

[2] *Ibid.*

States government often becomes involved in these conflicts as the respective rivals seek its moral and material support.

Intra-Latin American conflicts have a special significance for those who seek to understand the real interests involved in the foreign policies of the Latin American nations. That significance lies in the fact that the Latin American nations regard as "fighting matters" disputes that have little meaning for European and United States policymakers, who are both poorly informed of the historical and contemporary bases of such conflicts and inclined to deprecate the possible importance of any difficulties among the Latin American states. The world in which Latin Americans live possesses a dimension that is terra incognita in Europe and the United States.

The decisive element in intra-Latin American conflicts—the element that makes the game worth the playing—is the fact that the various disputants operate on a basis of rough parity in terms of international power. The conflicts assume tremendous psychological and political importance precisely because they allow the Latin American countries (as they are *not* allowed in disputes with the great non-Latin American powers) to act out the role of sovereign, independent states in accord with their nationalistic aspirations. These intra-Latin American contentions, other than those today involving Cuba, have no direct relationship with the cold war; nor are they linked to the general political objectives of the Latin American nations in dealing with the great powers. To most Latin Americans their own disputes are far more vital than a cold war between superstates with which they are altogether unable to identify emotionally. The United States must not fail to take this into account if it wishes to have a realistic understanding of the interests of the Latin American nations—an understanding upon which any viable United States policy must rest.

## The International Latin American Hierarchy

Intimately related to past and present Latin American conflicts is another political concern based upon the hierarchy of powers that has developed in Latin America since its independence. Rank in this hierarchy is determined by such variables as population, size of territory, wealth, degree of modernization, quality of literary and artistic production, national unity, victories in war, and political stability. Brazil, Mexico, and Argentina are presently bunched together at or near the top of the pyramid. Brazil's position rests largely upon the size of its population and territory, its São Paulo industrial complex, its architectural contributions, and the optimism with which the country's articulate sectors regard its future. Mexico's high rank is derived in part from its large territory and population but perhaps even more from the apparent success of its social revolution and its successful expropriation of the oil properties of powerful United States interests. In addition Mexico has scored points for three decades of political stability, for its rapid strides toward industrialization, and for its tremendous cultural vitality. Although Argentina's position is somewhat less clear, its persistently high opinion of itself, its wealth, population, and territory, its past achievements, and the fact that it has traditionally challenged the hemispheric leadership of the United States entitle it still to a position near the top of the hierarchy of Latin American nations.

It is evident that the three nations that now occupy the top of the power pyramid have special quasi-vested interests in foreign affairs, and they cannot maintain their prestigious leadership positions in Latin America merely by echoing Washington's policies. This accentuates the demand of the Latin American countries for independent policies, formulated in accord with their national interests as they themselves see them and not as paternally interpreted by other powers. Those states seek, moreover, to assert what they regard as an earned right and proven ability to act autonomously in the sphere of foreign affairs. This conviction is strong not only among the "big three" but also in such countries as Chile, Uruguay, and Costa Rica which have achieved a high degree of political development, national consciousness, culture, and modernization, but which lack the wealth, population, and territory of Brazil, Argentina, and Mexico.

## Common International Interests

The relative impotence of the Latin American countries, their development needs, their nationalism, their rivalries with one another, and their desires to play meaningful and respectable international roles—all these factors not only influence foreign policy formulation in the Latin

American nations but also give those states certain common interests in their relations with the United States. All wish, for example, to obtain from that country the maximum assistance possible, in order to become more developed and thereby to become stronger domestically and vis-à-vis the outside world. But at the same time, all those countries wish to obtain the assistance of the United States without succumbing to its preponderant power. The same considerations apply, in varying degrees, in their interests toward all non-Latin American powers that are stronger than they. A major common objective of the Latin American nations has therefore been the development of techniques appropriate to the achievement of those ends.

Three general avenues of approach have served the Latin American states in dealing with the stronger nations of the world: exploitation of great-power rivalries; the obtaining of self-denying commitments from outside powers; and cooperation among themselves in the effort to create a counterpoise to the strength of the great powers. The first of those approaches, which has been in use since the Latin American countries achieved independence, is exemplified by the way in which Colombia played upon the rivalries among Great Britain, France, and the United States in the nineteenth century to maintain control of the potentially valuable isthmus of Panama. More recently Mexico employed the threat of supplying oil to Nazi Germany to force the United States into a settlement of disputes produced by Mexico's expropriations of the properties of United States oil interests.

In seeking to obtain from the great powers self-denying commitments that would limit the use of their superior force, Latin Americans have supported such international organizations as the League of Nations, the United Nations, and the Organization of American States, all of which sought an international rule of law in which might would not necessarily be right. Above all, Latin Americans have been pressing for acceptance, in international law, of their doctrine of nonintervention.

## The Nonintervention Doctrine

During the nineteenth century the Latin American nations, with the exception of Mexico, were generally successful in assuring their security as independent states, partly because of their will to resist great-power domination and partly because of great-power rivalries that combined with a lack of vital interests in the area to hold in check the extension of great-power political influence in Latin America. Consequently the failure of Latin American nations to gain great-power acceptance of the Calvo Doctrine prohibiting intervention was not, then, of decisive importance. However, when the United States achieved undisputed hegemony in the Western Hemisphere, it became impossible to maintain a great-power equilibrium and the countries to its south found themselves confronting an expanding, immense, and frightening power to which there was no effective counterpoise.

Following long and strenuous efforts, the Latin American states finally wrested from the United States acceptance of the doctrine of nonintervention. That acceptance was embodied in the Additional Protocol Relative to Non-Intervention, signed at the Inter-American Peace Conference in Buenos Aires in 1936 and ratified the following year by the United States. In that protocol the United States government joined with the governments of Latin America in stipulating as international law for the American nations that ". . . The High Contracting Parties declare inadmissible the intervention of any one of them, directly or indirectly, and for whatever reason, in the internal or external affairs of any other of the Parties."[3] Achievement of that doctrine's acceptance established a power structure theoretically favorable to Latin American interests, for at the same time that the United States was obligated not to interfere in Latin America's affairs, it was sure to protect that area against domination by any non-American power. In the foreign policies of the Latin American nations and in the minds and emotions of Latin American leaders the doctrine of nonintervention came to hold an almost sacred role, analogous to that of the Monroe Doctrine in the foreign policy of the United States and the minds of United States citizens. Just as the Monroe Doctrine sought to limit European activity, the doctrine of nonintervention attempted to limit United States activity. Just as the Monroe Doctrine was in time modified in response to the changing interests of the United States (as in the case of the Roosevelt corollary), so too has the doctrine of nonintervention been modified since its acceptance in 1937 by the United States.

The doctrine of nonintervention was originally considered by the

---

[3] Robert N. Burr and Roland D. Hussey (eds.), *Documents on Inter-American Cooperation* (2 vols., University of Pennsylvania, 1955), II, 114.

United States government as merely a ban upon the unilateral use of armed force to impose the will of a stronger upon a weaker nation. However, the need shortly developed to broaden the scope of the doctrine. In the first place the Latin American nations made the crucial decision to preserve and develop the inter-American system instead of abandoning its power of original jurisdiction over Western Hemisphere affairs to the United Nations. Several motives were involved in that decision, including the desire for a preferential position in United States foreign aid programs; more significantly, Latin America's oligarchic, conservative governments feared that Russia might use its United Nations veto power to interfere with security measures for the Western Hemisphere.[4]

In retaining a regional system as the court of original jurisdiction in Western Hemisphere affairs the Latin American nations voluntarily limited the use of their historic technique of playing off one great power against another. It thus became urgent to restrict further the extent to which the preponderant power of the United States could be used by Washington in its dealings with the Latin American countries. Moreover, it was by now altogether clear that although Washington was committed to refrain from armed intervention except under multilateral auspices, it might easily use its economic and political power "indirectly" to intervene in the weaker Latin American states.

Motivation for and reaction to a Uruguayan proposal of 1945 pointed up the need for further revision in the doctrine of nonintervention. Montevideo, disturbed by the severe repression taking place in Peronist Argentina, proposed that the inter-American system adopt a principle that would make it possible to intervene collectively in behalf of the "elementary rights of man"; and Washington, itself involved in a serious political conflict with Buenos Aires, seconded that proposal. While Uruguay's suggestion was not approved, it did inspire fear that future attempts might be made to intervene collectively against a member government that happened to be following unpopular policies. Such an interventionist possibility might, it was feared by Latin Americans, lead to degeneration of the inter-American system into a weapon with which the United States could intervene in the affairs of the Latin American nations, wounding their sovereignty and independence.

[4] Arthur P. Whitaker, *The Western Hemisphere Idea* (Cornell University, 1954), p. 172.

To avoid both that possibility and the danger of intervention through nonmilitary means, the Latin American governments insisted that the OAS Charter include provisions outlawing both collective and unilateral intervention and both military and nonmilitary coercion. Thus, Article 15 stipulates that ". . . No State or group of States has the right to intervene, directly or indirectly, for any reason whatever, in the internal or external affairs of any other States. The foregoing principle prohibits not only armed force but also any other form of interference or attempted threat against the personality of the State or against its political, economic and cultural elements." The charter nevertheless made it clear that enforcement measures called for in the provisions of the Inter-American Treaty of Reciprocal Assistance for the preservation of the peace and security of the Western Hemisphere would not constitute intervention. However, it left undefined and subject to consultation the nature of the aggression, other than armed attack, that might permit intervention under the terms of the treaty.

## Cold War Position

Since the signing of the Charter of the OAS, the international power structure has been drastically modified. In 1948 the nuclear monopoly of the United States gave it uncontested military hegemony, both hemispheric and global. Now, with the Soviet Union's nuclear power providing a counterpoise to the influence of the United States and with the constantly increasing importance of Communist China, the Latin American nations are once more in a position to use the technique of exploiting great-power rivalries to their own advantage. In view of the tempting possibilities provided by the problems of the United States in its relations with China and the Soviet Union, it is remarkable that only Fidelista Cuba among the Latin American states has sought to counteract Washington's power by developing a strong counterrelationship with either Moscow or Peking. The explanation for that lies less in Latin American fear of Soviet aggression—for it is clear that the United States would not tolerate that—than in Latin America's preference for the United States' goal of a world order of "free and independent states" rather than the Sino-Soviet system of totalitarian communism. That predisposition has been reinforced by gradual disenchantment of many sympathizers with the Cuban experiment. And Castro himself has not only chafed under restraints imposed by Moscow but openly attacked Peking for its allegedly exploitative treatment of Cuba.

Yet if a world order of "free and independent states" is to come about, the international implications of the Latin American nations' relative weakness must be taken into account. Those countries believe that they cannot be "free to choose their own futures and their own system so long as it does not threaten the freedom of others" while any possibility of great-power intervention in their destinies exists. While they have supported the United States when it seemed clearly menaced by outside aggression, they have been reluctant to approve United States proposals to give the OAS even limited powers to facilitate possible collective intervention in their affairs. Though the Inter-American Peace Committee of the OAS was authorized to investigate tensions in the Caribbean, including Cuban-supported subversion, it was required to obtain the assent of affected governments prior to entering their territory—a requirement that seriously impeded any effective field investigation at the same time that it protected national sovereignty. Brazil, Mexico, and other nations made clear their opposition to intervention in 1962 when they both supported United States action to remove Soviet missile installations from Cuba and stated that they would oppose the use of force to bring about the overthrow of Castro. Latin American fear that a proposed inter-American peace force might become an instrument of United States intervention has aroused sufficient opposition to convince the United States not to press for a decision on the matter.

The rigid adherence of the Latin American nations to the doctrine of nonintervention is due basically to their relative weakness. It is strengthened, however, by the conviction of progressive elements that any United States intervention would support conservative or reactionary sectors and thus delay urgent reforms.

Latin American opposition to virtually any kind of intervention, stronger than ever in the wake of the Dominican episode, makes it highly unlikely that the United States can in the near future build the OAS into an effective security instrument. Four alternative approaches to hemisphere security matters thus remain to Washington. It can adhere to the nonintervention doctrine and rely upon collective action under the Inter-American Treaty of Reciprocal Assistance, perhaps in this way risking the further encroachment of antagonistic elements in the Americas. It could develop a compromise position in which, under specified circumstances, unilateral intervention might be permissible if promptly followed by collective control. Or the United States might reevaluate its present policies with a view to finding new ways of achieving its ultimate objective—ways that would obviate the use of intervention. Or, finally, the United States might continue its currently announced policy of unilateral intervention when deemed necessary by Washington. The last course would almost certainly arouse constantly growing opposition among the Latin American nations, forcing them away from cooperation with the United States and into alternative policies consonant with their self-respect and their emphasis on sovereignty and independence. Among the alternative policies open to Latin American nations would probably be a strengthened movement for cooperative action exclusive of and inherently opposed to the United States.

## Inter-Latin American Cooperation

From the time of their independence the Latin American nations, and especially those of Spanish origin, have sought to build upon their common historical, cultural, and institutional heritage a structure of cooperation. In the nineteenth century several of those states attempted at various times but without success to counteract the power of the greater countries by combining their military and political forces. Much more recently, and with greater success, the Latin American nations have concertedly advanced their common economic interests. In 1948 they succeeded in securing creation of a Latin American-controlled United Nations Economic Commission for Latin America, which in turn became an important tool for further economic cooperation and paved the way for an important movement toward economic integration.

The movement for economic integration has had political as well as economic implications. Institutionalized with the General Treaty on Central American Economic Integration and in South America with the twelve-member Latin American Free Trade Association, economic integration has become a prime objective of many Latin American leaders, including those of the Christian Democratic parties which are assuming growing importance in several Latin American nations. The 1964 meeting in Caracas of the Sixth Latin American Congress of Christian Democracy revolved about the theme of economic integration in Latin America and approved a declaration that sharply emphasized the close connection between economic integration and politics. That Caracas declaration not only asserted that political integration was essential to economic and social integration but also proposed that steps be taken toward political union through the establishment of two supranational councils—one in the field of education, the other in economics—and of a Latin American parliament representing the legislative bodies of all the Latin American nations. At Caracas it was also advocated that the Latin American countries work within the framework of the OAS, in spite of its asserted inefficiency, to achieve several objectives, among them ". . . a unified attitude of vigorous defense by the Latin American States of their common interests in relations with the United States."[5]

Christian Democrat Eduardo Frei, President of Chile, took the occasion to insist that the United States intervention in the Dominican Republic had dramatized the need for economic integration as a way of achieving sufficient strength for the Latin American nations to act effectively in world affairs. In particular Frei urged that ". . . the twenty poor and disunited [Latin American] nations [form] a powerful and progressive union which can deal with the United States as an equal,"[6] and in addition play an important role in the OAS which, according to Frei, presently serves only the interests of the United States. It is evident that the growing number of Latin American statesmen who are of Frei's persuasion see in economic integration the basis for combined political action whose primary target is no other than the United States.

Such a view was clearly reflected in 1966, at a meeting held in Panama to discuss reorganization of the OAS, when the Latin American representatives combined to seek approval of a document opposed by the United States that would place United States social and economic assistance to Latin America upon a contractual basis. Whatever the outcome of that effort may ultimately be, it is a clear indication of a growing readiness of the Latin American nations to act in concert against what they consider to be the unacceptable hemispheric posture of the United States. It is evident that further deterioration in United States-

[5] *DECE*, Ano I, No. 1, Junio de 1964, Santiago de Chile.
[6] *Política y Espíritu*, March-April, 1965.

Latin American relations will serve to accentuate that tendency and perhaps ultimately to create a deep chasm whose effects upon the world position of the United States would be grave indeed.

## Conclusions

It is clear that the Latin American states consider themselves to be genuine nations with distinct interests that do not necessarily coincide with those of Washington and that, moreover, they are resolved to uphold their interests, most especially when they relate to or clash with those of the United States. This applies particularly to those more highly developed and politically sophisticated countries that the United States considers most closely to approximate the kind of free and independent state that a peaceful Western Hemisphere community would be composed of.

In seeking both such a community and its own security, the United States balances delicately upon a tightrope. If, because of its citizens' attitudes of superiority or lack of empathy for foreign cultures, or because of inadequate information, the United States fails to deal with the countries of Latin America as if they were already fully free and independent nations while simultaneously helping them further to develop, the nationalistic sentiment of the Latin American states will propel them away from cooperation with the United States and threaten its security. If, on the other hand, the Latin American nations are not truly free and independent, in the sense of being able to maintain their independence against internal subversion, then also the security of the United States may be endangered.

In seeking to place its relations with Latin America upon a sound basis, the United States must deal with twenty governments whose foreign policy decisions are just as subject to domestic political considerations as are its own. Intelligent diplomacy therefore requires a more than superficial comprehension of the domestic politics of the Latin American nations.

# V

# Domestic Politics in Latin America

In their domestic political activities the peoples of Latin America, like peoples everywhere, endeavor to manipulate the power of government for personal economic and social goals and for ideological purposes. However, certain historical patterns that strongly condition Latin American political behavior tend to distinguish it from that of the Anglo-Saxon world to which the United States belongs.

## Codification Versus Tradition

Whereas Anglo-Saxon cultures tend to conform to written codes governing political activity, in numerous Latin American countries there has been considerable disparity between written statutes—often expressed as "universals" rather than as individualized approaches to particular national situations—and practical traditions. Political change has frequently occurred violently or through procedures unanticipated in written constitutions, although those documents have generally provided for representative governments responsible to and subject to change at the will of a given electorate. Most Latin American codes have in some manner guaranteed the right of individuals to participate in the struggle for political power, but in practice free elections have been infrequent, political liberties at least partially restricted, and governments imposed and deposed by might rather than right.

### The Political Role of the Military

The frequent use of force as a political instrument in Latin America has led to the open and persistent involvement of the military, often with civilian support and encouragement, in the government of many Latin American countries. Such a condition is closely related to the long-existing tendency in Latin America to accept strong authoritarian leadership and to concentrate political authority in the person of an individual caudillo. Caudillismo and personalism have manifested themselves in benign form in strong presidencies as well as in cruel, violent, and despotic military rule and in varying intermediary degrees. While presidents in Chile, post-Peronist Argentina, and Colombia have exercised less power than many of their Latin American counterparts, and although Uruguay has utilized the collegiate executive system, presidencies in general tend to be extremely strong not only on the national level but in regional and local government as well.

### Men Versus Ideas

The strength of personalism further differentiates Latin American from Anglo American politics in party matters, for while in the latter politically active segments have tended to support organizations and programs rather than individuals, in the former the individual *líder* has been the focal point of political struggle. The Latin American tendency to give personal loyalty to an individual caudillo has facilitated the creation and perpetuation of strongman governments and has simultaneously impeded the establishment of impersonal parties. In Cuba, for example, Fidel Castro claims to be implementing certain socioeconomic doctrines, but the loyalty that he commands actually centers in his person and his followers passionately rally to the banner of Fidelismo rather than to that of socialism or communism.

### Image Versus Reality

Latin America's failure to adhere strictly to written codes, its tendency to accept authoritarian rule and to use force to induce political change, together with the highly personalistic nature of its politics, have all contributed to an Anglo American image of Latin American political life as highly unstable, unpredictable, and violent. As in the case of most stereotypes, this image is distorted. In the first place the "violence" of political change is usually superficial, with the number of participants limited and the life of the ordinary citizen little disturbed. In such cases governments merely pass from one group to another with little alteration in basic ideational content. In the second place the image is distorted because it has been indiscriminately applied. Chile, Uruguay, Costa Rica, and Mexico, which have for several decades enjoyed relatively peaceful political conditions, can hardly be classed with Bolivia and Ecuador, which have suffered frequent bloody upheavals during the same period. Nor can Chile, Uruguay, and Costa Rica, which have shifted power from one sector to another while maintaining stable constitutional regimes, be compared with Paraguay or Nicaragua, where internal stability has been imposed by the same force that quenches all political opposition.

Nevertheless, the pattern of political behavior in many Latin American states over a long period is reasonably well reflected in an image of uncertainty and the frequent use of force. This pattern of behavior today affects several nations in spite of their professions of faith in representative government. Even in nations with impressive records of constitutional government, violence and instability may not be sufficiently obliterated to prevent their reemergence under stress. But, lastly, it is important to realize that the nations involved have generally been able to function as free and independent, if not necessarily democratic, states, however unstable, violent, or unpredictable their domestic politics may seem to the non-Latin American observer.

## Rule by Elite

Historically Latin American political activity has also differed from the Anglo American in the degree to which it has been monopolized by a restricted elite. The latter, during the nineteenth and early twentieth centuries, moved toward increased popular participation, while in most of Latin America, even in countries with fairly liberal constitutional suffrage provisions, politics remained the private preserve of a privileged elite whose most important elements included the landed aristocracy, the upper members of the church hierarchy, and the higher ranking officers of the military. It was those elements that shortly after independence assumed control of the Spanish American governments. They were able to take power because the wars for independence were not social revolutions and left virtually intact the hierarchical authoritarian societies that had taken root in colonial times. Except in Brazil where it lingered for more than half a century, monarchy as a universally accepted source of political authority was replaced by written documents which, being not people but paper, failed in their role of substitutes for the monarchical tradition.

Those written constitutions sought to create impersonal government for peoples whose political orientation had been for centuries conditioned by a hierarchical system of personal relationships extending from the monarchy through the aristocracy down to the meanest level of society, for peoples who therefore found it difficult to transfer their loyalty from an individual to a codified abstraction. Moreover, the constitutions were symbols of nations, and nations did not yet exist in the minds of their supposed citizens whose feelings of patriotism centered upon the *patria chica,* that is, upon a restricted locality or region. Finally, constitutions that provided for representative government were not in accord with the social and economic realities of the time. In Latin America of the early nineteenth century a virtually unbridgeable chasm divided the upper classes from the lower. The latter, barely subsisting, lacked the will for self-improvement and accepted their traditional dependency upon and subordination to the elite—a relationship that seemed at least to offer some hope of physical survival. In each new country there was generally, however, a small emerging group of people whose profession, superior education, or less inadequate income cast them into an intermediary class. Those people, largely teachers, lawyers, physicians, and small businessmen, were seldom accepted as social equals by members of the ruling elite, and while some of them pursued egalitarian political goals, many sought incorporation into elite elements.

*The Elite Power Base*

In sum, when the theoretical, impersonal form of government that replaced the power of the Spanish ruler proved uncongenial to American peoples, that monarchical power came to reside in elite elements enabled to govern either because of their wealth or because their leadership was supinely unquestioned in a hierarchical society oriented toward personalism. The strong position of the large landowners rested upon their control of many dependent *campesinos* and their social prestige, accumulated wealth, and extended family connections with other members of the elite. High churchmen commanded obedience through spiritual influence over the masses, authoritarian ecclesiastical organization, and control of immense landed and other riches. While the power of landowners and churchmen had already been established in the colonial period, the independent influence of the military emerged during and after the long and triumphant struggle for independence when individual officers gained tremendous personal prestige. In wartime the principle of military subordination to the civilian collapsed and populations became accustomed to resolution of political issues by force. Upon the cessation of war, military caudillos in command of large and loyal contingents assumed positions of authority in the new states that they had helped to bring into being.

The ecclesiastics, generals, and landed aristocrats who governed the new Spanish American nations did not, however, constitute a monolithic oligarchy, for they differed upon such matters as specific bureaucratic assignments, central versus regional primacy, and the desirable relationship between church and state. Acquisitive landholders might seek to enlarge their estates at the expense of the church through government action; clerics might attempt to increase church stature by opposing state patronage and vigorously upholding special clerical privileges. Nevertheless, both groups shared an overriding desire to retain their privileges and therefore to maintain the social and economic status quo. Since many military officers had risen from nonelite ranks, their concerns were somewhat different. They tended, however, to seek higher social status through acceptance by and intermarriage with the landed aristocracy and thus in the nineteenth century seldom used their power to challenge the more traditional elite.

## Modernization and the Challenge to Elite Rule

With the onset of modernization, doubts arose regarding the viability of policies oriented to semifeudal agrarian societies, and new social and economic groups emerged to defy the political monopoly of the elites. The irregular and complex, but clearly discernible, drive toward modernization in Latin America began in the latter half of the nineteenth century and gathered momentum in the twentieth. It brought the Latin

American states into increasing contact with and likeness to the developed nations of the Atlantic world and placed mounting stress on existing economic, social and political structures.

Modernization was stimulated partly by the exploitative drive of non-Latin Americans and was in that respect a phase of first European and later United States expansionism. But modernization was also actively encouraged by certain Latin American elites seeking both greater wealth and a material and cultural milieu comparable to that of the world's more respectable and prestigious nations. Those two groups cooperated to bring about improved technological and material levels in several Latin American states. There was an influx of direct and indirect foreign investment in mining, agriculture, transportation, communications, and public utilities. Technically skilled United States and European citizens migrated to Latin America. Corporations were established, under primary control of the foreign sector, to operate mines, oil fields, railroads, telephones, electric and other utilities, and large agricultural holdings. The foreign sector was socially separate from, but in reality subject to the control of, the elite, and in the political realm the two elements became closely allied in efforts to maintain the status quo. Thus foreign modernizers became part of the entrenched power structure of certain countries.

While modernization tended at first to strengthen the elite, it eventually created new social elements that sought to smash the political monopoly of the elite and to participate in the material benefits of economic development. Gradually certain states lost their simple feudal agrarian nature and became more complex. The small middle sector of intellectuals, artists, teachers, government employees, and professionals became more numerous and was broadened by the addition of technicians, managers, and business entrepreneurs, many of whom were the sons of non-Spanish speaking immigrants. Moreover, modernization sired an altogether new social grouping of nonagricultural labor, whose most significant elements were mining, transport, processing, and manufacturing workers.

## Political Practices

The process of material modernization not only broadened and strengthened outgroups but, by means of the concomitantly developing mass media, whetted their desire for such exotics as decent housing and apparel, better health care, and education, and for social, economic, and political reforms in general. Even the traditionally inert peasantry of some countries began to yearn for an improved status and to see in political action the possibility of achieving it. At the present time, therefore, in significant portions of Latin America many different groups, ranging from the traditional elite through the middle sectors and factory and mine laborers to the peasantry, are involved in a fierce political struggle to capture the government in order to protect and advance their own interests.

## Dictatorship

The opportunity for such groups to pursue their political objectives, the techniques they employ, and their ability to influence government policies vary greatly from country to country. Dictatorships like those in Paraguay, Cuba, Guatemala, Nicaragua, and Haiti severely limit oppositionist activity in spite of the fact that they may occasionally permit elections whose fraudulent nature makes their outcome predictable. In countries with dictatorships, elements seeking influence sometimes choose to curry favor with the ruler; but more effective methods of attaining goals unacceptable to tyrannical government have been (1) encouragement of dissatisfaction within military circles so they will withdraw support of the current dictatorship, and (2) fomentation of strikes, passive resistance by socially or economically significant groups, violent street demonstrations, or revolution.

## Official Parties

Some Latin American countries provide reasonable opportunities for competing groups to press for their goals and to influence government decisions through means generally associated with representative institutions. However, where a single dominant "official" party has become domesticated, the possibility of direct oppositional influence is severely limited. Free speech, a free press, and even opposition parties may all exist and the opposition may even be permitted to hold a few seats in the legislature as a result of elections absolutely controlled by the official party, but competing groups must seek their goals largely within the ruling party, abandoning any thoughts of capturing the government. America's oldest and most successful such system is the Mexican, which offers divergent elements the opportunity to vie for influence within a political framework sufficiently disciplined to prevent any radical or unanticipated alteration in policy or personnel. Prior to a 1964 revolution, Bolivia operated briefly under a similar system, and Colombia may move in that direction if it can consolidate its present Liberal-Conservative coalition.

*Military Influence*

In another type of restrictive political system the military defines the limits of competition, posing as guardian of the national welfare and often justifying its intervention with the claim that a particular governmental or electoral decision "threatens constitutional order." There are numerous examples of such intrusion into political processes. In Argentina in 1962 the military demanded nullification of Peronist votes, alleging "disturbance" of the constitutional order, and ultimately deposed anti-Peronist President Frondizi for failure to form a coalition government of all anti-Peronist parties. Finally, after ruling for a time through a puppet and then accepting a legally elected president for three years, the military assumed control of the government again in mid-1966. In Peru a major political party, APRA (Alianza Popular Revolucionaria Americana), was bitterly opposed by the military which, when a count of the 1962 presidential ballots showed APRA candidate Haya leading, declared the election fraudulent, ousted a dissenting president, and assumed control of the government. When President Quadros of Brazil resigned in 1961, military elements delayed transfer of power to Vice President Goulart until the constitution had been altered to weaken the presidency; and then in 1964, with some civilian support, the military deposed Goulart and installed one of its own in his place.

*Representative Government*

In three Latin American nations—Uruguay, Costa Rica, and Chile—orderly representative government has existed over a relatively long period. Their citizens are thus assured that they can seek their objectives with relative freedom and influence decision-making without fear of military intervention.

## Pressure Groups

In all Latin American countries, but especially in those free of dictator-ship, individuals from competing groups attempt to further their inter-ests by banding together into organizations that range in nature from pressure groups to formal political parties. Some such aggregations are very loosely organized; others possess complex institutional structures but do not function primarily for political purposes.

### The Extended Family

Noteworthy among the former is the extended family which em-braces not only distant cousins and relatives by marriage but large numbers of godchildren and godparents, faithful servants, old friends of the family, and useful hangers-on. It is generally assumed that indi-viduals in power wield it to benefit members of their extended family, and certain families attain great influence over government policy. The status of the extended family engenders an exaggerated form of nepo-tism, with its attendant evils. But it also provides a stabilizing and mod-erating element in political life, softening the impact of frequent or violent governmental change, for certain extended families may encom-pass all or most of the political spectrum, thus creating within any party in power a brake upon excessive political revenge.

### The Military

More formally organized are chambers of commerce, agricultural so-cieties, trade and professional associations, labor unions, peasants' leagues, student organizations, the church, and—especially where they do not control government—the military. The pressure of military spe-cial interests, for example, accounts for the disproportionately large military allocations in most national budgets. Both foreign observers and Latin Americans believe that a substantial part of the funds ex-pended for "defense" should be shifted to economic and social develop-ment, and yet in most countries such a change might provoke open in-tervention by the military to preserve its privileged position.

## The Church

While many Latin American churchmen still cherish and strive for continuance of the old order in which the church was a powerful elite governing element, others are acting in harmony with a liberalized papacy to forward social, economic, and political reform. Clerical influence has expressed itself in various Christian Democratic parties and in the labor movements of several countries, and certain prominent individuals in the church hierarchy have taken strong and effective public positions against various dictatorial governments.

## Students

Competing organizations of university students have tended to reflect the national political scene. Some students are members of elite families and have influence for that reason; but increasingly, especially in the better developed countries, more students belong to the expanding middle classes. Students' influence as a whole results less from family than from the fact that they comprise an educated minority in countries where higher learning is at once respected and exiguous and where youth is numerically predominant and highly valued. Students are recognized as the nation's future political leaders and their generally well-structured organizations put them in a position, through strikes, demonstrations, manifestos, and agitation, to exert influence upon government policies—a position to which certain authoritarian governments have reacted by purging or restricting student organizations and even closing entire graduate schools and universities. Students tend to be both highly nationalistic and opposed to any type of imperialism, whether political, economic, or cultural, thus standing in a posture of opposition to the United States. The implications of that fact are especially important in view of the imminent significant expansion of enrollment in Latin American universities in response both to rapid population growth and the demand for broadly available higher education.

## Labor

In the more highly developed countries of Latin America organized labor has become a powerful pressure group. Even where the number of organized workers is small, labor can affect vital national matters precisely because it is an organized entity operating in a relatively unorganized agricultural environment. In some countries, such as Argentina, the fortunes of organized labor are related to those of political parties. In others, such as Mexico, labor is dependent upon government support and cooperation. In still others, such as Bolivia, it has come to wield power totally disproportionate to its numbers, virtually holding a knife at the throat of the nation. Everywhere organized labor is becoming an increasingly important factor in national politics.

## Political Parties

Expert observers disagree widely about the basic nature of Latin American political parties, particularly their ideological content and degree of institutional permanence. Frank Tannenbaum has recently written:

> There have been changes in Latin America in the last generation which have complicated and obscured the political scene without really changing its character. The spread of doctrines such as Nazism, fascism, socialism and communism and their adoption as party names have given foreigners and even some culturally Europeanized nationals the impression that something strange has happened in Latin American politics, that what had always been a personal phenomenon has become a matter of ideals, with the party and the ideology displacing the individual, the slogan more important than the leader, the law of greater significance than personal influence, and matters of principle taking precedence over friendship, family, and political clan. Those who have let themselves believe all this have simply lost their bearings. . . .
>
> The one thing that has not changed has been the caudillo, the leader, he who has "la suma del poder," who governs because he can, not because he was elected. . . . Leadership is personal. The basis of authority is customary rather than constitutional. The political unit is not the individual; it is the gang, the extended family, the community, and the Indian village, each with its own "natural" leader, each endowed with unlimited authority and each possessing the complete loyalty of his immediate followers.[1]

Robert Alexander, however, believes that ". . . personalistic groupings are becoming less and less important" and that ". . . political parties increasingly tend to be organized around ideas and philosophies, or

[1] Frank Tannenbaum, *Ten Keys to Latin America* (Knopf, 1962), pp. 137-38.

as an expression of some particular interest group in the specific Latin American country. Although individual leaders may play a key role in establishing this more doctrinal type of party, the party itself can go on without a leader. . . ."[2] Kalman Silvert, tending to agree, states that ". . . in contemporary Latin America, the emergence of impersonal political institutions is everywhere clearly visible to one or another degree."[3]

Such differences partly reflect the unavailability of reliable information, which in turn stems from both a Latin American disinclination to pursue the objective study of politics and a lack of interest in Latin American politics on the part of non-Latin American students. Nevertheless, it does seem clear that personalism importantly affects party organization in spite of the fact that some parties have moved toward an impersonal basis in some common interest or ideology. It remains to be seen whether they can survive any significant loss of leadership.

### Democratically Oriented Traditionalist Parties

It is impossible to describe in detail the multitudinous parties, quasi-parties, and coalitions—fleeting, semipermanent, or of long duration—of Latin American politics. They may, however, be differentiated on the basis of their degree of association with either democratic or totalitarian governmental systems. The democratic may be defined as those that advocate while out of power, and uphold while in power, competitive political systems in which governments change as a result of free elections conducted according to standards established in written law, and that permit freedom of political activity for opposition groups. While most Latin American political parties have at one time or another succumbed to the temptation to curb opposition expression, several have maintained a fairly consistent democratic orientation, among them certain elitist traditional parties founded in the nineteenth century and generally called Conservative or Liberal. Such parties are still active in Argentina, Chile, Colombia, Ecuador, Honduras, and Paraguay. Of more recent origin, but embracing both older elite segments and professionals, government employees, white collar workers, and businessmen, are the moderate Radical parties of Argentina and Chile. Also oriented to-

[2] Robert Jackson Alexander, *Today's Latin America* (Doubleday, 1962), p. 148.
[3] Kalman H. Silvert, *The Conflict Society: Reaction and Revolution in Latin America* (New Orleans: Hauser Press, 1961), p. 13.

ward political democracy are the noncommunist Socialist parties of many Latin American countries; Socialist parties are most influential in countries that have had heavy non-Spanish European immigration such as Brazil, Uruguay, Argentina, and Chile.

### Populists and Christian Democrats

Also democratic in their general line are two classes of political party of much more recent origin: the Populist and the Christian Democratic. The Populist parties claim to be indigenous to America and advocate those basic social and economic reforms that seem most appropriate in the given nation, seeking broadly based support primarily in the non-elite sector. Of these the most prominent have been APRA of Peru, Acción Democrática of Venezuela, and Liberación Nacional of Costa Rica.

Christian Democratic parties seek to implement the principles of social and economic justice embodied in the papal encyclicals Rerum Novarum and Quadragesimo Anno. Tending somewhat further to the left than their European counterparts, Latin American Christian Democratic parties favor government action to better the social and economic conditions of the less privileged, advocate meaningful land reform, and support anti-imperialist policies including nationalization of those foreign-controlled resources that do not contribute to domestic development. Of the seventeen nations in which Christian Democratic parties exist, those in which they have so far played the most striking roles have been Venezuela, Peru, and particularly Chile, where their candidate Eduardo Frei was elected president in 1964 by the absolute majority denied to his three predecessors in office who received only pluralities. Christian Democratic parties will assume increasing importance in the future because they operate within a framework of traditional religious and social values at the same time that their programs embrace the nationalism and reformism that are major contemporary trends in Latin America.

### Totalitarian Parties

Easily identifiable among Latin American parties with totalitarian tendencies are those inspired by European fascist models and active in Chile, Brazil, and Bolivia during the 1930's. Of these only the Falange

Socialista Boliviana survives, its leaders claiming to have adopted democratic principles.

Communist parties, notwithstanding their demands while out of power for the maintenance of democratic liberties, fall into the category of those with totalitarian orientation since they do not themselves grant such liberties when in power. They exist, legally or illegally, in most Latin American countries, but even where they are their largest their memberships are absolutely and relatively small. However, because of disciplined organization, ability to exploit crises, support of certain popular causes, influence in some labor unions, and the willingness of other parties to accept their help in highly competitive political struggles, the Communist parties have been relatively effective.

Less easily identifiable as totalitarian are the parties of the Jacobin left which, alleging an indigenous inspiration, purport to seek radical transformation of the social and economic structure through seizure of total power. The Peronist party of Argentina has been the most successful of these, inspiring and supporting similar but less successful parties throughout Latin America. Now operating clandestinely, Peronism continues to exercise great influence in Argentina in spite of its leader's exile and governmental and military efforts to restrict or suppress its activities. A similar party of more recent origin is the Fidelista party of Cuba which began as an indigenous party of the Jacobin left before making common cause with elements of international communism. Early Fidelista triumphs encouraged the establishment or expansion of similar groups such as the Frente Unida de Acción Revolucionaria of Colombia, and the Partido de Abril y Mayo of Ecuador. These and other such parties are still small, but they do have determined leadership and espouse programs that appeal to distressed masses.

## General Political Characteristics

No mere listing of some of the groupings in Latin American political life can convey the infinite complexity and subtlety of Latin American politics or indicate the difficulties that outsiders must surmount in order to grasp the essence of Latin American political behavior. The region's domestic politics cannot be described in simple, easily understood terms. They must be experienced to be grasped. Moreover, the influence in politics of the various elements varies from nation to nation, as do the traditions and patterns that condition contemporary political life. Ideologies and slogans that mean one thing in one country or to members of a particular social group may have an entirely different connotation in another environment. Since politics reflect a continuing and evolving struggle to advance complex and shifting individual or group interests, generalizations concerning the political role of any segment of Latin American society must be viewed with cautious skepticism, not excepting the remarks to follow.

The political struggle in contemporary Latin America tends to be interwoven with issues related to two widely and fervently held aspirations: the desire for socioeconomic modernization and the nationalistic ambition for meaningful independence and status. Those goals are intimately linked, for modernity establishes status which in turn inspires citizens' pride which enhances ability to maintain independence. While the politically articulate of all Latin American countries share these aspirations, they disagree over both their precise definition and the best means for their achievement. Some think of modernization in the purely material senses of industrialization, or the application of science and technology to agriculture, or the improvement and expansion of communications and energy production, or exploitation of various natural resources, or a combination of two or more of these. Others insist that social development must come first, that a prerequisite of modernization is the eradication of the attitudes, hierarchical class relationships, and inequalities of opportunity and wealth associated with the traditional semifeudal order in Latin America. Questions raised by such differences of approach are generally resolvable only within the precincts of practical politics; they include: Should industrialization be given priority over agricultural development? Should the expansion of education take precedence over increased energy production? Should drastic land reform be instituted immediately to destroy the traditional socioeconomic pattern, or should land policy seek to augment food production through forcing cultivation of presently idle lands and introduction of scientific farming? Should the state or should private enterprise play the dominant role in promoting modernization? What should be the nature of foreign capital and enterprise in a developing country? Can modernization be attained through evolution or is violent revolution necessary? Are totalitarian or representative institutions the better vehicles for rapid modernization?

Does independence consist merely of the right to exercise sovereignty without interference from other nations; or does it require that a nation be economically diversified and strong; or that it be relieved of all foreign control over its basic economic activities? Is it sufficient for an individual nation to find its place in the sun within the Latin American community or should it aspire to play upon a larger stage? Can independence and status best be gained through alliance with and cooperation with the United States, through nonalignment or neutralism, or through cooperation with the Soviet Union or China?

Attempts to resolve these questions arouse bitter political feelings because they affect the individual fortunes, social position, power, and life style of those who exert political power. A decision to industrialize may promise great wealth to those favored with government allocations of capital and with tariff protection; but this may threaten the interests of importers of the items to be manufactured nationally, or increase the price of a necessity and thus reduce the real income of wage earners. The efficient and equitable collection of a fairly graduated tax may be opposed by those who will be required to pay higher taxes as well as by those who have previously evaded their obligations altogether, and this in spite of the fact that such tax revenues are desperately needed to provide sufficient government revenues for development projects that will ultimately benefit the taxpayer.

These and other conflicts of philosophy and interest promise mounting political strife in most Latin American nations both because of the nature of the differences themselves and because pressure for their early resolution is constantly mounting. Lack of a firmly rooted institutional process for the establishment of consensus or compromise in many countries will, moreover, encourage the increased use of force, in either repression or revolution, as a political tool.

## United States Entanglement

The United States must view increased political conflict in Latin America with concern, for wish it or not, it is inextricably enmeshed in the domestic politics of the Latin American countries. The involvement of the United States stems from the fact that its government and citizens are ubiquitous and vital elements in the process of modernization which contributes so heavily to domestic political strife in Latin America. The rate and nature of any given nation's modernization are certain to be influenced by loans and technical assistance from the United States government or by the thrust of United States private enterprise. In favoring one methodological approach over another, United States agencies and personnel inevitably take positions that coincide or conflict with those of various domestic groups and they may thus unintentionally or intentionally influence the course of politics. The persistence of the cold war accentuates the United States' involvement, for its policies may be automatically denounced as imperialistic even where they relate to strictly technical problems. Moreover, United States private enterprise may become involved in local politics, particularly where it controls large basic industries affected by and affecting domestic conflicts.

Defense pacts further entangle the United States, for in the prevailing atmosphere of intense nationalism, they pull the United States into almost any controversy touching upon the aspiration for political independence. Latin American politicians, like their counterparts everywhere, find it useful to accuse their opponents of "selling out the fatherland," or *entreguismo.* Although nations other than the United States have in the past been the alleged purchaser, or recipient, the wealth, power, and position of the United States, together with its present relationships with the Latin American countries, make it the preferred target for that charge.

### Attitudes Toward the United States

The utility and effectiveness of political attack upon the United States are variable and are influenced by attitudes of politically articulate elements toward the United States. Those attitudes may be described as an ambivalent compound of admiration, respect, liking, envy, contempt, hostility, and fear. The civic virtues of the people of the United States, their willingness to assume responsibility on the community level, their ability to compromise differences, and their relative honesty as public officeholders are admired and respected. Latin Americans are impressed by the stability of United States political institutions, the relative freedom accorded to large groups of the population, and, in particular, the economic productivity and high standard of living of the people.

On the other hand many Latin Americans deeply resent the arrogance of some United States citizens with whom they come in contact. Others are especially critical of what they believe to be a strong racist element in the United States national character. Many who strongly favor fundamental economic, social, and political reform are convinced that the United States government and business interests seek to maintain the status quo in Latin America. While the Alliance for Progress has led some to conclude that Washington has seen the error of its ways, others see the Alliance as an instrument of United States penetration and control or as simply a defensive program forced upon Washington by Fidelismo. Even those who believe that the United States is sincere feel that it does not go far enough toward reform.

In contrast, those Latin Americans eager to preserve their privileges are equally hostile to the United States, believing that its influence disrupts the social system and values that they cherish. Presently privileged traditionalists denounce "Yankee materialism" and object to the contagion of democratic and egalitarian doctrines from the United States. Some elite elements regard the Alliance as a United States instrument for the subversion of established and desirable order.

*Fear of United States Power*

Underlying such contradictory hostile attitudes is fear not of being politically or territorially conquered in the traditional mode of imperialism but of being submerged psychologically and overwhelmed politically, economically, and culturally by the brute mass of United States influence that makes itself felt with or without the conscious will of the United States government and people. That diffuse anxiety stimulates—and is in turn stimulated by—extreme nationalistic hypersensitivity to "outside" interference. Lastly, the generalized anxiety of the Latin American peoples over United States influence on their lives and fates is heightened by their conviction that the United States knows little and cares less about their concerns and problems.

It is generally felt in Latin America that citizens of the United States view Latin American nations solely in terms of trade and security. Consequently, it is feared, the United States is inherently disposed to use its power to mold those nations into useful units in its own security and economic systems, suppressing the emergent international personalities of the Latin American countries. This view is strengthened by their interpretations of recent relations with the United States—that the United States lost interest in Latin America after gaining its cooperation against the Axis in World War II, and that it came courting again only when the Castro revolution extended the cold war to the Western Hemisphere.

Latin Americans' fear of United States domination is further reinforced by their universal feeling that the people of the United States consider themselves vastly superior. It is clear that such sentiments could in and of themselves encourage the subordination of "inferior" Latin American interests to those of the "superior" United States. This occurred, in fact, when under the Roosevelt corollary to the Monroe Doctrine the United States assumed unasked the role of policeman of the Caribbean, and again in 1965 with the Dominican intervention. Such fears are obviously sharpened by existing weaknesses, for peoples whose sense of inadequacy is great have a corresponding need to be treated as equals.

*Charges of Imperialism*

Fear of domination by and hostility toward the United States are constantly expressed in the tireless reiteration by politicians of a pejorative semantic complex centered about the term "imperialism." In addition to the traditional use of "imperialism" to refer to extension of political, commercial, or territorial control, contemporary Latin American politicians use the term and its variations to describe any foreign activity whatsoever that appears in any way to damage their own or to enhance their opponents' personal or political position. The deliberate distortion and misapplication of the term not only creates an atmosphere of unproductive tension in foreign relations but threatens to prevent the identification and successful handling of real threats of an imperialistic nature. However, the charge of imperialism is very useful politically, for although its precise meaning is hazy, it is certainly a "bad thing." Its use is calculated to exploit the conviction that "something is wrong"—which it is—while simultaneously placing the blame at the doorstep of some detested foreigner and avoiding the need for action on the personal or national level. For the many adherents of the conspiratorial view of history, the charge "imperialist" plays in Latin America a role identical to the cry of "communist" in the United States.

# VI

# United States Involvement in Latin America's Politics

The United States, whether it wishes to be or not, is involved in the domestic politics of the Latin American nations. The effects of that involvement vary from nation to nation. The reactions within a particular country to United States policies and activities, however, are somewhat predictable according to the degree of development of the country. This chapter discusses the domestic politics of several Latin American nations as a means of illustrating United States involvement at various stages of the development process in Latin America.

## Argentina

A review in some historical depth of the politics of Argentina outlines the experience of a significantly developed Latin American nation. It illustrates well the conflicts that may arise en route to modernization and the way in which the United States may become involved in domestic politics.

### The Oligarchy

In the late nineteenth century Argentina was dominated by a small elite composed primarily of large landholders whose political arm was the National Autonomous Party, forerunner of the present National

Democratic Party. To its opponents this elite was and is specifically known as "the oligarchy." Seeking both to better the financial and social status of its members and to make Argentina a nation it could be proud of, the oligarchy cooperated with foreign interests in the material development of the country; it followed a foreign policy designed to expand world markets for Argentine livestock and cereals, to emphasize Argentine political sovereignty and independence, and to acquire leadership of the Spanish American nations in international affairs. Foreign investors and technicians, primarily European, were encouraged to build and operate railroads, telegraphic and telephonic communications, and other public utilities that both developed resources owned by the elite and provided the status symbols of national modernity.

In foreign affairs the oligarchy sought to prevent the transformation of economic dependence upon Europe into political dependence by (1) demonstrating that Argentina was a civilized nation capable of meeting its protective and financial obligations to foreign nationals, and (2) seeking to establish principles of international law, such as the Calvo and Drago doctrines, that would restrict the right of great-power intervention. The elite attempted to achieve a position of leadership for Argentina within Latin America by (1) maintaining sufficient military and naval power to contest Chilean and Brazilian strength in South America, and (2) challenging the supremacy of the United States in the Pan American movement.

In internal politics nationalism played a definite role. Elite politicians based their campaigns for office on a claimed ability to make of Argentina a *nation*. "This is no mere election contest," wrote Julio Roca during his 1880 presidential campaign, "but a question of whether we are an organized united nation, not just one of those 'South American places' upon which the world sneers."[1]

## Irigoyen and the Radicals

The exclusive rule of the oligarchy was challenged, beginning in the 1890's, by primarily middle class elements that formed two parties, the Socialist and the Radical. The former, although vociferous, remained relatively small; the latter ultimately became Argentina's majority party. In 1916 a Radical, Hipólito Irigoyen, became president, initiat-

---

[1] As quoted in Thomas F. McGann, *Argentina, the United States and the Inter-American System, 1880-1914* (Harvard University, 1957), p. 28.

ing a fourteen-year period of Radical dominance. But the party's objectives were less clearly defined than those of the oligarchy. Following achievement of the unifying desire to unseat the elite and gain control of government, various conflicting interests emerged in such Radical subgroups as professionals, shopkeepers, agriculturalists, government employees, and artisans, making difficult the adoption of a platform acceptable to all. In spite of certain limited advances in the spheres of social welfare, labor legislation, and education, Radical administrations left basically unaltered the economic and social structure that had been solidified under oligarchic aristocratic rule. In fact, many middle class elements appeared to be using the Radical Party more as a social ladder than as a means of fundamental reorientation of Argentine life.

*Introduction of Economic Nationalism*

Those Radicals represented by Irigoyen did, however, differ from the traditional elite in favoring economic nationalism as opposed to the use of foreign capital and skills in national development. Irigoyen sought both to enhance the power of the state through government ownership and control of public utilities, including petroleum resources, and to implement an anti-imperialist policy of eliminating foreign control over the economy. Toward the latter goal he took but one major step—the establishment in 1922 of a government organization, Yacimientos Petrolíferos Fiscales (YPF), to develop Argentina's oil resources. Notwithstanding its many rises and declines in fotrune, YPF became and continues to be a major symbol of Argentine nationalism and independence. Irigoyen Radicalism exploited the concept of economic nationalism for internal political ends by claiming that the oligarchy had sold out Argentina to foreigners, mostly British, sacrificing Argentine political independence in order to increase its own excessive wealth and power. Hence, the oligarchy was—according to Irigoyen—in league with foreigners, anti-Argentine, and unworthy of being entrusted with the government.

*Military Coup of 1930*

In 1930, after many decades of accepting its subordination to the civilian and remaining aloof from politics, the Argentine military led a successful revolt against the Radical government, taking its first step toward assumption of a major and at times decisive role in Argentine politics. Since then the military, whose only consistent policy has been to prevent any reduction in its share of the national budget, has supported now one and now another approach to the solution of various national problems. This lack of a political line is a result of the multisegmental nature of the Argentine officer corps which encompasses many varying social and economic groups differing widely in their views both of the role of the military in politics and the desirable posture of Argentina in Latin America and the world. The position of "the military" at any given time reflects the attitudes of its momentarily dominant group and may change with shifts within the military power structure.

Influential sectors within the military have favored such varied approaches to the solution of Argentina's problems as establishment of a fascist state, cooperation with rightist Catholic Action groups, a mass-supported dictatorship promoting rapid economic and social reform, liberal democracy with military guardianship, and oligarchic rule. In foreign affairs some military elements have stressed development of the economic and military capacity to dominate southern South America; others have favored a "third position" in world affairs; still others have advocated alliance with the democracies both in the Western Hemisphere and internationally. Whatever the military position, however, it has invariably been justified by fervent appeals to nationalist sentiment.

## The Concordancia

The 1930 anti-Radical coup was designed to establish a fascist-style dictatorship, but mounting civilian and military opposition forced a presidential election in 1932 that in effect restored the traditional elite to power through the election of the candidate of a coalition of the Conservative Party and the conservative wing of the Radical Party. This coalition, known as the Concordancia, managed—largely through fraud and corruption—to control Argentina until 1943. Domestically the Concordancia, seeking to combat the effects of the world depression, abandoned the relatively liberal economic policy of the oligarchy and moved toward economic nationalism, instituting various government controls and strengthening the YPF.

In foreign policy, however, the Concordancia differed little from the traditional elite of the late nineteenth and early twentieth centuries. It consistently appealed to nationalistic pride through political measures that appeared to enhance Argentine independence, to assert Argentina's role as a leader in Latin America, and to buttress its status in world affairs. Argentina rejoined and became active in the League of Nations, took the lead in settling the Chaco War, and opposed United States efforts to develop an effective inter-American peace and security system.

The anachronistic foreign policies of the Concordancia were, however, contrary to the trend toward economic nationalism. Instead of striving for the reduction of foreign influence, the Concordancia appeared willing to drift with the earlier pattern of cooperation with foreign interests for the achievement of economic development. It saw Argentina as primarily an exporter of agricultural products to Europe, leaving nonagricultural modernization to foreign capital and technicians. The notorious Roca-Runciman Treaty of 1933, embodying that view, agreed, in return for England's promise to purchase a specified annual amount of beef, to (1) restrict export sales by Argentine beef *processors,* thereby leaving this profitable activity in the hands of British and United States interests, (2) permit duty-free importation of British coal, and (3) grant favorable treatment to British investments. The Roca-Runciman pact permitted the foes of the Concordancia to charge with good effect that the government had sold out to exploitative foreigners who would keep Argentina forever in thrall in order to enrich the landholding, cattle-raising elite.

## Military Government of 1943

In 1943 a military officers' group known as the GOU (Grupo de Oficiales Unidos), disturbed by the growing military power of Brazil that resulted from aid received from its ally the United States in World War II, took advantage of the Concordancia's lack of popularity to bring about its downfall. This time the military itself formed a government whose major purpose was to make Argentina capable of competing militarily with Brazil and dominating South America. The new administration's overt sympathy for fascism and its failure to control fascist activities in accord with Argentina's inter-American commitments soon brought it into conflict with the United States.

As various GOU officers vied for supremacy in the new government, they sought civilian support. Thus a faction led by Colonel Juan Domingo Perón commenced to organize both rural and urban workers, instilling in them a high degree of political consciousness and a sense of their own power. Those *descamisados* were also encouraged to hope for an improved standard of living and greater opportunities for personal advancement, so that they were transformed ultimately into a potent collective political force demanding drastic economic and social change in Argentina. With their support Perón first won a dominant position within the GOU and then, in 1946, was elected president.

## Peronismo

Perón broadened and strengthened the labor-military basis of his following by constant and skillful exploitation of anti-United States sentiment. Before his election, when the United States government was using diplomatic pressure and economic coercion to force Argentina's abandonment of a pro-Axis policy, Perón accused the United States of intervention in Argentina's domestic affairs and assumed the role of defender of the national sovereignty against Yankee imperialism. In 1945, after United States Ambassador Spruille Braden publicly expressed his opposition to both the existing military government and Perón, the latter accused the United States of trying to influence the outcome of the election and adopted with effective results the campaign slogan "Perón or Braden."

The popularity of the Perón regime was due to a program that combined nationalism with economic and social development. Ideas that had only been mouthed by Irigoyen were now implemented. The railroads, largely under British control, were nationalized and British interests purchased. The constitution was amended, providing for extensive controls over private property and economic activity, declaring that mineral and other energy sources belonged to the nation, and stating that public services should be owned and operated only by the national government. Steps were taken to expropriate foreign-owned utilities and to develop state-owned and -operated power facilities. The Perón regime sought also to accelerate industrial development, in particular heavy industry, in order to reduce dependence upon imports of equipment. With the help of his wife Eva, Perón went beyond these measures, which were well within the confines of conventional economic nationalism, to make the social and economic betterment of the underprivileged working groups—the *descamisados*—an alleged prerequisite to the nationalist goal of a great and powerful Argentina. Only if the *descamisado* were adequately fed, clothed, housed, and trained, Perón maintained, could the nation become independent of foreign imperialism and lead in Latin America.

Wage increases, low-cost housing, social security, and recreational opportunities for the masses; tariff protection, subsidies, and other inducements for industrialists; and position, power, equipment, and pay for the armed forces gave many different groups and individuals a personal and real interest in cooperating with the political party that Perón established. In addition, many others were attracted by his attacks upon the oligarchy and still others by an independent foreign policy that aligned Argentina with neither the Western nor the communist powers but sought to cooperate with whichever seemed momentarily best able to advance Argentine interests. Perón sought, moreover, to create a "third force" in world affairs, and in particular to form a bloc of Latin American nations that would cooperate in international matters. In using as his rallying cry the need of Latin America to unite against Yankee imperialism, Perón merely followed in a more emphatic manner Argentina's traditional policy of challenging United States leadership in Western Hemisphere affairs.

Perón's downfall in 1955 resulted from the superimposition of economic and other failures upon a base of discontent that had existed since the beginning of his regime among those who either wished a return to traditional representative government or personally despised the "upstart" Peróns, or both. The regime's serious economic difficulties were the effect of (1) attempts to achieve economic self-sufficiency rapidly and at all cost, (2) a decline in the world market price of Argentine exports, (3) the high cost of worker benefits, and (4) excessive graft and corruption. As his regime skidded toward fiscal disaster, Perón declared a moratorium on pay increases and other worker benefits, causing his *descamisados* to lose some of their enthusiasm. Seeking, apparently, to distract national attention from the economic crisis, Perón turned upon the Catholic church, losing still more support in the process. Then, desperately seeking operating funds, Perón committed the cardinal sin of negotiating a contract with the Standard Oil Company of California for the exploitation of certain oil resources that had been considered since the days of the Irigoyen regime to be sacred to the YPF. Finally, Perón lost any chance of retaining power when he alienated the armed forces both by his inept policies and his transparently disguised attempt to arm the *descamisados* as a counterpoise to the professional establishment.

## Military Caretakers of 1955

The officers who succeeded in deposing Perón wished to reestablish civilian rule in Argentina. Toward that end they established a "caretaker" government, headed and controlled by themselves but cooperating closely with civilians, which was to relinquish power following a constitutional convention and the subsequent election of a new congress and president, for which a target date of 1958 was established. The caretaker government, headed during most of its existence by General Pedro Aramburu, sought as a necessary prelude to the restoration of representative government the extinguishment of Peronism. Its leaders were imprisoned or exiled, its party outlawed, its labor movement (the General Confederation of Labor) placed under government control. Government economic controls were somewhat eased and private foreign capital was welcomed in certain types of enterprise. Perón's nonaligned third position was abandoned and it was declared that Argentina would cooperate with the democracies in international affairs. Finally, to encourage the reactivation of virtually atrophied civilian political life and civilian participation in government, the caretakers established an advisory committee representing all major Argentine political parties.

## Problems of the Caretaker Government

The provisional government encountered serious obstacles to the implementation of its programs. From the previous regime it inherited an empty treasury, a gigantic foreign debt, an unfavorable balance of trade, and a national economy severely crippled by lack of transport facilities and energy—both of which had been disastrously neglected following their nationalization. However, Argentina might be rescued from its economic plight, it was reasonably theorized, by the effective development and utilization of its oil resources, for the nation was importing more than half of its petroleum at a cost about equal to its unfavorable balance of trade. The exploitation of petroleum resources was, however, a political rather than a technical problem, for Argentinians violently disagreed about the degree of national or foreign, government or private, participation in a process that all agreed was necessary. In order to arrive at a solution of the problem, normal political processes would have to be reestablished.

Argentine politics, as the caretaker government moved to restore representative civilian government, was a compound of pre-Peronist patterns and the more recently developed articulateness of the lower and lower-middle classes. Supporting caretaker efforts was the tradition of democratic government that had developed in the early twentieth century; parties of that era were reactivated. The largest of these was at first the Radical Party, which had survived in a vestigial form during the Perón dictatorship; but in 1957 that party split into two rival groups—the Intransigent Radicals headed by Arturo Frondizi, and the Peoples' Radicals under Ricardo Balbín. Other parties with democratic tendencies were the reactivated National Democratic Party and the Socialist Party, along with a relative newcomer, the Christian Democratic Party. But while the membership of those groups was predisposed toward a democratic system, it had so lost contact with the procedures and practices of representative government that it was unable to act effectively.

Another considerable part of the population was either uncommitted to representative government or actively hostile to it. While this group included small numbers of communists and fascists, its members were primarily those who had been politically educated under Perón. They were grateful for the concrete benefits and increased status they had enjoyed under Perón and were determined to retain and increase them. This group was, moreover, still strongly influenced by its emotional conditioning to the symbols and mystique of Perón. Perón had fused emotions of intense nationalism with goals of social and economic reform by insisting that betterment of the *descamisado* was necessary to the achievement of a great and powerful Argentina. From this the *descamisado* deduced that any program that did not help him directly was antinationalistic and that any non-nationalistic act, such as the leasing of oil properties to foreign interests for exploitation, was contrary to his personal interests.

Elements thus conditioned were an important and unpredictable variable in the politics of the caretaker period. With Perón in exile, his party illegal, and his labor union under government control, Peronists became both a dangerous political iceberg and a potential source of support for those who could manage to win their confidence. Although it is impossible to estimate the number of Peronists, it is clear from the way they were courted that Argentine politicians considered them numerous. Several extreme nationalist and neo-Peronist parties sprang up to attract their vote, and several of the reactivated democratically oriented parties competed for it, the Intransigent Radical Party of Arturo Frondizi most successfully. In his campaign for the presidency Frondizi emphasized nationalism and social and economic "transformation." He expressed the convictions that Argentina must be strong, independent, and sovereign; that the obstacles to this were the foreign imperialist nations and the grasping international monopolies that were allied with Argentina's traditional oligarchy; and that the provisional military government was also secretly and probably treasonably allied with the foreign interests and the oligarchy.

Making this catechism applicable to all urgent issues, Frondizi attacked the caretaker government's sponsorship of a 1957 Conference for the Defense of the South Atlantic to consider tactical aspects of the Inter-American Treaty of Reciprocal Assistance—a conference in which Brazil, Uruguay, Paraguay, and representatives of the Inter-American Defense Board took part. Denouncing Argentina's participation in the cooperative defense of the South Atlantic as subordination of its defense needs to those of the United States, the Intransigent Radicals insisted that agreements binding Latin American nations to the United States should be replaced by pacts leading to ". . . Latin American integration and avoiding the imperialist penetration favored by the dispersion of our economy and culture."[2]

### Oil and the Presidential Campaign

But the petroleum question proved to be the most explosive issue during the presidential campaign. The provisional military government had reactivated the YPF and ordered it to proceed immediately with an in-

[2] "La conferencia del Atlántico Sur lesiona la soberanía nacional," *Conducta*, June 6, 1957, p. 8.

crease in production. Among many obstacles to that, however, was lack of capital which it was proving impossible to secure either from the United States government, which insisted that private capital should be given the first opportunity to exploit Argentina's resources, or from the International Bank for Reconstruction and Development, whose charter prohibited loans when private capital was available, as it was in this case. Provisional President Aramburu was thus in a dilemma, for he had too severely criticized Perón's Standard Oil of California concession to consent to private foreign participation.

In answer to this problem a former cabinet minister in the provisional government, Alvaro Alsogaray, began publicly to recommend granting of concessions to foreign oil interests in *previously unexplored* areas, under the supervision of and in cooperation with the YPF. Alsogaray claimed that such an arrangement would ease immediate economic problems by reducing exchange shortages and providing capital for YPF's expansion. Moreover, running against the xenophobic tide, Alsogaray managed to attract a sufficiently large nucleus of support to organize a political party whose major platform was his approach to the oil question.

Alsogaray's plan encountered strong opposition from both the Intransigent Radicals and other traditional parties such as the Popular Radicals and the Socialists. All denounced Alsogaray and his followers as *entreguistas* and insisted that they were paid tools of foreign imperialist monopolies. Frondizi made a paramount issue of the matter, stating that "Petroleum is not only of interest for the development of the Argentine economy: it is of profound interest to its foreign policy. Scarcity of combustibles affects the military power of a nation. A country without petroleum can be pressured more easily; it is a weak country subject to the dictates of foreign political or financial powers. But a country dominated by a foreigner is also a weak country because its progress, its welfare and its self-determination are dependent upon that power which controls that essential factor of its economic life."[3]

Relying upon more than nationalistic appeals to attract ex-Peronists, Frondizi promised that workers' benefits would be maintained and increased and that, if elected, he would restore political rights to Peronist

[3] Arturo Frondizi, "YPF y la defensa de la soberanía nacional," text distributed at a news conference, May 22, 1957, and reprinted as a supplement in *Programa Popular*, Buenos Aires, June 10-16, 1957, pp. 2-3.

leaders (although not to Perón himself) who had been stripped of them by the caretaker government. This promise, combined with other facets of his program, seems to have been decisive in Frondizi's overwhelming victory in the presidential elections of 1958.

### Frondizi's Presidency

In spite of a legislative majority, Frondizi's position in the presidency was extremely difficult from the beginning. An important sector of the armed forces deeply mistrusted his flirtation with the Peronists; inflation was raging; export income was declining; capital for economic development was unavailable; poor economic conditions in general made it likely that the high expectations of the *descamisados* would be disappointed. To meet these problems Frondizi adopted two somewhat contradictory programs that were ultimately to corrode his domestic support. In foreign affairs he enunciated a more moderate policy, calling for cooperation among the Latin American nations; participation in the United Nations; unenthusiastic acceptance of the Organization of American States (OAS); and correct, if not warm, relations with the United States. His actions belying his words, however, Frondizi promptly developed very intimate economic relations with the United States—relations that seemed to his critics to subordinate Argentine interests to those of the United States and to sacrifice middle class and *descamisado* interests to those of the "imperialist monopolies."

Deciding that Argentina must be rapidly developed and that this would be impossible without United States financial aid, Frondizi turned to the orthodox solutions that Washington was currently advocating for underdeveloped countries. Frondizi early retreated from his position on petroleum, issuing a decree permitting contract negotiations with foreign interests. Oil production rose; imports declined; and much foreign exchange was saved. But the nationalists who had supported Frondizi considered themselves betrayed.

### International Monetary Fund Agreement

Seeking both a basis for long-term economic development and a solution to the immediate economic crisis, the Frondizi government signed a stabilization agreement with the International Monetary Fund

(IMF) under whose terms private foreign investment was to be encouraged, free enterprise—as opposed to state intervention in economic life —was to be developed, and inflation was to be stemmed through a series of austerity measures. It was understood that upon acceptance of the IMF agreement Washington would provide the financial assistance necessary to carry it out in the belief that Argentina would become a Latin American showcase of the efficacy of free enterprise as a means to development. A few months later free-enterpriser Alvaro Alsogaray entered the Frondizi cabinet.

According to orthodox economic criteria Argentina commenced to make progress. The number of government employees was reduced, government expenditures cut, and the budget balanced; there was an increase of investment and productivity, and growth in the gross national product; prices and wages moved toward stabilization and the rate of increase of the cost of living declined. But while the government's economic program was winning praise and financial support from the United States, it was bringing on disastrous domestic political consequences. Because the IMF austerity program placed restrictions on wage and salary increases and removed price-reducing subsidies on consumer goods, the heaviest burden of the program fell on salaried and wage earning groups, whose real income fell. The austerity program also halted governmental expansion of social benefits and threatened curtailment of those already in effect. Moreover, it was widely and correctly believed that Frondizi's new economic orientation had been adopted to please the United States and obtain its assistance. Frondizi had, in fact, begun to behave in a manner contrary to the deep currents in Argentine politics that he had exploited and aggravated in order to gain the presidency.

The congressional elections of 1960 found Frondizi no longer with Peronist support and his Intransigent Radical Party in a decidedly minority position. Although under attack from all sides—Peronists, the anti-Peronist military, and many conflicting Argentine elements who nevertheless shared the nationalist conviction that Argentina must follow an independent and unfettered course in world affairs—Frondizi found himself forced to take steps that weakened his position even further. To appease the Peronists he lifted a prohibition against their holding important posts in the powerful General Confederation of Labor (CGT), which promptly fell under Peronist control, and thus further alienated the armed forces from Frondizi.

## The Cuban Question

Another crisis was created by Washington's attempt to secure collective hemispheric action against Castro. Early in 1962 the United States sought formal condemnation of any American nation's control by international communism, together with the expulsion of Cuba from the Organization of American States (OAS). The Argentine government, while still maintaining polite diplomatic relations with Havana, was not sympathetic to Castro. It was under great pressure, however, to abstain from drastic anti-Cuban action, both from Peronists who identified with the domestic reforms of the Cuban revolution and from Mexico and Brazil, the latter having just agreed to buy a large quantity of Argentine wheat. On the other hand the armed forces and various conservative elements bitterly opposed Castro. After failing to secure approval of a resolution that might satisfy the United States on one hand and Mexico and Brazil on the other, Argentina agreed to condemnation of communist domination but abstained from voting upon the Cuban exclusion matter.

Frondizi may have momentarily placated the Peronists and other pro-Castroites, but he further antagonized the military which now threatened to intervene in forthcoming provincial and municipal elections. Before this threat Frondizi broke with Cuba, and several weeks later it was announced that Washington had granted Buenos Aires a cheap long-term loan. Frondizi's enemies promptly charged that he was a pawn of the United States State Department, that the loan was a payment for the break in relations with Cuba, and that Washington now sought to keep Frondizi in power by shoring up the Argentine economy. In short, it was charged that the United States was intervening in Argentina's domestic politics.

## Military Intervention of 1962

A few weeks later, in elections for provincial offices and the national congress, Peronists ran candidates who secured 35 percent of the vote together with control of many provincial governments, including Buenos Aires, and several congressional seats. The alarmed military now made certain demands upon Frondizi for anti-Peronist action and when he failed fully to comply seized him, imprisoned him, and replaced him with another civilian, José María Guido, whom it instructed to rule by decree.

For more than a year the military, while promising to hold elections that would restore constitutional government, ruled through its puppet. During that period the United States, which had granted prompt recognition, continued to be a factor in Argentine politics. During the October 1962 United States-Soviet confrontation over Cuba, Argentina not only supported Washington's request for OAS approval of a "quarantine" of Cuba but sent two destroyers and a squadron of planes to help maintain a blockade. The new government attempted to return to the IMF stabilization program that Frondizi had felt it necessary to discard, calling Alvaro Alsogaray to the cabinet to reinstate the austerity program. And petroleum concessions continued to be granted to private foreign interests.

On all of its policies the new regime aroused heated criticism, criticism that Arturo Illia of the Popular Radical Party echoed in his winning campaign for the presidency in 1963. But upon assuming office Illia found himself confronting precisely the same apparently insoluble problems that had faced his post-Perón predecessors—problems that he had not been able to solve by August 1966 when he was ousted from office by force and a military government was established.

### United States Involvement

It is obvious that, intentionally or not, the United States has long been deeply involved in Argentine domestic politics as a result of activities affecting both the country's modernization and its foreign policy. Washington's insistence upon modernization by means of private enterprise has been forced upon reluctant governments that have then found themselves running counter to the deep tide of economic nationalism favored not only by Peronists and "leftists" but by the majority of politically articulate Argentines who have persistently associated it with the decline of the power of the oligarchy and with Argentine independence and sovereignty. Again, Washington's support of the IMF stabilization and austerity program has inspired the wrath of injured middle class and labor elements whose real income has been adversely affected by restrictions on wage and salary increases, by curtailment of social benefits, and by higher prices for certain necessities. It should therefore be no surprise that vast numbers of Argentine citizens view the United States in the doubly villainous role of obstacle to economic, social, and political modernization and the cause of their own personal hardships.

# Chile

In comparison with Argentina, Chile is poor in per capita wealth and small in population and territory. However, its well-functioning political system has historically adhered more closely to the ideal of representative government than has that of Argentina. During almost fourteen decades the constitutional order of Chile has been significantly disturbed only two times, and since 1931, under extremely adverse conditions, representative institutions have been preserved and strengthened. Chile has shared with Argentina such problems as malnutrition, illiteracy, lack of housing, and dislocations of rapid urbanization. But in contrast to Argentina, Chile has sought their solution by peaceful constitutional methods and without military intervention.

## Political Parties

The Chilean political panorama is cluttered with a plethora of parties and factions thereof, of varying ages and degrees of permanence, no one of which has until recently been able to command a meaningful electoral majority. Government by coalition has therefore been the normal situation, with Chilean political life characterized by continually shifting alliances formed first to nominate, then to elect, and finally, if successful, to legislate and govern.

For purposes of schematic simplification only, Chile's major political groups may be classified as belonging to the right, center, or left—categories that should not, however, be necessarily identified with similarly denominated European political parties. On the right stand the Conservative and Liberal parties, to one or the other of which the traditional landed aristocracy has tended to adhere. The major issue dividing those two parties has generally been the relationship between church and state, with the Conservatives taking an ultramontane and the Liberals an anticlerical position. The Conservative Party has recently been weakened by the strong emergence of the Christian Democratic Party. The Liberal Party, the stronger of the two, perhaps more than any other single political grouping represents the interests of business. From 1958 to 1964 the presidency, which is nonreelective, was exercized by Liberal Jorge Alessandri.

The Radical Party is centrist, moderate, middle class, and profoundly anticlerical, drawing substantial support from provincial landowners and businessmen and from white collar employees. Beginning in 1938 three successive Radicals were elected to the presidency, heading governments of center-left coalitions that adopted expanded social legislation and implemented a policy of economic nationalism and rapid industrialization. By 1952 the failure of that economic program could no longer be disguised; the Radicals suffered a severe defeat in the presidential election amidst serious inflation and the growing discontent of salaried employees and middle class business and professional people. Six years later, in 1958, Radicals and Conservatives combined with Liberals to elect the latter's candidate, Jorge Alessandri.

On the left stands the Christian Democratic Party whose extraordinary expansion has carried it from minute beginnings before World War II to brilliant victory in the presidential election of 1964. In that vote Eduardo Frei received the first majority, as opposed to plurality, gained by a presidential candidate since the end of World War II. That majority was not at the time, however, considered a true indication of strength, for both the Conservatives and Liberals had thrown their support to Frei in order to defeat Salvador Allende, the favored candidate of a Socialist-Communist coalition. The following year's congressional elections proved that the Christian Democrats had won massive support in their own right, for running on their own against Conservatives and Liberals as well as against candidates of other parties, they won nearly 56 percent of the seats in the Chamber of Deputies and twelve of the twenty-one seats then at stake in the Senate. The impressive legislative victories since won by the Christian Democrats leave no doubt they have become a major force in Chilean politics. The party's platform advocates implementation by direct political action of the social goals of Catholicism as expressed in the papal encyclical Quadragesimo Anno. According to Frei, fundamental and radical change in the economic and social structure is sought at the same time that both solely "free enterprise" and exclusively statist solutions of national problems are rejected. Within those guidelines the Christian Democrats do not for a moment hesitate to use all possible power of the government to achieve needed social reforms and to promote economic development.

All of the remaining parties on the left, when combined, possess a strength slightly less than that of the Christian Democrats. The two most important are the Communist and Socialist parties whose coalition, when in effect, is known as FRAP (Frente de Acción Popular). Those and the several other parties and fringe factions of the left favor somewhat more drastic reform of Chilean society than does the Christian Democratic Party.

## United States Involvement

Chilean political struggles revolve around issues of the social and economic reforms necessary to bring about modernization and the method of implementing reforms. Although the immediate welfare of Chileans and not questions of the cold war most often excite the interest of the politically articulate Chilean, the United States is nevertheless enmeshed in the country's domestic politics. This is partly because Chileans possess a high degree of nationalism born and nurtured by pride in a tradition of peaceful, constitutional, progressive government; important nineteenth century military victories over South American neighbors; and relative ethnic homogeneity. Nationalism sensitizes Chileans to interference in their affairs, and this, combined with moderate endemic anti-United States sentiment, encourages politicians to charge that their opponents' policies subordinate Chilean interests to those of the United States. Also involving Washington in domestic Chilean politics is the heavy investment of United States business in the copper and nitrate industries which are vital to the Chilean economy in general and to government revenues in particular. Differing approaches to modernization, because of their relation to issues of the cold war, may also affect the United States. For instance, Chilean politicians of the left may advocate solutions based upon the experience of communist nations, while those further to the right may look to the example of the United States and Western European nations; when Washington supports the latter as opposed to the former, it becomes directly involved in domestic affairs.

For example, FRAP has advocated the nationalization of United

States copper interests along with other basic Chilean industries, whereas a recent Radical, Liberal, and Conservative coalition had no misgivings about foreign exploitation of Chilean resources as long as the government received its reasonable share of the profits. The Christian Democrats, while favoring ultimate nationalization, have adopted the moderate approach that nationalization is not the sine qua non of good government and that copper may be cooperatively controlled and produced by the Chilean government together with United States interests. In December 1964, less than four months after assuming office, the Frei administration reached an agreement with United States copper companies under which the Chilean government would become a partner in several existing and all future operations, and their goal would be to double ore production and triple processing within the succeeding five years. That advantageous arrangement encountered so much congressional opposition from both left and right that Frei withdrew the implementing legislation pending new elections. The opposition objected to the tremendous political advantage that would accrue to the Christian Democrats who would not only win a victory for nationalism by bringing powerful foreign interests under national government control but also, by increasing copper production, would create significantly larger government revenues that could be utilized to carry out other aspects of the Christian Democratic reform program and in that way gain even further political support. In April 1966, following the decisively victorious elections of 1965, Frei gained approval of the copper agreements.

Differences over modernization methods have affected the development program worked out by the Chilean government under the Alliance for Progress. FRAP has criticized the Alliance as an instrument of United States imperialism, denouncing the administration that first accepted it. Christian Democrats deem the Alliance ineffective but do not see it as an imperialist tool; on the contrary, they have welcomed it as evidence of a change in Washington's Latin American policy. The Liberal-Conservative-Radical coalition regards the Alliance as an instrument for solving serious problems whose neglect might strengthen more radical and leftist elements. Importantly, however, the Liberals, Conservatives, and to a certain extent the Radicals have emphasized production and stabilization aspects of the Alliance in preference to fundamental reform of the social and economic structure. Parties of the left have demanded immediate tax and land reforms and have emphasized social as opposed to economic regeneration. Elements of the left have effectively denounced the stabilization program of the government as a sellout to the International Monetary Fund which they consider to be an imperialist instrument of the United States.

## The Cuban Question

As it has throughout the hemisphere, the Cuban matter has involved the United States in Chilean domestic affairs. Because the question is related both to modernization policy and to Chile's role as an independent nation in world affairs, it is particularly controversial. The social and economic reforms of the Cuban revolution have provided prototypes for some Chilean parties of the left, parties that claim that only through violence and/or drastic legislation can Latin American problems be solved. The Christian Democratic Party, at first somewhat sympathetic to Castro, has become disenchanted with both his foreign and domestic tactics; it continues to approve the goals of the Cuban revolution, however, and to uphold the right of the Cuban people to support any type of regime they wish to have. Parties of the right and center have favored neither the ends nor means used by Castro. The question of Cuba has therefore intensified the domestic conflict over how best to proceed with the modernization of Chile.

Washington's efforts to dislodge Castro have also affected Chile's international reactions to the Cuban question. The Alessandri government received much direct and indirect financial assistance from Washington, and since, despite the Alliance for Progress, the United States is widely believed to oppose all social and economic reform, leftist opponents of Alessandri charged that any Chilean action against Cuba was not only a move against social and economic reform and an attack upon the sovereignty of the Cuban people but was evidence that the Chilean government was willing to sell out Chile's independence for a few *Yanqui* dollars.

Chile's abstention on the vote to exclude Cuba from the OAS, while due partly to pressure from the left, did not satisfy FRAP which demanded that Chile quit the OAS upon Cuba's ousting. Eduardo Frei's Christian Democratic Party, on the other hand, found the abstention a satisfactory way of indicating sympathy for the aims of the Cuban revolution but disapproval of its methods. But the Conservative Party, one of the coalition supporting Alessandri, called upon the government to suspend trade with Cuba. Again, at a July 1964 foreign ministers' conference called by Venezuela to ask sanctions against the Cuban government for supplying Venezuelan revolutionaries with arms to foment a rebellion, the Chilean government found itself in a difficult position. The presidential campaign of 1964 was in progress and FRAP candidate Allende was openly sympathetic to Castro. The coalition that had elected Alessandri had crumbled and some of its parts were flocking to the banner of Christian Democrat Frei. In addition, a Radical faction was demanding that the government get tough toward Cuba. Alessandri had promised to be strictly neutral in the election of his successor, but obviously he could not wish to tip the scales in favor of FRAP and feared that if Chile voted for sanctions against Cuba in the Venezuelan case, the FRAP candidate might gain favor through the accusation that Chile had submitted to United States pressure. In maintaining a tough nationalist policy, Chile's representatives at the foreign ministers' conference made clear their dilemma and argued that it would be dangerous from the long-term point of view to threaten the balance of Chilean domestic politics in order to give stronger backing to the Venezuelan resolution. Chile abstained, only a few weeks later to break relations with Cuba on the ground that it was legally obligated to do so under the terms of the Inter-American Treaty of Reciprocal Assistance.

## Mexico

The political system of Mexico differs from that of either Argentina or Chile in being dominated by a single official party that since 1930 has given the Mexican nation remarkable stability. Above all, Mexican politics carries the stamp of the historical experience of the revolution—a movement that had some of the same objectives as contemporary Latin American reform movements and that had even before World War I begun the violent restructuring of the nation's social and economic system. The Mexican revolution sought land reform; social, economic, and educational benefits for the deprived; integration of the Indian into national life; industrialization and diversification; and nationalization of subsoil resources, the latter goal culminating in 1938 in expropriation of foreign-owned oil interests. Many of Mexico's reforms were, it should be noted, frequently denounced as socialistic or communistic in the United States press.

## The Official Party

The early stages of the Mexican revolution were marked by violence and governmental chaos which began to decline when, in 1930, the National Revolutionary Party was established, gradually to evolve into the present Party of the Institutional Revolution (PRI). From its beginnings the official party has been organized along functional lines and now contains sectors representing the major groups in society—agriculture, labor, and the urban masses—each of these divided into subgroups such as the Petroleum Workers Union, civil servants, small merchants, industrialists, etc. Conflicting groups struggle within the framework of the party and accept its decisions so that a united front is presented to those who challenge PRI's control of the government. At least token political opposition is generally permitted, and freedom of speech, political organization, and campaigning are ordinarily provided for. PRI, however, retains firm control of the legislative and executive branches of government not only through its control of election machinery but because it is both sensitive to the complaints of discontented groups and able to meet their demands if it seems wise to do so. The official party provides a mechanism both for maintaining stability and implementing a program of social and economic development that responds to the needs of the community.

This is not to imply that the PRI functions perfectly and that there is no criticism of its program and operations. In any nation with an average per capita income of less than $300, some elements will feel strongly that they are not getting their fair share. The PRI has in the past been able to resolve most such conflicts, but there have recently been open manifestations of discontent with government policies. Charges have been made that the party has lost its revolutionary impetus, has come under the control of capitalists and imperialists, has forgotten the agricultural sector, and has provided an atmosphere in which the rich have become richer and the poor poorer.

*United States Involvement*

Internal Mexican conflict has had repercussions upon Mexican-United States relationships, creating disputes that have been aggravated by a long history of strife between the two countries. That strife has left a residue of suspicion among people who live in close proximity to a richer, more populous, and stronger nation than their own, a nation moreover that not only has deprived them of much territory but that intervened during their revolution in order to protect the interests of United States citizens whom some Mexicans regarded as cruel exploiters.

A turning point in Mexico's relations with the United States came in 1938 when, following Mexican expropriation of foreign oil interests, Washington demanded prompt and adequate compensation but did not heed the oil interests' demands for intervention, and instead of upholding their claims for compensation, which Mexico considered excessive, submitted the matter to a mixed United States-Mexican commission for settlement. Washington's conciliatory attitude, coupled with Mexico's desire to consolidate the revolution, led to improved relations that prospered particularly during their cooperation as allies in World War II. Once again private United States investment began to flow into Mexico, this time under strict regulation by the Mexican government, so that by 1960 more United States private capital was invested in Mexico than in any other Latin American nations save Venezuela, Brazil, and Cuba; and trade between the two nations had expanded to the point where approximately three-quarters of Mexico's foreign trade was with the United States.

Although relations were on a satisfactory basis during the 1950's and 1960's, many Mexicans remained uneasy about the tremendous economic and political power of their northern neighbor. Moreover, aware of their nation's great prestige in Latin America, Mexicans felt able and entitled to play an independent role in world affairs. This attitude was reflected in Mexico's United Nations voting record which, except for Guatemala's, was more independent of the United States than any other Latin American nation's. Individual, influential Mexicans sought to develop some form of Latin American cooperation outside the Pan American movement as a counterpoise to the influence of the United

States; within the OAS the Mexican government upheld the strictest possible interpretation of the doctrine of nonintervention in order to contain possible expansion of United States political influence. Thus, at the Inter-American Conference of 1954 Mexico, by abstaining, showed its opposition to a United States-sponsored resolution opening the way for collective action against any American government that might come under the influence of international communism. However, it was the Cuban revolution that brought about a serious political controversy between the United States and Mexico.

## The Cuban Question

At stake in the Cuban controversy was the domestic political power of the moderates who controlled PRI and, consequently, the government of Mexico. The Cuban revolution had aroused widespread sympathy among Mexicans, who believed that Cubans were following their example. Moreover, as in Chile, policy toward Cuba became a focal point for a struggle over the best road to modernization. Leaders of the PRI's radical agrarian wing and of several labor unions sought to use sympathy for Cuba to increase their own influence in the PRI and to reorient its development program. This became especially clear when former President Cárdenas returned from a visit to Cuba with praises for Castro's reform program. But moderate elements lost enthusiasm for Castro as he moved into the Soviet orbit and began to encourage Mexican and other Latin American extremists. However, to denounce Castro openly or join in any OAS collective action would only play into the hands of the opposition who would accuse the government of abandoning Mexico's revolutionary tradition and becoming a collaborator of Washington with its reputation for enmity toward reforms that might disturb the status quo in Latin America. Mexico therefore adopted a policy of speaking favorably of the reform aspects of the Cuban revolution and upholding Cuba's right to carry out in Cuba any type of revolution it might desire; at the same time, however, the government restrained potentially troubling pro-Castro elements within Mexico.

In inter-American affairs Mexico sought to secure a compromise settlement between the United States and Cuba. Failing this, Mexico opposed not only collective OAS action but, by abstaining, the exclusion of Cuba from the OAS. In October 1962 Mexico did support United

States demands for the withdrawal of Russian missile bases from Cuba, but made it clear that it would not approve any invasion of Cuba aimed at overthrowing the revolutionary regime. Since that time Mexico has been reluctant to approve any coercive action against Castro. It opposed creation of an OAS committee to investigate Cuba's involvement in Fidelista subversion in other nations, unless it were provided that the committee must obtain the involved nation's consent. Mexico abstained on the resolution of the foreign ministers' July 1964 consultation adopting sanctions against the Cuban government; it has so far refused to comply with that resolution, although according to the Rio treaty, it is obligated to do so.

## Common Characteristics
## of Argentina, Chile, and Mexico

Notwithstanding their significant political differences, Argentina, Chile, and Mexico share certain crucial characteristics. In each a variety of interests representing the relatively complicated social, economic, and institutional structure of the nation struggle openly to influence the government. In each less privileged elements possess the means of making their influence felt upon government decisions. In each nationalism has been a dynamic force; and this dynamic nationalism has been not the property of an elite but has been broadly diffused and has acted not only to further the implementation of various national programs but also as a cohesive force for maintaining unity and stability and as a standard for determining the success or failure of competing groups and policies in contributing to the "good of the nation." Among the other Latin American nations these characteristics are already possessed by Uruguay, and it appears that Venezuela may be on the eve of acquiring them in a permanent form.

## Venezuela

Venezuela is of particular interest not only because of its strategic Caribbean location and its vast petroleum and iron resources, but also because it has been undergoing a nationalistic social and economic revolution peacefully within the framework of a democratic political system. Its success to date has served to contradict the Castro thesis that violent revolution is essential for Latin American development, and Fidelistas and other enemies of the United States have therefore attempted to sabotage the Venezuelan democratic regime.

In dealing with its problems Venezuela is in some respects better equipped and in others less well equipped than are Chile and Mexico in dealing with theirs. Venezuela, as one of the world's largest petroleum producers, has the advantage of great wealth that endows it with Latin America's highest per capita income and with sufficient government revenues to undertake a program of significant reforms intended to raise living standards, diversify the economy, and increase agricultural productivity. On the other hand, the present democratic Venezuelan political system, in sharp contrast to those of Chile and Mexico, has not yet passed the test of time and may at any point prove incapable of resisting a military establishment that remains almost as strong today as it was during Venezuela's long epoch of despotism.

Until 1958 Venezuela had been ruled largely by harsh military dictators who governed in the interests of a privileged minority. That tyrannical system gave way to a constitutional government with a multiparty structure in which no single group was to have a majority and which was perforce a coalition government. All Venezuelan parties have advocated nationalistic programs for development, although differing in the details and degree of nationalization and government intervention they support. The oldest and most influential party, supported by labor and the middle class, is the Democratic Action Party (AD) which was founded in the late 1930's and has held power briefly in the 1940's and since 1958. The two presidents elected since 1958—Rómulo Betancourt and Raúl Leoni—have been members of AD, the party that has provided the major impetus to the moderate reform program of Venezuela. In 1958, when AD received 49 percent of the vote, it was close to a majority party; but its influence has so declined that in 1963 it received only 33 percent of the ballots cast in the presidential election.

One of the beneficiaries of AD's decline was the nation's second largest party, the Christian Democratic (Copei), whose program does not differ greatly from that of AD, with which it has worked in coalition. Copei, polling approximately 20 percent of the votes in 1963, has prospered both because of its appeal to student and youth groups and because of the successes of its Chilean counterpart. Venezuela's third largest party is the Republican Democratic Union (URD) which won nearly 19 percent of the 1963 vote. URD is largely the personal creation of Jóvito Villalba, a popular politician who seeks support among independent middle and lower class elements. Formerly in a coalition with AD and Copei, URD has since 1960 been in the opposition. Fourth largest in the 1963 election was a relative newcomer, the conservative Independent Party, with 16 percent of the vote. Two other parties of importance in Venezuela are the Movement of the Revolutionary Left (MIR), formed in 1960 by discontented left wing elements in the Democratic Action Party, and the Venezuelan Communist Party (PCV). These two parties remain active, although they were denied participation in the 1963 election because of their agitation for violence against the government.

As in other Latin American countries the struggle for power among these parties revolves around issues of modernization and foreign policy and involves the United States because of the economic interests of its citizens and its foreign policy objectives. Although United States companies own most of Venezuela's oil resources, the United States government, bowing to pressure from domestic oil interests, restricts the importation of Venezuelan oil, for which the United States is the major market. Venezuela's economic vitality is therefore highly dependent upon the United States. Democratic Action and Copei believe in encouragement of strictly regulated foreign investment in petroleum and other activities, along with entrance of the Venezuelan government itself into the oil business. The Republican Democratic Union is more critical than they of United States economic activities, although it does not propose nationalizing foreign oil interests. The Independent Party, on the other hand, favors greater and freer activity by foreign investors, while the Movement of the Revolutionary Left and the Communist Party advocate nationalization of Venezuela's resources, particularly of petroleum.

The struggle among Venezuela's political groups over the means for modernization is also reflected in attitudes toward Cuba. Leaders of MIR and PCV claim that modernization can be achieved only through violent revolution. They accuse the government coalition of Democratic Action and Copei of being subservient to the United States because of its anti-Castro and pro-United States policies, and they advocate the violent overthrow of the government, accepting help toward that end from the Cuban regime. URD, while disassociating itself from the extreme left, is also critical of government policy, tending to be sympathetic to Castro and hostile to Washington.

## Brazil

Until 1964 Brazil presented political characteristics similar to those of Argentina, Chile, and Mexico. Since then, however, its political system has been undergoing important modifications whose ultimate significance is impossible to predict. The country appears to be vacillating between a multiparty and a single party system dominated by the military. The armed forces have controlled the government since the 1964 political collapse that resulted from successive administrations' failure to cope adequately with pressing post-World War II problems. Those problems, similar to the ones faced by Argentina, Chile, and Mexico, were the pressures, tensions, and dislocations resulting from the attempt to accelerate the transformation from a traditional to a modern society. But Brazilians aspired to even more than rapid modernization. They began to envision their nation as a major factor in both inter-American and world affairs—a role for which they considered Brazil potentially suited as the world's fifth largest nation territorially and eighth largest in population. The aspiration of many Brazilians to achieve the transformation of the nation into a great power through the instrumentality of representative institutions was handicapped in several ways.

*Domestic Politics*

In the first place the government was not really representative because literacy qualifications for balloting and officeholding disenfranchised about 50 percent of Brazilians of voting age. The interests of this element could not therefore be articulated through ordinary political channels; instead they were made known by the agitations of the Peasant Leagues of northeastern Brazil, by the labor unions of urban centers, and by middle and upper class leaders who wished either demagogically to enhance their own political power or genuinely to improve the lot of the disenfranchised.

Even for those who might participate in Brazilian politics, there were major weaknesses in the political system. One was the assumption by the armed forces of the role of "guardians of the constitutional order"— a role assigned them constitutionally only by direct order of the president, but seized by them on four crucial occasions after their forcing of Dictator Vargas' resignation in 1945. Moreover, the system of political parties was too amorphous to provide either the long-range planning necessary to solve Brazil's problems or the discipline necessary to implement proposed solutions. Post-World War II Brazil had neither the effective one-party system of Mexico nor the national multiparty systems with roots in the past of Argentina and Chile. Brazil's multiparty system on the national level came into being only after World War II. From the overthrow of the Empire in 1889 until 1930 there were no national political parties in Brazil; state political machines selected representatives to the Brazilian congress and negotiated among themselves for the presidency and other high national positions. Even such regional activity was curtailed from 1930 to 1945 during the Vargas dictatorship so that parties organized subsequently were political novices venturing upon totally untrod territory.

Among national parties active between 1945 and 1965 were the moderate Social Democratic Party, the centrist National Democratic Union, the Labor Party, Socialist Party, and Communist Party. Lacking in the cohesion that can sometimes result from tradition and experience, the newborn national parties were torn by both regional and personal factionalism, and because no single party could elect a majority in congress, government programs were at the mercy of highly unstable coalitions.

### Modernization and Inflation

Brazil's inadequate political system was severely strained by the attempt to rapidly accelerate economic transformation. The process of modernization reached a dizzy pace after President Kubitschek assumed office in 1956 and attempted to fulfill his campaign promise to bring about "fifty years of progress in five." Although Brazil's gross national product rose substantially, domestic tensions and dislocations increased even more.

Brazilians flocked from country to city seeking a better life, only to find themselves swelling the filth-covered, degrading, poverty-perpetuating slums, under conditions of "modern" life that they could neither understand nor alter. Their misery was accentuated by government policies based upon the belief that inflation provided the best environment for rapid development. Heavy borrowing and reckless use of the printing press provided the money for economic development and such grandiose projects as the creation from the ground up of a new capital city, Brasilia. The cost of living rose yearly by such staggering amounts as 59 percent in 1959 and 84 percent in 1964, and with its ever more worthless money Brazil was at times unable either to service its foreign debt or pay for vital imports.

*Political Collapse*

Amid mounting popular discontent and fiscal chaos the shaky representative political system commenced to collapse. In 1961 President Janio Quadros abandoned his predecessor's policy of cooperation with the United States for an "independent" posture, at the same time enunciating a reform program that combined austere anti-inflation measures with land and tax reforms. Blocked by both leftist and rightist elements in congress, Quadros resigned, precipitating the intervention of the armed forces.

Powerful elements of the armed forces, fearing the leftist tendencies and political opportunism of Vice President "Jango" Goulart, a protege of former Dictator Vargas, demanded that the constitution be changed to diminish presidential power. Goulart was then permitted to assume office. During the next sixteen months the new government continued to follow an independent foreign policy but did little to solve Brazil's domestic problems because of factionalism in the congress and because Goulart's efforts were directed primarily toward restoration of presidential powers. Early in 1963 this was achieved through a plebiscite and Goulart began to attack inflation and to set in motion reforms which he claimed were designed to solve Brazil's basic problems and which his opponents charged were planned to win support from laboring and other underprivileged groups. Among other things his program called for land reform, prevention of tax evasion, subsidization of food production to reduce prices, and extension of suffrage. Blocked by congress, Goulart became increasingly reckless, taking steps that convinced many that he was attempting to set up a Peronist-like dictatorship based on the support of the underprivileged. When he openly asked enlisted soldiers for their personal loyalty, armed forces officers organized a revolt that by April 2, 1964, was successful in deposing him.

### Military Government

The military had cooperated with certain important civilians, including several state governors who accepted the revolution's stated purpose of defending "democracy" against usurpation by a president allegedly under communist influence. However, instead of stepping aside once the revolt had succeeded, as in past interventions, the Supreme Revolutionary Command of the military issued an Institutional Act that—without congressional approval—declared the armed forces the ultimate source of political legitimacy. The chiefs of staff of the armed forces were given the right to remove from their positions, upon suspicion of communism or subversion, a wide range of government officials including congressmen, state governors, and judges as well as to suspend individuals' political rights for ten years. A new president was to be chosen by congress within ten days, according to the act, and he was to be given very broad powers, including the right to declare a state of siege that would enable him to rule by decree.

Under the sword, congress, on April 11, 1964, named as president General Humberto Castello Branco. He immediately announced a reorientation of Brazil's foreign policy toward cooperation with the Western nations and the United States and away from his predecessors' "independent" policy. In domestic matters Castello had to follow a middle course between one group within the military that wished to restore constitutional government and another that wished to follow a hard line of dominating the government in order to assure the stability needed to solve some of Brazil's pressing problems. After a period during which many alleged communists and other subversives—including forty congressmen and former President Kubitschek—were jailed, exiled, and deprived of their political rights, it appeared that the constitutionalists in the army might succeed, for the government was able to proceed with its program of slowing down inflation and developing the economy with considerable success and without further political repression. But when Kubitschek followers won a number of victories in state elections, indicating serious discontent with the government, the administration began a series of moves that made clear that the "hard liners" were in the ascendency. President Castello dissolved all existing political parties and announced the formation of a government party, the National Renovating Alliance. The constitution was then further modified to provide for the indirect election of the president, state governors, and other officials, with the justification that such changes were necessary to assure the tranquility needed to carry out the objectives of the revolution. The election in 1966 of the candidate of the National Renovating Alliance—the Minister of War, General Artur Costa e Silva —indicated that the military intended to retain control of the government of Brazil.

Brazil's political history makes evident the inadequacy of its political system for achieving rapid economic development within a framework of representative institutions. Before the coup of 1964 the unstable representative political system was unable to cope with domestic tensions and dislocations. Under a military regime inflation has been slowed and limited progress made toward solution of some economic and social problems. However, the less privileged elements in Brazil have continued to bear a heavy burden as prices still rise faster than wages, and aspirations for representative government are frustrated.

### United States Involvement

Brazil's political struggles reflect differences over policies of modernization and foreign affairs; and because the United States' interests and policies affect both, it becomes involved in Brazil's domestic politics. Direct links are provided primarily by large private investments in Brazil, by government assistance programs, and by the treaty obligations of the inter-American system. These links bring the United States and its citizens into contact with a political environment in which a pervasive and intense spirit of nationalism provides political leaders with a useful tool for advancing their own programs and undermining those of their rivals.

By 1963 United States private investments in Brazil surpassed those in all other Latin American nations except Venezuela, with nearly 60 percent of that investment in manufacturing and almost 28 percent in utilities, petroleum distribution, and mining. Since the 1930's there has been a growing tendency to restrict and regulate foreign investment in Brazil. The exploitation of petroleum resources became a state monopoly in 1953 and it is planned ultimately to bring all public utilities under government control. But stronger measures have been demanded by various groups and individuals opposed to foreign private investment. For example, Governor Miguel Arrais of the state of Pernambuco claimed in 1963 that underdevelopment in Brazil could not be eliminated without putting an end to exploitation by foreign capital. And the governor of the important state of Rio Grande do Sul, Leonel Brizzola, who in 1962 formed a coalition with the Peasant Leagues of the northeast and the Brazilian Socialist Party, not only nationalized three United States companies in his own state but also advocated that the government take over all foreign investments. Moreover, late in 1962 conservative industrial interests, seeking to reduce competition, joined the left in supporting legislation limiting the profits foreign investors could receive; this legislation, it was believed, would discourage foreigners from participating in the development of Brazil's industry. In December 1964 anticommunist Governor Carlos Lacerda of the state of Guanabara denounced a decree of the military government that called for private development of Brazil's large iron resources, charging that the Minister of Planning was in the pay of the Hanna Company, a United States concern.

## United States Assistance

Of even greater importance than private investments in involving the United States in Brazil's domestic politics has been the foreign aid program of the United States government. It is not that Brazilians do not want such assistance; during the 1950's one of the sources of ill-feeling toward the United States was its allegedly insufficient aid. Moreover, Brazilian governments have on several occasions since World War II been willing to be rescued from financial crises by the United States. But Brazilians do object to strings that restrict their leaders' freedom of action. The United States has generally insisted upon anti-inflationary conditions intended to facilitate orderly economic development. Washington has also used its economic leverage to support what it considers to be friendly as opposed to unfriendly political groups, and many Brazilians have criticized this use of foreign aid as intervention in their internal affairs.

One example of such reactions occurred during the Goulart regime, when the Brazilian government was under pressure from the left and Washington sought to strengthen moderate elements by making financial assistance available. When negotiations were undertaken in Washington by a Brazilian moderate, San Tiago Dantas, in the winter of 1963, leftist and nationalist elements in the Brazilian congress, led by Leonel Brizzola, denounced the talks and demanded that Brazil either "go it alone" or get help in Eastern Europe. Then, while discussions were still in progress, a United States congressional committee report quoted Lincoln Gordon, United States Ambassador to Brazil, as stating that communists had infiltrated the Brazilian government. In Brazil, opponents of the Washington aid negotiations demanded that the government respond to the ambassador's charge by halting the talks and recalling Dantas. When the United States State Department denied it believed that communists exercised substantial influence on the Brazilian government, discussions continued and led to an agreement providing, among other things, for anti-inflationary measures. Nevertheless, when Dantas returned to Brazil he was eliminated from the Goulart regime and the anti-inflationary program was forgotten.

*Brazil's Foreign Policy*

Brazil and the United States are allies under the Inter-American Treaty of Reciprocal Assistance and cooperated on cold war issues until 1961 when, with the presidency of Quadros, a major shift occurred that lasted until the military coup of 1964. Brazil, rejecting the lead of the United States, commenced to make foreign policy decisions exclusively on the basis of its own interest and consequently assumed a nonaligned position. The Quadros regime established diplomatic relations with Russia and other communist-governed nations, sought to increase Brazil's trade with those countries, and supported the admission of mainland China to the United Nations. President Goulart's similar policy was notably apparent in early 1962 when Brazil led the unsuccessful opposition to United States efforts to expel Cuba from the OAS. Brazil did not, however, renounce its OAS commitments, and it supported the United States naval blockade of Cuba during the missile crisis of October 1962.

The reorientation of Brazil's foreign policy is important to an understanding of its domestic politics because it was partially motivated by the need to gain the support of two major sectors—one reflecting Brazil's growing nationalism and the desire for a more important role in world affairs, the other the anti-imperialist, anti-United States left. Quadros hoped that in return for his policy of nonalignment and acceptance of the communist world the opposition left would support an anti-inflation program burdensome to Brazil's less privileged groups.

Although the independent policy was popular with a broad spectrum of Brazilians, the Goulart regime's significant shift toward leftist nationalism produced a domestic reaction. The military regime that seized power in April 1964 moved toward collaboration with the United States, breaking relations with Cuba, supporting the United States' intervention in the Dominican Republic, and agreeing to austerity measures advocated by the United States to control inflation. But that eagerness to cooperate with the United States produced its own domestic repercussions, leading to popular discontent with the military regime. Aware of the political risks involved in close collaboration with the United States, the Brazilian military hoped to counteract them with a successful domestic program of orderly development.

## Colombia

Colombia seemed in the 1930's and early 1940's to be en route to the establishment of stable representative government. Between 1910 and 1948 no civil wars disturbed its internal peace; governments changed hands peacefully as a result of elections that, beginning in 1930, were relatively free and honest. Although its Liberal and Conservative parties struggled hotly for office, each represented an elite of landowners, churchmen, commercial people, and industrialists, differing at first largely over the question of the relationship between church and state.

## Political Development

In the 1930's, however, Liberal Party leaders began to advocate and effect certain basic reforms. The previously disenfranchised mass of Colombian males was given the right to vote; labor was permitted to organize; constitutional changes permitted the government to expropriate property that was either foreign-owned or not being used in the national interest. These programs alarmed elite groups within both parties and they succeeded in slowing them, but not before less privileged groups had begun to harbor hope that their lot might be bettered. After World War II, inflation worsened the piteous condition of the Colombian masses and the political machine collapsed amid controversy over how best to modernize.

The dominant Liberal Party was badly divided as it faced the 1946 presidential election: one faction was meliorist; the other, led by charismatic Jorge Gaitán, proposed to rescue the masses through prompt and radical alteration of the social and economic structure. The Liberal split handed the presidency to the Conservatives but with a congressional minority. And now the Conservative Party was split between the Laureanistas (followers of Laureano Gómez), who favored a Franco-type state, and the Ospinistas (followers of Mariano Ospina, the newly elected president), who argued for gradual modernization.

In the ensuing political paralysis the plight of the Colombian masses remained as severe as ever, and popular discontent was at the boiling point in 1948 when Jorge Gaitán was assassinated. Colombia exploded into political chaos. Gaitán's supporters, believing that he had been murdered for political reasons, wildly rioted and pillaged in Bogotá and other cities; communist agitators joined in the orgy of destruction and looting, and it was weeks before order could be restored sufficiently to assess the physical and political damage. That disaster added to the Latin American political lexicon a new word—bogotazo—whose specter has since haunted many governments. Colombia seemed unable to regain its political or societal footing after the trauma of the Gaitán killing. It sank into a period of fratricidal conflict, severe political repression, banditry and other crime, and guerrilla warfare that cost thousands of lives and flooded the country with mounting hatred and despair.

*Military Intervention*

In 1953 the military finally intervened in an attempt to halt crime and bloodshed. The conflicting factions accepted General Gustavo Rojas Pinilla as a caretaker president until order could be restored and a civilian constitutional regime reinstated. But Rojas was ambitious and, inspired by the example of Perón, set about the creation of a personal following among both civilian and military elements. In 1957 Rojas' decision to retain the presidency for another four years precipitated a successful united Conservative-Liberal drive to unseat him through passive resistance with the aid of discontented army groups.

*The National Front*

The Conservative and Liberal parties then went a step further, forming a coalition called the National Front, which agreed upon a sixteen-year program of cooperative and unified political action. Under the terms of their agreement (still honored in 1967) the two parties would alternate in the presidency and share equally ministerial and other administrative positions.

The Colombian National Front vaguely resembles Mexico's official party, the PRI, in one respect: it shelters various conflicting political interests that together manage to effect political control. Within the front these interests attempt privately to reconcile their differences while retaining a monopoly of power through cooperation in elections and in governmental administration. But there are important differences between the Mexican and Colombian systems. Colombia has a stronger tradition of congressional independence so that the front is not always able to secure passage of its legislative programs. Moreover, Colombia has had relatively free elections, in line with the tradition established in the 1930's and 1940's, whereas the PRI has generally been able to manipulate elections. Finally, whereas the Mexican party represents a broad range of economic and social sectors, the Colombian National Front is essentially a coalition of the traditional elites.

In spite of its elitist character, the National Front appeared to recognize Colombia's need for social and economic change and sponsored mild land and tax reforms and a long-term development plan under the Alliance for Progress. Massive assistance was obtained to carry out this plan when the United States decided to make Colombia a showcase of the Alliance for Progress. Yet the National Front experienced difficulties that became increasingly acute as time passed. The development program's implementation was accompanied by inflation that adversely affected working and middle class groups. To many it seemed that the government was moving too slowly in the areas of social and economic reform. Yet attempts to move more rapidly or even to enforce existing laws, such as those for the payment of taxes, met strong resistance in congress. Discontent was apparent in the 1962 presidential elections when a faction of the Liberal Party refused to abide by the National Front agreement and instead of supporting Conservative Guillermo Valencia nominated Alfonso López Michelsen on a Liberal Revolutionary Movement ticket. López, campaigning on a platform that denounced the rising cost of living and strongly criticized the front's development program, lost, but he polled more than a third as many votes as the government candidate. The congressional election of March 1964 produced an even greater fissure in the National Front, for the fact that 70 percent of the voters failed to exercise their franchise was understood by all to indicate strong and widespread displeasure with the government's approach to Colombia's economic and social plight. The election gave the coalition precisely the two-thirds of the seats necessary to pass legislation—not one vote more—putting the administration's program at the mercy of dissidents in both parties. Conditions deteriorated even more rapidly. Growing discontent in military circles was openly displayed at the end of June 1964 when the minister of war attacked the government publicly, charging that elite pressure groups were halting the progress of the development program, claiming that agrarian reform was coming to a standstill, and calling for social justice for the less privileged members of Colombian society.

Colombia was finding it increasingly difficult to meet its foreign exchange needs, but when the president sought legislation to solve the problem, he encountered serious opposition. Because the Colombian congress seemed unlikely to pass legislation considered essential for the country's financial and economic health, in December 1964 the United States government and other foreign interests that were helping to finance Bogotá's development plans announced that they would assume no new commitments until Colombia's financial house had been put in order. But even that ultimatum did not inspire Colombia's leadership to cope constructively with the nation's problems. Student riots of May 1965 frightened the president into declaring a state of siege that enabled him to rule by decree without the consent of congress. During the next few months steps were taken to stabilize Colombia's finances and sufficient progress was made to convince the United States and other foreign lenders to resume assistance to Colombia.

The renewal of foreign aid did not, however, solve the political problems of the National Front. In congressional elections of March 1966 it failed to win even the two-thirds majority necessary for passage of basic legislation. Although the National Front candidate, Carlos Lleras Restrepo, won the presidency two months later, less than four of every ten eligible voters had participated, many casting ballots for a nonofficial candidate who had entered the race at the last moment. A significant aspect of the 1966 elections was the revelation that the opposition was tending to look toward the leadership of the former dictator, General Gustavo Rojas Pinilla, who, although deprived of political rights in 1958, was exercising influence through the new and surprisingly strong Popular National Alliance Party; its success was, however, interpreted as deriving substantially from a protest vote against the National Front.

## United States Involvement

The United States plays a less obvious role in the domestic politics of Colombia than of Argentina or Chile. Nevertheless, anti-United States and anti-imperialist sentiment has been deeply embedded in Colombia since the beginning of the twentieth century when Washington supported and encouraged the secession from Colombia of its strategic Province of Panama and transformed the newly "independent" country into a United States protectorate. And anti-United States sentiment is sufficiently strong to have political value. For example, the Colombian government owns majority stock in the nation's major airline, while New York-based Pan American Airways owns a noncontrolling 40 percent. However, when a private Colombian airline's request for added routes was rejected by Bogotá, that airline charged that the administration was "controlled from New York."[4] Again, after a devaluation of the Colombian peso in accord with IMF recommendations, the left charged that the devaluation "was imposed by the International Mone-

[4] *Hispanic American Report*, XV, 55.

tary Fund in order to benefit United States imperialists and the national oligarchy."[5]

The opposition of some Colombian political factions to cooperation with the United States is connected with their attitudes toward modernization. The Laureanista wing of the Conservative Party has long detested United States egalitarianism and Protestantism and has distrusted both the Alliance for Progress' promotion of social change and its sponsorship by the United States. The moderate wings of both the Conservative and the Liberal parties, which form the major strength of the National Front, favor cooperation with the United States and support the Alliance for Progress; they have been willing to approve all the sanctions against Cuba that Washington might desire, short of armed intervention. The dissident Liberal Revolutionary Movement, which opposes the National Front, is divided on both domestic and international policy. With respect to the latter its minority left-wing group decried the United States blockade of Cuba, has opposed Colombian participation in any action against Castro, and has given other evidence of hostility toward the United States. Another anti-United States group is the small United Front of Revolutionary Action (FUAR) which considers itself to be Fidelista and is reportedly receiving Cuban aid. FUAR not only opposes any action against Cuba but denounces any cooperation between United States "imperialists" and the Colombian "oligarchy."

## Comparison of Colombia
## with Argentina, Chile, and Mexico

Although some Colombian political slogans sound like those employed in Argentina, Chile, and Mexico, and although conflicting interests struggle for control of the government and political influence, the Colombian political system differs from those of the other three nations in several major respects. The less privileged elements in Colombian society find it difficult to influence government decision. Whereas in both Argentina and Mexico, and to a lesser extent in Chile, the traditional elite has lost its position of dominance, in Colombia it is still firmly in control of the government. The membership of labor unions is small and ideologically divided. The Fidelista FUAR, in spite of its

[5] *Ibid.*, 56.

program of reform, attracts chiefly a very restricted group of intellectuals. Although the Liberal Revolutionary Movement and the Popular National Alliance Party have shown a disposition to advocate more governmental action in behalf of the less privileged, neither has demonstrated great ability to influence government.

A further difference from Argentina, Chile, and Mexico is the relatively weak sense of nationalism in Colombia. Regionalism has so long been a dominant characteristic of Colombian culture and history that loyalty to the *patria chica* sometimes transcends loyalty to the nation. Moreover, until recently most Colombians have accepted the existence of a traditional hierarchical society, and this kind of society militates against the broad diffusion of nationalism. Important in this connection is the fact that the church in Colombia is much more influential politically than in Argentina, Chile, Mexico, Uruguay, Brazil, or Venezuela and that an important conservative wing of the church gives strong support to the traditional order.

## Peru

The political systems of such countries as Ecuador, Bolivia, Guatemala, and Peru differ even more from those of Argentina, Chile, and Mexico than does that of Colombia. In Peru, for example, there exists a small organized labor group but those groups that have until very recently been most influential in governmental decision making are the large economic and financial interests of the coast, the large landholders of the sierra, and the army officer corps which has sided with them on most issues.

### APRA

Although several small political parties, such as the Socialist, Communist, and Christian Democratic, have claimed to represent the less privileged elements in Peru, until very recently their chief spokesman has been APRA (Alianza Popular Revolucionaria Americana). Primarily a middle class and labor party, APRA has advocated a moderate program of social legislation, agrarian and land reform, national economic development, and "anti-imperialism." The Apristas have never managed to gain complete control of the Peruvian government, for the army officer corps, as well as members of the ruling elite, have opposed it strongly and managed to thwart its activities. However, APRA did have some influence in the formation of the governments of 1945-48 and 1958-62 when it supported and cooperated with elite-led administrations. During the first period opposition elite elements who feared Aprista power supported a successful revolution. In the second, Aprista leaders failed to press their program and at the same time the elitist government decided that some reform was necessary. There was neither real crisis nor genuine reform, for the government failed to gain passage of even a mild agrarian reform law. However, in 1962 when it appeared that APRA would win the presidency, the army intervened and, alleging fraud, annulled the elections.

*Acción Popular*

Meanwhile, during the six years preceding the thwarted 1962 election a rival had emerged to challenge APRA's claims to speak for the downtrodden of Peru. This party, Acción Popular, advocated a reform program similar to the Aprista program, and its charismatic leader, Fernando Belaunde Terry, kept pace with APRA's candidate in the annulled election of 1962. Belaunde won election the following year and, because he was acceptable to the military of Peru, was permitted to assume the presidency. However, in the same elections APRA won more congressional seats than Acción Popular, making Belaunde dependent upon its support for passage of his legislative program.

Both APRA and Acción Popular were deeply committed to reform; thus one of the new government's earliest achievements was an agrarian reform law whose dual purposes were the immediate one of halting illegal land seizures by making land legally available and the longrange one of achieving basic land reform. In spite of this measure, the Belaunde administration has followed a moderate course which may reflect the continuing power of the Peruvian elite. If Belaunde actually wishes basic change (which many observers doubt), he may feel unable to effectuate his ideas. Questions of the rapidity of reform and its nature are a source of conflict within both reform parties. Belaunde found it expedient to remove a member of Acción Popular's directorate who criticized the president's failure to take strong action against the United States-controlled International Petroleum Company which has been involved in a dispute with the government of Peru over royalties and taxes. A group within APRA has also criticized its leadership for excessive moderation and for softening its anti-imperialist position.

### Critical Problems

In short, critical Peruvian political issues relate to modernization policies, involving the United States because (1) United States citizens have large oil and mining investments in Peru, (2) close ties exist between the Peruvian elite and those interests, and (3) the United States is in a position—should it choose to do so—to affect the world market for Peru's important exports of lead, zinc, and cotton and thus to curtail or augment governmental revenues needed for development.

Although both APRA and Acción Popular profess dedication to the cause of Peru's depressed sectors, neither possesses adequate institutional means of affecting government policy. A major fact of Peruvian life is the large and hard core of wretchedness among the Indians of the sierra who are generally unintegrated into national life and play little or no role in either APRA or Acción Popular, both of which are predominantly urban. Acción Popular is a Belaunde-centered personalist group with little effective organization. APRA is still fairly well organized but its influence has been steadily weakened by internal divisions and persistent military opposition. Moreover, APRA has for decades been dominated by the now elderly Victor Raúl Haya de la Torre whose disappearance may prove APRA to have been a far more personalist party than has been supposed.

Like Colombia, and for the similar reasons of exaggerated regionalism and hierarchical social structure buttressed by ecclesiastical conservatism, Peru lacks the propulsive force of a highly developed sense of nationalism. While nationalism does manifest itself among certain urban elements, personal loyalty seems more important to most Peruvians. Altogether untouched by nationalistic sentiment is the vast unintegrated Indian population that is hardly aware of being Peruvian.

## The Dominican Republic

Further removed from the political systems of Argentina, Chile, and Mexico than those of either Peru or Colombia is that of the Dominican Republic. Eighty percent of its three million people are largely illiterate peasants and rural workers. Together with urban workers they comprise a poverty stricken mass that has been generally impotent to affect government decisions. During most of its history the Dominican Republic has been tyrannized by self-enriching despots, the most recent of whom—General Rafael Trujillo, who ruled from 1930 to 1961—was perhaps the most oppressive. Following Trujillo's assassination an attempt was commenced, after several transitional governments, to create representative institutions, and several political parties have since come into being; those that have survived tend to be highly personalistic. Among those that were outlawed or became defunct were such parties of the left, in which Castro-communist sympathizers were either active or dominant, as the 14th of June Party, the Dominican Popular Party, the National Revolutionary Party, and the Dominican Popular Socialist Party which was early outlawed. The three parties most influential in the five years following 1961 were the National Civic Union (UCN), the Dominican Revolutionary Party (PRD), and the Reformista Party. The UCN, supported largely by middle class and professional people, and the PRD, led by Juan Bosch and appealing to the less privileged classes by its program of social and economic reform, were the leading contenders in the presidential election of 1962 which Bosch won because he was able both to organize the rural vote and to win support from urban elements. After his inauguration in early 1963 Bosch alienated many followers by his uncertain leadership and frightened Dominican conservatives by his proposed reforms. Within seven months the real power in the Dominican Republic—the military—reasserted itself, sending Bosch into exile and supporting a civilian junta that governed until the spring of 1965.

By then a split within the armed forces had developed and a group of officers turned against the junta, seeking to restore Bosch. Their revolt was frustrated by conservative opposition and the intervention of the United States, which with the aid of the OAS set up a provisional government pending new elections. The major contenders in the election of June 1966 were Juan Bosch and Joaquín Balaguer, a former Trujillo supporter who had organized the Reformista Party to support his candidacy. Balaguer was elected chiefly because he won the vote of the rural population which appears to have become disturbed by the turmoil of both the Bosch regime and the revolution that attempted to restore him to power.

The future of Balaguer's government is as unpredictable as the new and untried political system of the Dominican Republic. Dominicans have not yet developed the skills and the variety of competing interests and institutions that might keep the military under control and maintain orderly government. Moreover, most Dominicans are not imbued with the type of nationalism that motivates development programs and acts as a cohesive stabilizer. Under conditions of virtual collapse the Dominican Republic becomes a political vacuum—a fact that, combined with its strategic location, has sucked the United States into Dominican politics. The United States' primary interest has been to keep the island out of hostile hands; only secondarily has it sought to better the lot of the Dominican people and to develop representative institutions.

During most of the period between 1930 and 1961 Washington beamed upon the stability and order maintained under Trujillo. A mutual defense agreement was signed with his regime in 1952; and the Dominicans profited from a liberal sugar quota. Although private United States opposition to Trujillo mounted in 1956 following the abduction and murder of Jesús Galíndez, an exiled critic of the Trujillo regime who was a scholar at Columbia University, no official action was taken until 1960 when the United States joined other OAS members in both condemning the Dominican Republic and adopting sanctions against it for violating human rights and for intervention in the affairs of Venezuela.

Upon Trujillo's assassination the United States government encouraged the establishment of constitutional government, going so far as to station naval vessels off Dominican shores as a warning to Trujillo's followers who were contemplating the establishment of a new dictatorship. When Bosch was elected, the United States government provided him with heavy assistance to help carry out his reform program and to strengthen the democratic regime. When Bosch was overthrown in 1963 the United States withheld aid from the regime that supplanted him until the new Johnson Administration assumed a hard line policy in early 1964 and recognized the militarily supported junta that ruled the island until just before the United States intervention of 1965.

## Implications for United States Policy

The foregoing survey of the domestic politics of various Latin American countries demonstrates that while the peoples of Latin America and the United States share similar political objectives, their respective political systems differ in many ways and that nowhere in Latin America is there a system closely resembling that of the United States. These facts are important because United States policy has allegedly been to encourage the development of democratic institutions; in the absence of any generally accepted definition of "democratic institutions," both policy makers and the general public find it easy to project their private image of a democratic society as a basis for deciding whether or not a nation is democratic. Yet, in most of the countries of Latin America the concepts, institutions, and economic and social conditions that the United States system comprises are still underdeveloped.

The question therefore arises: how can the United States government implement its policy of promoting democracy if no Latin American nation will follow the model of the United States? It would seem necessary, first, to devise a new and more flexible definition of democracy that instead of stressing form and procedure emphasized values and life styles and, second, to study intensively the political system of each Latin American nation to determine how these values and conditions might flourish in each individual case.

Differences in the political systems of the Latin American nations make it obvious that it is impossible for the United States to develop one "Latin American" policy applicable to the entire area. Each nation's policy making process is the product of its unique environment and historical experience. Consequently any specific policy toward a given country cannot be based upon glib generalizations about the role of the "Latin American nations" in the cold war or about the nature of "Latin American" politics. Such generalizations confuse the issues and perpetuate a distorted view of Latin American political realities. If policy is to be based upon mutual interests, decisions must be made only after consideration of the policy's implications for the domestic concerns of each nation affected.

*National Cohesion*

The preceding political survey has also emphasized the fact that Argentina, Chile, and Mexico, though their political systems differ, have certain characteristics that distinguish them from other Latin American nations, with the exceptions of Uruguay and possibly Venezuela. In each of these countries a variety of interests representing a complicated social and economic structure struggles for influence over government, in each less privileged groups have some means of affecting governmental processes, and a dynamic force in the political system of each of them has been a highly developed and widely shared sense of nationalism. These countries thus conform more closely than any others in Latin America to the United States ideal of free and independent states, for the sum of those special factors makes their possessors viable, internally cohesive nation-states.

An important consequence of cohesion is sensitivity to foreign intervention, a desirable characteristic from the point of view of the United States because a cohesive, nationalist nation is able to cope with subversion more effectively than one that is fragmented. However, such a nation resists United States political and economic influence, creating the illusion that those nations best able to govern and protect their peoples constitute the greatest problems for United States policy. Nations with limited cohesion, such as Colombia and Peru, have more easily than Argentina or Chile bowed to the wishes of the United States and followed its lead in Western Hemisphere affairs, but because of the tensions building up within those less cohesive nations and the awesome magnitude of their problems, they may provide greater potential for subversion than countries that stoutly affirm their independence of United States desires.

*Economic Nationalism*

It is of special significance that politics in Latin America revolve around the issues of modernization and political independence. At stake in both spheres are the interests of individuals, their fortunes, political positions, and personal reputations. These domestic matters, although of greater moment to Latin America than cold war issues, nevertheless have international repercussions. The desire of *obreros* (industrial and mining workers) and *empleados* (white collar employees) for social and economic betterment clashes not only with the interests of traditional elites but also with stabilization policies urged by the United States. Those who benefit from economic nationalism—among them industrialists, middle managerial and technical personnel, and government officials as well as the less privileged—advocate the extension of governmental economic activity, restriction of foreign interests, and state ownership of basic national resources and utilities. This brings them into conflict not only with domestic elites whose wealth is based upon more liberal economic systems, but also with the United States which advocates free enterprise and wishes both to protect the existing interests of its citizens and to provide them with new and greater opportunities for profit. In these situations Washington finds itself accused of supporting reactionary, elite exploitative interests and opposing social and economic reform. On the other hand, elite groups desperately seeking to preserve the status quo clash not only with *obreros, empleados,* the distressed classes, and economic nationalists, but with the United States which, much to the distress of the traditional elite, is insisting upon tax and land reform as a basis for expanded economic assistance.

The United States' involvement in Latin American domestic politics combines with its goal of an international community of free and independent states to create a serious policy dilemma. The majority of the populations of all Latin American nations necessarily consists of less privileged elements. They tend to favor government policies designed to bring them immediate and perceptible benefits, and the politically articulate among them tend to seek such benefits within a framework of economic nationalism. The needs and wishes of the deprived, and the methods they advocate, blend into a long-term trend toward nationalistic social and economic revolutions in Latin America. This trend began with the Mexican and Uruguayan experiments and was greatly accelerated by the depression and the postwar "revolution of rising expectations." It is also the trend of the immediate future. The economic plight of the less privileged is being constantly intensified by an uncontrolled, rapid population increase; and no alternative has yet been found to the national government as the principal agency capable of acting quickly and effectively to solve increasingly desperate problems.

### United States Action

If the United States wishes to deal with the nations of Latin America as free and independent states, it must recognize that they have the inalienable right to solve their problems as they see fit, as long as they do not menace the rights of the United States. While, however, at first glance this may seem a wise course to follow—for if the United States insists upon adopting Latin American policies contrary to existing trends, it may permanently alienate those nations—it must be remembered also that no matter what the United States does, its action or lack of action will have political impact within the Latin American nation involved. If Washington helps Latin American nations to implement what it considers to be unsound or even absurd economic or social policies, it may be helping to create even greater problems than those already existing. Rather than pressing policies it approves that are contrary to the trend toward nationalistic social and economic revolutions, *the United States must help find new solutions* to Latin American problems, solutions that are compatible both with those trends and with sound policy. To do so the government and people of the United States must clearly comprehend the nature of the problems that provide the explosive issues in the politics of the Latin American nations and upon whose solution the future of Latin America hangs.

# VII

# Latin American Problems

Latin America faces numerous obstacles in its development efforts. Each nation has its unique constellation of problems, but many types of problems are shared to some extent by most of the nations. The ultimate aim of all of the Latin American countries is to raise the standard of living of their people to the point where they may play active roles in viable modern societies. The present chapter attempts to describe the attendant problems and to indicate the basis of the United States' vital interest in their solution. In the course of the analysis it will become apparent that the obstacles to a higher standard of living in Latin America are not only economic but social, cultural, and political as well.

## Poverty

One fundamental problem of Latin America can be simply expressed: most of its people exist in abject poverty. The average daily caloric intake is below the minimum necessary for healthy survival; housing is inadequate in space, sanitation, and protection against the elements; the incidence of disease and death is high. The extreme poverty of the Latin American nations is apparent when their annual per capita gross domestic product is compared with those of more highly developed nations. In 1960 this figure for the United States and Canada, respectively, was $2,976 and $1,993; the average for all the Latin American nations was $366. Thus Canada's gross domestic product was more than five times the average of Latin America's and that of the United States more than eight times. Latin America does not compare badly, however, with certain other countries. Its average gross domestic product is slightly higher than those of Greece and Spain and vastly larger than those of India and Indonesia, which together contain about a sixth of the world's population and have average per capita gross domestic products less than one-fifth of the average Latin American.[1]

The average per capita gross domestic product for Latin America as a whole, although it is very low, fails to indicate the poverty of individual nations and the extent of deprivation of the mass of people. There is a vast difference between wealthy Venezuela, with its per capita gross domestic product of over $1,100, and Bolivia, Haiti, Paraguay, and Peru, each of which has a per capita gross domestic product of less than $150. Moreover, no average figure for any country indicates how small the real income of most people is. In Venezuela, for example, the 2.5 percent of the population who work in the oil export sector of the economy are estimated to receive an average annual per capita income of approximately $3,000, whereas the average annual income of the farm workers who constitute a large proportion of the population varies between $10 and $100. Moreover, the average per capita gross national product figure does not necessarily indicate a nation's state of development. Argentina, for example, with a figure lower than Venezuela's, has a more evenly distributed income; some economists even consider it no longer underdeveloped.

## Effect of Population Increase

Not only is the standard of living in Latin America very low, but the present high rate of population growth makes improvement very difficult. Between 1953 and 1962 the population of all Latin America increased at a rate of approximately 2.8 per cent annually, ranging from a low of 1.2 percent in Haiti to a high of 4 percent in Costa Rica. It is estimated that by 1980 Latin America's population will reach 334.1 million—an increase of approximately 67 percent over the 1960 total of 199.5 million. Merely to keep pace with population growth, the gross

[1] Based upon Victor L. Urquidi, *The Challenge of Development in Latin America* (Praeger, 1962), pp. 162-63.

national product will also have to be increased 67 percent by 1980; it will have to be raised even more if the standard of living is to be improved. Current intergovernmental planning under the Alliance for Progress has set as a minimum goal an average annual increase of 2.5 percent in the per capita gross national product. Since 1950 the average annual increase has reached this goal only twice. From 1950 through 1957 the average increased annually at the rate of approximately 2 percent but began declining toward the end of the period. In 1958 the figure was less than 1 percent and it hovered around that through 1963. Only in 1964 and 1965 was the goal of 2.5 percent increase attained. But these figures are averages for all of Latin America; in 1964 and 1965 only about half of the nations achieved or surpassed the growth rate of the Alliance.[2]

## Adequacy of Physical Resources

The low standard of living in the Latin American nations and their failure to increase their per capita gross national product rapidly is due partly to lack of physical resources. As one economist has pointed out, Latin America, in spite of its reputation for wealth, is less fortunate than other areas of the world.[3] For example, 37 percent of Europe's land and 20 percent of the United States' is suitable for agricultural production; but a mere 5 percent of Latin American land is arable with current techniques. The area is reputedly rich in petroleum, but the reserves of both North America and Russia are nearly 90 percent larger.

Nevertheless, physical resources are not the major problem of the Latin American nations. In comparison with other areas, Latin America —which encompasses about 15 percent of the earth's land mass but only 7 percent of its people—is relatively sparsely populated. The ratio of resources to population should continue to be favorable for some time, although a lack of certain basic resources may prevent Latin America's ever achieving the standard of living of the United States.

In contrast to the nations of Africa and the Near and Far East, the states of Latin America seem somewhat better prepared to develop their resources because of their greater political sophistication and ex-

[2] *New York Times,* March 18, 1966.
[3] Simon G. Hanson, *Economic Development in Latin America* (Washington: The Inter-American Affairs Press, 1951), p. 36.

perience, because they have fewer—though formidable—cultural barriers to technological innovation, and because their institutions more closely resemble those of the world's more highly developed nations. Some Latin American countries have already reached an intermediate stage of economic development and, according to some experts, are well along the route to self-sustained economic growth.

## Economic Factors

Some of the problems of Latin American economies stem from their dependence on the production of one or very few minerals, basic foodstuffs, or raw materials that are exported primarily to industrialized nations. In 1960 a single item accounted for 50 percent or more of the exports of eleven of the twenty Latin American countries. Coffee made up 56 percent of Brazil's total exports and 71 percent of Colombia's; 70 percent of Chile's sales abroad were in copper; petroleum made up 90 percent of Venezuela's exports. Of the more diversified countries, six depended upon only two items for over 50 percent of their exports. Nearly 60 percent of Argentina's exports were in meat and cereals. Only Mexico, Paraguay, and Peru had a greater diversity of exports, but these consisted of unprocessed minerals, foodstuffs, and raw materials.

Although manufacturing makes the most important contribution to gross national product for Latin America as a whole, exports of commodities in the agriculture and stockraising or mining and petroleum industries provide the mainstay of the economic life of most Latin American nations. Taxes on these commodities produce a substantial portion of governmental revenues. Sales of exports secure the foreign exchange needed to import capital or consumer goods. Profits, salaries, and wages flowing from the production of exports provide purchasing power that sustains the domestic economy in general. Above all, returns from exports furnish capital that may be used for development.

### Dependence on World Market

In an economy heavily dependent upon a limited group of exports, the facts that prices are set in a world market beyond the seller's control and that both price and demand fluctuate widely create major problems in long-range governmental and business planning. Unfortunately, from 1953 through 1963, when the need for development funds was increasing, export prices generally were declining while prices paid for imports were rising. As each year passed, a larger amount of real income was required to purchase the same amount of imports. Between 1954 and 1961, coffee prices dropped from 52 to 35 cents and the fifteen coffee-producing nations of Latin America lost about $600 million annually, or a total of $3,600 million (by 1963 the price had fallen to 30 cents). During the first year of the Alliance for Progress the same countries that lost that huge amount received from the United States a total of $707.5 million in economic assistance; naturally enough, their leaders often point out that the decline in the price of coffee cost them more than they received in aid from all sources. A recent rise in the prices of some basic Latin American commodities neither promises to be maintained nor offers evidence that the problem of cyclical fluctuation has been eliminated.

*Foreign Trade Barriers*

Several demand-limiting factors adversely affect Latin America's trading position; one factor is a nationalist tendency in important customer nations. In the United States this is reflected in restrictions on imports of cattle and beef, lead, petroleum, and sugar, which special interest pressure groups have succeeded in forcing through Congress on grounds of national interest. If barriers on these products were suspended, it has been estimated, Latin American nations would be able to increase their exports to the United States by roughly the amount they now receive from it under the Alliance for Progress.[4] Another demand-limiting factor is the growth of competition from the new African countries; because of their former colonial connections with either the British Commonwealth or the European Economic Community, they are generally given preferences that impede the expansion of Latin American sales of competing commodities.

Finally, Latin American economists believe that there has been and

[4] Louis O. Delwart, *The Future of Latin American Exports to the United States: 1965 and 1970* (Washington: National Planning Association, Inter-American Research Committee, 1960), p. 99.

will continue to be a long-term deterioration in terms of trade for Latin American nations as long as they continue to rely heavily upon the exportation of raw materials. These economists believe that it is inherent in the relationship between manufacturing and raw-material-producing nations that the prices received for exports of raw materials will decline in relation to prices paid for manufactured goods. Although the majority of economists outside the underdeveloped world contest this view, it is based upon sufficient evidence to merit serious consideration. If it proves to be even partially valid, the problem of Latin American dependence upon the export of basic raw materials and foodstuffs is even greater than it appears to be now.[5]

## Unbalanced Economies

Heavy reliance of the Latin American nations on a few export commodities has contributed to the creation of lopsided economies. Historically, in the nations that became more closely integrated into the world economy beginning in the late nineteenth century, rapid modernization took place in those sectors that produced for export, while there was little or no advance in those that produced for domestic consumption. Consequently many Latin American countries developed economic systems that were partly modern and partly archaic. In Peru, modern technology was introduced into mining and into the coastal plantations supplying world demand for tropical agricultural products such as citrus fruits and cotton. Domestic food production, however, continued to be carried on under either the colonial hacienda system or an even more primitive indigenous method particularly prevalent in the sierra region. Because of its profitability, the export sector attracted capital, foreign and domestic, while producers for the home market found it virtually impossible to finance expansion or the initiation of new operations.

## Industrialization and Diversification

Attempts begun in the 1930's to correct economic imbalances merely created different, more complicated types of imbalance in several na-

[5] Raymond Vernon, *The Dilemma of Mexico's Development* (Harvard University, 1963), pp. 142-43.

tions. Such efforts were stimulated by the effects of the world depression during which prices for primary commodities dropped drastically and Latin Americans found their government revenues and economic activities curtailed to the point of disaster. To prevent repetition of catastrophe, they determined to diversify, and, although they gave some attention to previously unexploited resources, they placed far greater emphasis on industrialization—a process that many saw as a panacea for all conceivable economic ills. In several nations industrialization did not advance sufficiently to balance the primary commodity export sector, but did go far enough to cause severe dislocations in traditional, unmodernized domestic agriculture. Farm workers were attracted to cities whose populations therefore expanded far more rapidly than did food production so that several nations which had always supplied all of their own basic food needs had to import food products whose higher prices added fuel to the already raging inflation.

Another major problem exposed, if not created, by efforts to industrialize and diversify was the lack of a sufficiently large domestic market to support efficient industrial operations in certain types of products. Most Latin American nations have small populations (only Brazil and Mexico have populations in excess of 25,000,000) among which wealth is distributed so unequally that only a minute proportion can entertain the idea of purchasing even such a "modest" item as a small electrical appliance. In 1960 when the average hourly wage in the small appliance industry in the United States was $2.50, the average wage of all workers in the same industry in nine Latin American nations ranged from a high of 47 cents in Argentina to a low of 15 cents in Chile. Since agricultural wages are even lower, the bulk of Latin America's population are not prospective buyers of manufactured goods.

A further inhibiting factor is the inability of some Latin American industries to compete with the more highly industrialized nations in the world market, partly because their domestic markets are protected and partly because their productivity is lower as a result of smaller-scale operations and generally less efficient plants. Industries with profits from small domestic markets do not seem to feel that investment to increase efficiency is justified. In many cases they could not survive against foreign competition in the domestic market without protection, so that a vicious circle is formed. Assured of the domestic market, the national industry remains inefficient and unable to compete outside national boundaries, relying on high prices and gradual growth of the internal market to increase profits.

## Agricultural Production and Land Tenure

While attempts to diversify and industrialize have seriously aggravated agricultural problems, contributing to inadequate production for domestic consumption, at the root of low food productivity lie backward technology and a stagnating system of land tenure. Producers for the domestic market have generally neither mechanized nor applied available scientific knowledge to crop cultivation so that yield per man hour per acre is but a small fraction of its potential.

The problem of land tenure is complex in the extreme. Throughout Latin America a major form of landholding is the latifundium, or great estate, owned by an individual or family. A large proportion of Latin America's limited arable land lies within these large estates. Although the importance of the latifundia varies from area to area, it is estimated that in 1950 about 60 percent of the land was owned by 10 percent of the people. Those latifundia that produce for export are generally called plantations and are often efficiently operated. The remainder are termed haciendas and are generally the inefficient domestic producers.

The hacienda was not designed as a dynamic economic unit. Its purpose, broadly social, was to provide a self-sufficient situation for the large number of dependents usually associated with its operation, together with sufficient cash income to enable its owner to live stylishly in the big city, should he so wish. Those who work the hacienda usually do so in return for the right to use land. Under this system currency does not often change hands and the dependent *campesino* receives the use of barely enough land to meet minimal needs. As for increasing production or earnings, neither the owner nor the dependent sees the need. The owner seeks only sufficient income to maintain a status that could not be improved upon since he is already at the top of the social pyramid as a landed aristocrat. The dependent has no incentive to increase his production even if his limited knowledge were to make that possible, for he is a product of the hierarchical society and accepts its assumptions.

A further type of arable land unit, equally unproductive, is the minifundio—a plot of land that because of differences in soil fertility may vary in size but is sufficient only for the subsistence of a single family. It is the minifundio upon which most Latin American landowners dwell. Approximately 97 percent of the farms in Guatemala and 90 percent of those in Peru fall into this category. In the early 1950's, in the Dominican Republic, Ecuador, and Mexico (which, it should be remembered, had been undergoing a land reform program for more than three decades), over 25 percent of the farms consisted of less than 2.5 acres. More than 50 percent of the farms in Colombia, Ecuador, Honduras, and Panama were smaller than 12.5 acres. As examples of the numbers of agricultural units involved in these figures, it should be noted that over half a million individual farms in Colombia and over a million in Mexico are classified as minifundios. From the point of view of the gross national product the minifundio is too small to produce efficiently under the existing state of agricultural technology in most Latin American nations. Their owners exist on the margin of the economy, making little contribution to development.

The same may be said for the *comunidad*—a type of landholding that prevails in the Indian countries of Latin America. A *comunidad* consists of a group of extended families who collectively own a given area of land. Within the group individuals have limited property rights and may dispose of their holdings to other members of the group but not to outsiders. Much of the work within the *comunidad* is done collectively. It has been estimated that as many as five to six million people live in *comunidades* in the Andean region of South America and that half of the farmers of Mexico operate under a similar system.[6] From the point of view of agricultural productivity the *comunidad* is of minimal importance because of its rigid discouragement of investment and innovation.

The depressed condition of the agricultural sector has repercussions throughout the general economy. The rural population's lack of purchasing power serves, by limiting the market for manufacturers, as an impediment to industrialization. In addition, urbanization combined with low productivity creates food shortages which in turn produce, aside from malnutrition, rising prices and the necessity to import foodstuffs. This chain of events not only contributes to mounting inflationary pressures but diverts capital from development purposes,

[6] Albert O. Hirschman, ed., *Latin American Issues* (Twentieth Century Fund, 1961), p. 168.

for not only must governments faced with mass discontent on account of high food prices pay subsidies to keep prices down (thus perpetuating low productivity) but they must expend foreign exchange for food imports rather than for capital goods.

### Economic Infrastructure

Another obstacle to increasing the gross national product of most Latin American nations is an inadequate economic infrastructure. Particularly inadequate are internal transportation systems and electrical energy production. True, several Latin American nations have extensive railway and highway systems. Cuba, for example, has more railroad mileage per thousand square miles than does the United States. Roads suitable for heavy traffic are slowly being built in many countries. Transportation systems are inadequate for development needs not only because of insufficient total mileage but also because much of what exists is in the wrong place, many systems having been built to serve the needs of the export-import based economies whose replacement or diversification is now being sought. Cuba's rail system was built to serve the sugar industry; Peru's links its mining regions with the coast. Geographical factors have been a further obstacle to the development of rail and road transportation facilities, for expanses of dense forest and desert and masses of mountainous terrain make both construction and maintenance very expensive, above all in view of the fact that the territory served is often so sparsely populated as to promise minimal usage and revenues.

Insufficient electrical production is a problem shared by all Latin American nations even though several, such as Argentina, Brazil, Mexico, Chile, Uruguay, and Venezuela, have impressive capacities when compared to others. Argentina, with the highest installed per capita capacity for producing electricity, has only 15 percent of that of the United States and must carefully ration the use of electric power.

Nor does the use of other forms of energy compensate for lack of electricity. Estimates of the total per capita consumption of energy including coal, oil, and electricity indicate that although the majority of Latin American states are better off than most nations of other underdeveloped areas, their consumption is only a fraction of that in the

United States and Canada. For example, in 1963 twelve Latin American nations outdistanced India in per capita consumption, with eight of them consuming anywhere from three-and-a-half to seventeen times more energy. Among the African nations, excluding the Union of South Africa, Rhodesia, and Algeria, no one of them equaled those twelve Latin American nations. On the other hand, Venezuela, with the highest per capita consumption, used in 1959 less than 44 percent of the corresponding Canadian figure and 33 percent of the United States figure; Argentina, the second largest consumer in that year, used only 18 percent and 13 percent, respectively, of the Canadian and United States figures. And the United States and Canada, respectively, had per capita consumptions of energy 110 and 77 times greater than that of Paraguay, the second lowest per capita consumer of energy in Latin America.[7]

Shortages in the economic infrastructure are being decreased, but slowly and painfully. Railroads, roads, and electric generating and transmitting systems are expensive and not immediately profitable so that within the context of the Latin American value system they do not attract investment.

## Domestic Capital Resources

A major problem in economic development is securing an adequate supply of investment capital, either foreign or domestic, for productive enterprises. Between 1950 and 1957 about 90 percent of Latin America's growth came from domestic sources, and 10 percent from foreign. Under the terms of the Alliance for Progress, Latin American participants are expected to provide 80 percent of their capital needs and foreign sources the remainder.

Both public and private capital are major domestic sources of funds. Private capital has been concentrated in the hands of a minute proportion of the population who have had considerably more surplus capital than they have been willing to invest in productive domestic enterprise. Inflation and social, cultural, and political factors have encouraged the spending of surplus funds for luxuries, its investment in often unproductive real estate, or its deposit in foreign bank accounts. Institutional

[7] United Nations, *Statistical Yearbook, 1964,* pp. 330-32.

arrangements such as savings banks, savings and loan associations, and investment funds for mobilizing and channeling resources into productive investment have until recently been virtually nonexistent and are still too few to meet Latin America's needs for investment capital.

A number of problems hinder government investment in productive enterprise; the most obvious is the severely limited amount of most governments' revenues. The rich pay a negligible income tax by British or United States standards so that the government is unable to siphon off the surplus capital of the wealthy to invest it productively. The sources of Latin American government revenues are chiefly taxes on foreign trade or upon consumption together with scores of miscellaneous and onerous fees and charges for the legalization of a broad variety of transactions necessary to the conduct of everyday affairs such as the renting of an apartment or the paying of a debt. Although income taxes in some countries appear to be high, the method of their calculation and the laxity of collection virtually nullify them. Since property taxes have always been low in all Latin American nations, the tax burden, other than that upon foreign trade, falls upon the consumer, the *empleado* and the *obrero* whose pockets are not only empty but full of holes.

Nor do most Latin American governments effectively utilize their limited resources. Several governments have made up deficits in the operation of publicly owned enterprises such as railroads rather than raise fares and thus release funds for productive purposes. In a number of nations large shares of government revenues are allocated to defense instead of to economic development.

### Foreign Investment

In obtaining private foreign capital the Latin American nations must compete with other areas of the world; in 1962, for example, United States private investments in Latin America brought only 12 percent net return in comparison with a 14 percent return on investments in the nations of the European Common Market. Private investment in Latin America is discouraged by rampant inflation and by political conditions. The chief economic limitation on the supply of foreign public capital is the willingness and capacity of the more developed countries to produce a surplus available for investment in underdeveloped nations. Since the world's leading investor, the United States, uses merely $50 out of every $10,000 (0.5 percent) of its income for foreign aid, it does not seem that the bottom of the barrel of available foreign public capital has been reached. Political and ideological considerations are often the decisive factors in determining how much foreign public capital is made available to a given nation.

## Social and Political Factors

While economic problems have played their part in retarding the growth of the per capita gross national product and subsequently in preventing the raising of the standard of living in Latin American nations, social and political factors have been equally important. In the category of social factors are the abject living conditions of most Latin Americans. Housing is a major problem. A 1962 estimate indicated that about 14 million housing units were required to meet the current needs of all Latin American nations.[8] These needs have not been met and have undoubtedly increased along with the population so that larger numbers of Latin Americans live in increasingly overcrowded and deteriorating housing, if indeed they are fortunate enough to have any housing at all. In vast, crowded urban areas the sewage systems are inadequate or nonexistent and water is distant and often contaminated. In 1962 it was estimated that 35 million city dwellers lacked running water;[9] the situation in rural areas is certainly worse. Although in recent years public health conditions have improved considerably from the epidemiological standpoint, unhygienic, overcrowded living conditions combine with semistarvation to contribute both to human distress and to a high incidence of disease and mortality.

Aside from the tremendous suffering involved, which some would regard as sufficient reason for action, such degrading living conditions have many subtle adverse effects upon economic progress. Illness and undernourishment debilitate the human resources essential for development; peoples subsisting so meanly feel a gnawing sense of resentment that is subject to demagogic exploitation; even very young children must seek work, at the expense of an education which however

[8] Inter-American Development Bank, *Institutional Reforms and Social Development Trends in Latin America* (1963), p. 23.
[9] *Ibid.*, p. 34.

inadequate would better equip them for personal advancement and a broader national contribution. Thus, the whole complex of human wretchedness in Latin America is both cause and symptom of underdevelopment—part of a vicious circle that must somehow be broken if progress is to be achieved.

## Education

The generally inadequate educational systems of Latin America are but a further obstacle to development. The schools of Latin America educate too few people, educate them badly, and fail to educate them in certain vitally needed fields. It is everywhere assumed that people need to be able to read and write merely to survive in today's world. In the United States and Canada the illiteracy rate of the population over the age of ten years is only 2-3 percent. In Latin America the percentage of illiterates in this same age group varies greatly from nation to nation, ranging from 13 percent in Argentina to 89 percent in Haiti. In half of the Latin American nations over half of the population above ten years of age is illiterate as is a third or more of the population of another four countries. While the number of students entering school has recently increased, it is estimated that about 40 percent of all school-age children in Latin America do not attend school. Among those who begin, only 17 percent finish primary grades and only 4 percent complete secondary school (*humanidades*). Whereas the average United States resident spends nine years in school, the Latin American spends barely over two years.

Important areas of instruction are often neglected. In spite of the fact that low agricultural productivity is a severe problem in most Latin American nations, little attention is paid to agricultural science at any level of education. Rural areas, where even rudimentary technical education might be useful, are much less well endowed with educational facilities than are the larger urban centers. Although developing countries need technicians, administrators, economists, engineers, and scientists, the educational system does not train them in adequate numbers. Little attention is given to vocational training in either the primary or secondary schools where curricula are chiefly concerned with traditional humanistic studies and oriented almost exclusively toward preparation for the liberal professions. Limited attempts have been made to expand the character of higher education by founding various types of economic, social scientific, biological, and chemical institutes within traditional structures and by establishing separate schools of technology. Nevertheless, most university students are still preparing for the traditional fields of law, medicine, civil engineering, and the humanities—fields that are prestigious and are thought to pave the way to high position. (Half of all students in all Brazilian universities are studying law, philosophy, and letters; a quarter are in the social sciences, engineering, and agricultural sciences.)

Latin American educational systems generally fail to provide adequately even for the elite who are exposed to schooling. This qualitative weakness results from many factors, including outmoded methods of instruction, shortage of trained personnel, and insufficient financial resources. Teachers depend heavily upon rote learning from standard (and usually out-of-date) authorities; there are few first-rate technical books in Spanish or Portuguese; and there is a lack of well-organized, adequately stocked, accessible libraries. Moreover, there is a lack of research facilities, and there are few, mostly ill-equipped, laboratories. The shortage of trained educational specialists is due partly to the heavy demand in government and industry as the modernization process gains momentum for the few who now exist. Attracted to more lucrative or influential positions than are offered by schools or universities, these people either do not participate in the educational systems at all or do so on a part-time basis.

Both the shortage of trained personnel and the outmoded techniques that characterize most Latin American educational systems can be attributed in part to the lack of financial resources. Although a few good private institutions have been developed in Latin America, the traditional source of educational support at all levels has been the state, or in some cases the church. The inadequacy of that support is clear from the statistics on illiteracy and school enrollment; it is equally well reflected in the fact that in only a few Latin American universities are a few faculty members paid enough to live at a middle class level without the necessity of additional work to supplement their incomes.

It has been estimated that to correct deficiencies in Latin American educational systems from elementary school through the university by

1970 would require a total of $34 billion.[10] Since this amount will probably not be available, a decision must be made on how best to allocate the limited funds that will become available for educational purposes. For example, is a drive to educate the masses worthy of the major allocation, or should available funds be concentrated rather heavily upon the improvement of higher education?

### Cultural Values

The characteristic economic, social, and educational milieu of Latin America both reflects and creates the dominant cultural values and attitudes. These values, it must be noted, are held not only by traditional elite elements but by the emerging, modernizing middle sectors. Moreover, while these cultural values are major determinants of the behavior and attitudes of individual Latin Americans, they are little understood by the people of the United States.

Several widely accepted values that act to impede modernization are associated with (1) the ideal of a hierarchical society, (2) ideas concerning property, investment, and work, and (3) the question of birth control. The concept of a society composed of well-defined social layers neatly arranged in ascending order has deep roots in Latin America, reaching back to medieval Iberian institutions and the epoch of the conquest. In many conservative Catholic circles it is felt that such a social order is preordained and that the members of each class must perform their designated functions without question or protest. Other Latin Americans, while not attempting to justify such a system upon religious grounds, consciously or unconsciously accept the existence of hierarchical social relationships.

At the apex of the pyramidal society is the landed aristocrat whose immense hacienda is both a symbol of his position and an economic basis for its perpetuation. The landed aristocracy provides a reference group to be emulated by those less fortunate elements who daringly aspire to crawl up the sides of the pyramid. The values and attitudes of the landed aristocracy have therefore far broader influence than the combined influence of its individual members. Several of these aristocratic attitudes are particularly important to the question of economic

[10] Mildred Adams, *Latin America: Evolution or Explosion* (Dodd, Mead, 1963), p. 167.

development. Among them is the attitude that the ideal society is the *existing* society in which the landed aristocracy is a privileged element, or at most the existing society modified to strengthen and maintain aristocratic privileges by eradicating some of its more glaring evils—evils from the point of view of those who would challenge the privileged group. Moreover, education of the masses, in a hierarchical system, is unnecessary beyond the minimal point of bare literacy, so that broad public education is not supported by those who cling to aristocratic values. Even the masses in a hierarchical society become accustomed to being "kept in their place." No matter how naturally gifted he might be, the member of a depressed group is convinced that he has little to gain by performance beyond the traditionally expected, on any level whatsoever. The masses not only have no desire to increase production, but in some cases actively oppose innovation that might promote productivity because of their conservative anxiety that change generally results in disaster rather than improvement.

The low social value attached to manual labor is another cultural impediment to economic development. It is axiomatic in the traditional, hierarchical societies of Latin America that those with high position do not labor with their hands. This attitude has discouraged the development of the engineers and technicians required for modernization, since laboratory work requires the use and may even cause the disfigurement of the hands and is therefore demeaning. This attitude demands the maintenance of a large pool of cheap domestic labor and discourages this significant depressed element from attempting to improve its status.

The overriding importance of land ownership as a symbol of the highest social status has acted powerfully to restrict economic development. Aristocratic landowners, already in possession of extensive holdings, continue to accumulate land not primarily to increase their income, but as a way of life and to insure vast holdings for their offspring. Middle group elements immediately put some of their first surplus funds into land in order to ascend the social pyramid. The land resources of the Latin American nations are therefore inefficiently exploited and surplus capital that might be better invested elsewhere is poured into status investments.

The desire for land is not only the result of its symbolic value, but the reflection of an attitude that John Gillin aptly describes as "tangible materialism."[11] By this is meant preference for ownership of property that is itself valuable rather than of property that merely represents value that cannot be seen, touched, or displayed as one's own. Thus, to a Latin American it is more desirable to own a building than to own municipal bonds. Tangible materialism creates a sluggish securities market and makes it difficult to arrange for private large-scale industrial financing. It impedes capital accumulation through such institutions as savings and loan associations, insurance companies, and mutual investment funds. Loan funds are scarce and interest rates consequently high. Because of their suspicion of intangible assets, investors prefer immediate and high profits to long-term investments. Tangible materialism is reinforced by personalism, a value also important in political life. The fact that such intangible symbols of property as securities and other commercial paper are not associated with known and trusted individuals makes Latin Americans avoid such investments.

The pressure of Latin America's growing population upon its means of subsistence makes attitudes toward population control important from the development point of view. While mechanical or pharmaceutical means of birth control may possibly be practiced by a very small sector of the Latin American population, it appears that, if the Mexican case is typical, Latin Americans generally oppose the very "family planning" that might provide them a respite from this burden on their productive capacity. Opposition to birth control derives from the values of the Catholic religion, from the traditional Latin American concept of the family and extended family as institutions, from the peasant view of children as economic assets, from the symbolic role of children as proof of masculinity, and from sentiments of nationalism. It is particularly significant that major goal-defining groups in Latin America—journalists, lawyers, teachers, doctors, priests—seem almost unanimously to oppose birth control.

*Political Attitudes*

It is obvious that instability, based upon and perpetuating imperfect political institutions and nurtured by social and economic stresses, also discourages economic development. Investors both domestic and for-

[11] Richard N. Adams, et al., *Social Change in Latin America Today* (Vintage, 1961), pp. 38-40.

eign hesitate to commit funds to nations whose future seems uncertain. Moreover, regardless of the degree of political stability, where economic nationalism flourishes, it discourages foreign participation in national economic development. It also leads politically important sectors of the population to accept unquestioningly the idea that foreign enterprise has schemed against their nation's political independence and economic progress. Hence importation of capital is genuinely feared and therefore hemmed about with restrictive conditions that, together with the threat of possible expropriation, tend to discourage foreign investment.

## Conclusion

Such are some of the economic, social, and political impediments to the modernization of Latin America—impediments that at the same time are partly the result of past failure to modernize. It is evident that many of Latin America's problems, if they remain long unsolved, will create grave tensions that may lead to political explosions. For this and other reasons their solution is an important factor in the United States' achievement of its broad objectives in international affairs. A rising standard of living in Latin America would not only provide a larger market for the products of United States industry; it would remove some of the conditions that encourage frustration and despair among Latin Americans and foster antiforeign hostility toward the United States. Although improved living conditions would not necessarily lead to the establishment of democratic regimes, the solution of the multiple problems of the Latin American nations would enable them to conform more closely to the criteria for free and independent nations in the peaceful world community that it is the goal of the United States to establish. The following chapter reviews some of the steps that have been taken toward the solution of these problems.

# VIII

# The United States and
# the Alliance for Progress

Official interest in promoting the economic and social development of the Latin American nations first developed in the United States in the 1930's when the Export-Import Bank began its operations and the first technical assistance programs were undertaken. Since that time, the institutional basis for promoting development has expanded and increasing numbers of people have become involved in the modernizing process. Today many individuals and agencies participate on their own initiative, or as agents of the United States government, or in cooperation with the government. They include the private investor establishing manufacturing plants or exploiting the sea, forest, and subsoil resources of the Latin American nations; the university providing technical assistance, cooperating to develop a sister institution in Latin America, or carrying on basic research related to Latin American problems; the foundation giving financial assistance to help Latin Americans develop their human resources; the United States labor union seeking to strengthen its Latin American counterpart through educational programs; and a variety of specialized governmental departments and international agencies whose concerns range from agriculture and demography to education and public health. From the point of view of the United States government the major instrument for giving direction and meaning to the complicated Latin American development program is the Alliance for Progress which came into being in 1961.

In reality there was little new about the Alliance. Many of the ideas upon which it was based, and most of its administrative apparatus, significantly antedated 1961. The Alliance for Progress had several conceptual progenitors, including the portion of the 1948 Charter of the Organization of American States that established the Inter-American Economic and Social Council for ". . . the promotion of the economic and social welfare of the American nations through effective cooperation for the better utilization of the national resources, the development of the agriculture and industry and the raising of the standard of living of their people. . . ."[1] The council's 1960 Act of Bogotá listed the social reforms most needed, and those reforms became a basic feature of the Alliance for Progress.

Theoretical foundations for the Alliance were culled from the often conflicting schools of economic thought represented by such entities as the United Nations Economic Commission for Latin America (ECLA) on the one hand, and the United States government, the International Bank for Reconstruction and Development (World Bank), and the International Monetary Fund on the other. Operation Panamerica, suggested in 1958 by President Kubitschek of Brazil, provided the major new idea that an inter-American, government-sponsored crash program was essential to Latin American development.

The Alliance sought to marshall all the diverse existing development instruments and ideas under a single banner, to give the modernization program a set of common goals, and to provide the financial and technical assistance necessary to achieve them. The banner and statement of goals was the Charter of the Alliance for Progress, signed in Punta del Este, Uruguay, in August 1961 at a ministerial meeting of the Inter-American Economic and Social Council. The United States government envisioned the Alliance's program not as philanthropy but as a technique for implementing Washington's major foreign policy objectives of assuring the security of the United States and the way of life of its people and creating a community of free and independent nations. It was hoped that the Alliance would pave the way to a peaceful social

[1] Robert N. Burr and Roland D. Hussey (eds.), *Documents on Inter-American Cooperation* (2 vols.; University of Pennsylvania, 1955), II, 190.

and economic revolution that would go far toward solving Latin America's basic development problems and raising the standard of living of its masses. This would be, in short, an alternative to the Cuban model of violence and diversion to the Sino-Soviet sphere of influence. It would provide an alternative that, it was hoped, might prevent the remaining Latin American nations from straying from the fold. Moreover, when modernized, the Latin American nations would be more able both to conduct themselves as free and independent states in a peaceful community and to provide economic opportunities for citizens of the United States.

## Specific Goals of the Alliance

The Charter of the Alliance for Progress set forth certain goals to be attained, within the ensuing decade, by the nations of Latin America. It specified, for example, that each Latin American country should have a minimum annual per capita economic growth of 2.5 percent, which growth should be employed (a) to raise the relative standard of living for less privileged social sectors and (b) to increase the proportion of the national product devoted to investment so that eventually economic growth would become self-sustaining. Elevation in the standard of living was to be judged not alone by economic performance: adult illiteracy was to be eradicated and six years of primary education made available to all children; life expectancy at birth was to be extended for at least five years, and a certain percentage of total housing was to be supplied with potable water and adequate drainage; both the quantity and the quality of housing were to be improved.

Moreover, the Alliance's charter outlined the structure of a presumably more desirable Latin American economy. Product diversification, including rational industrialization, was to be sought. The latifundia and minifundia systems were to be replaced by more equitable systems of land tenure under which ". . . the land will become for the man who works it the basis of his economic stability, the foundation of his increasing welfare, and the guarantee of his freedom and dignity."[2] To avoid both inflation and deflation, stable prices were to be maintained domestically. Internationally, the Alliance was to move toward creation

---

[2] U.S. Department of State, *Bulletin*, Sept. 11, 1961, p. 464.

of a Latin American common market and promote the worldwide sale of Latin American exports at equitable prices.

## Means of Achieving Goals

In three major sections the charter of the Alliance described the means by which its goals would be reached. The section entitled "Economic and Social Development" was concerned with four major topics: (a) the comprehensive development plans required of each Latin American nation as a prerequisite for foreign assistance, (b) emergency measures pending formulation of those detailed plans, (c) sources of foreign aid for approved development programs, and (d) mechanisms through which these funds would be made available. According to the charter, acceptable national development plans would incorporate the principle of self-help and would provide both for the improvement of human resources and for more intensive exploitation of natural assets. Acceptable plans would also have to state in detail the measures that would be taken to strengthen the agricultural sector and to reform the taxation base and fiscal structure of the nation's economy. A program for the encouragement of foreign investment was also to be included.

It was agreed that a great deal of both public and private external support for national development plans would be required. It had already been estimated that in the ten years to 1971 a total of $100 billion capital would be needed to implement Alliance goals. Of this sum it was agreed that the Latin American nations themselves would supply $80 billion with the rest coming from such external sources as the World Bank, the Inter-American Development Bank, the United States government, and private investors. To supplement the efforts of the Latin American nations, the United States agreed ". . . to allocate resources which, along with those anticipated from other external sources, will be of a scope and magnitude adequate to realize the goals envisaged in"[3] the charter. The United States also agreed to finance technical studies necessary in drawing up the various detailed national plans for development and reform envisioned under the charter. Other suggested sources of technical assistance included the Organization of American States (OAS), ECLA, the Inter-American Development Bank, and the United Nations.

[3] *Ibid.*, p. 466.

*Economic Integration*

Special sections of the Charter of the Alliance for Progress dealt with "Economic Integration of Latin America" and "Basic Export Commodities," both subjects considered of the utmost importance by Latin Americans. In the section on economic integration it was agreed that expansion of existing markets was essential to the growth of both industrialization and general productivity. To further that objective the Montevideo Free Trade Treaty and the Central American Treaty on Economic Integration were designated as appropriate instruments. The delegates also accepted the principles that (a) Alliance funds could be used to promote economic integration, (b) national enterprises should be conducted so as to be able to compete with foreign enterprises, and (c) free enterprise should be encouraged.

*Expansion of Exports*

Even greater attention was given to the question of exports. It was accepted that Latin American trade must be expanded, cyclical fluctuations minimized, and deterioration in terms of trade reversed. Among many ways listed for accomplishing these objectives, four were of major importance. The first stated that "importing member countries [obviously the United States and other developed nations were intended here] should reduce and if possible eliminate . . . all restrictions . . . affecting the consumption and importation of primary products. . . ."[4] The other three called for (a) international cooperation to counteract the effect of the preferential treatment accorded by Western European nations to their former colonies, (b) support of the United Nations Commission on International Commodity Trade in its efforts to stabilize commodity prices, and (c) the convening by the OAS of a special conference of experts to recommend ". . . effective means of offsetting the effects of fluctuations in the volume and prices of exports of basic products."[5]

[4] *Ibid.*, p. 468.
[5] *Ibid.*, p. 469.

## External Financing

Three major international financial agencies from whom assistance might be expected were in existence when the Alliance came into being. Two of them, the International Bank for Reconstruction and Development and the International Monetary Fund, had been created in the immediate post-World War II period. The third, the Inter-American Development Bank, was established in 1960.

### World Bank

The International Bank for Reconstruction and Development, commonly known as the World Bank, of which the Latin American nations are members, had been primarily interested in augmenting the infrastructures of the underdeveloped nations and in encouraging private investment. From the time of its formation through 1964 it invested approximately $1,438 million in Latin America, much of that in electric power production and in transportation. To stimulate private investment the World Bank created an affiliate, the International Finance Corporation. IFC was provided ultimately with a capital of about $400 million to promote development through joint investment in private enterprise with nationals who would also provide competent management. By 1966 IFC had loaned $86 million to enterprises in Latin America which amounted to 57 percent of all its loans.

As intended by its founders, the World Bank operated virtually as a commercial institution, lending only to projects that would repay promptly and with interest. It was even able to borrow money from private investors on its own account, so well run were its development operations. In spite of the fact that the World Bank was performing as it was supposed to perform, it became the object of Latin American criticism that it failed to support absolutely vital development projects that could not meet its standards of eligibility. Because of the United States' considerable influence upon World Bank policy, some Latin Americans charged that Washington used the Bank to implement its policy that private capital and enterprise should bear the main burden of financing the development of Latin America. Whether or not this charge was true, World Bank operations changed considerably under the pressure of criticism. In the first place, in 1960 the World Bank established a new affiliate lending institution—the International Development Association—which was empowered to make loans for important development projects even if they could not be expected to produce a profit. Although most of its funds were made available to Asian and Middle Eastern nations, five Latin American countries were given credits of about $35 million in the period 1962-64. In the second place, the World Bank itself began to devote an increasing proportion of its funds to Latin America. From 1947 through 1956 about 18 percent of the Bank's net loans were for Latin American projects, whereas the $1,001 million authorized for Latin American plans in the period 1961-64 accounted for about 35 percent of the total loans made by the World Bank.

### International Monetary Fund

The second major international financial agency with an interest in Latin America is the International Monetary Fund (IMF) which provides loans of foreign exchange to members to enable them to overcome balance-of-payments difficulties. In the 1950's because of the fluctuations in the prices of exports of primary products and because of heavy imports for development and other purposes, the Latin American nations began to have serious balance-of-payments problems. They have received considerable assistance from the IMF, owing it a balance of $625 million at the end of 1962.

In the late 1950's, however, the IMF became the butt of mounting Latin American criticism, for it had begun to insist, as a prerequisite for its help, that borrowing nations adopt reforms that would remove the alleged causes of their difficulties. The purpose of the reforms was to create conditions of financial stability and responsibility of the type generally prevalent in the world's most advanced nations. Their undertaking usually required painful austerity programs that produced hostile political reactions to the governments involved. The IMF came under even greater attack when both the World Bank and the United States government began to require, as a condition for loans, that the prospective borrower comply with the standards of the IMF.

*Inter-American Development Bank*

The third major international financing agency of importance in Latin American development was created in response to Latin American demands for a source of funds that would be used for their problems exclusively and that would not only supplement existing lending entities but would make loans on a more flexible basis. This instrument —the Inter-American Development Bank—was established in 1960 with an authorized capital of $1 billion to be raised through subscription from all the American nations; it was empowered also to raise additional money in the open market. Of the original capital, 85 percent was to be devoted to regular banking operations and the remaining 15 percent to a Fund for Special Operations that would make soft loans in support of non-self-liquidating but necessary projects. The United States accepted 41 percent of the capital stock for regular banking operations and 66 percent of the Special Operations Fund. The remaining capital was subscribed by all of the Latin American nations, with Argentina, Brazil, and Mexico assuming the greater share. In addition, the bank was made responsible for a Social Progress Trust Fund, previously established to implement the Act of Bogotá, in which there remained $394 million pledged by the United States for use in stimulating Latin American social development. Felipe Herrera of Chile was elected president and under his direction the bank has played a vital role in forwarding the objectives of the Alliance not only through its loans, but also by assisting Latin American governments to obtain funds from other sources. During the first five years of its existence its own operations have been expanded and it has developed sufficient standing to borrow money on its own account in the open market.

Between the adoption of the Alliance and the end of 1964 the Inter-American Development Bank made loans totalling $1,165 million to all the Latin American nations except Cuba—an amount representing 25-30 percent of the international public development financing that went to Latin America. In accord with the principle of self-help, partial rather than total underwriting has been provided by the Bank itself, chiefly from borrowing governments. In 1963, because of very heavy calls upon the Bank's funds, member governments increased its authorized resources for regular banking operations to $2.15 billion. At the same time the Fund for Special Operations was increased to $219 million.

In administering the Social Progress Fund the Inter-American Development Bank, between 1961 and early 1964, financed a variety of projects including low-income housing, water supply and sewage systems, assistance to low-income farmers, and improvement of higher education. Because of heavy calls upon the fund, the United States increased its original allocation to $525 million. Then, in 1964, in order to make possible the financing of more of these social projects, the bank was authorized to use the Fund for Special Operations for these purposes. The United States agreed to provide an additional $750 million over a three-year period and the Latin American nations pledged a contribution of $150 million in their own currencies.

In addition to its own direct financial operations, the Inter-American Development Bank has actively engaged in working out methods by which the European nations could contribute to Latin American development through long-term financing of European-produced capital goods.

### Export-Import Bank

In addition to international financial agencies there are other external public sources of capital for Latin American development. Two major United States entities are the Agency for International Development and the Export-Import Bank, neither of which, however, is exclusively concerned with Latin American development. The Export-Import Bank was founded in 1934 to promote United States sales abroad. Between 1940 and 1961 it authorized loans of $12.5 billion of which about 36 percent were made to Latin Americans for the development of transportation, steel mills, and electrical production, among other things. (The Brazilian and Chilean steel mills at Volta Redonda and Huachipato, respectively, for example, were partially financed with Export-Import loans.) Since the beginning of the Alliance for Progress the bank has continued to provide hard loans primarily for the purchase of United States products to be used for Latin American development projects, but it has become relatively less important as a source of funds for Latin American development partly because of a reduction in the amount of its loans to the Latin American nations and partly because of the greater availability of funds from other sources such as the Agency for International Development. Although the Export-Import Bank authorized loans to Latin America of $671 million between August 1961 and the end of 1965, this amounted to an average of less than $160 million annually compared with an average of about $200 million a year in the period 1940-61.

*Agency for International Development*

The Agency for International Development (AID) was established in 1961 to consolidate an existing Development Loan Fund and other agencies concerned with foreign aid into one organization that would give greater emphasis to long-term development and economic and social planning on the part of recipient nations. As a branch of the Department of State, AID can coordinate its activities with United States policies. Although its activities encompass the entire underdeveloped world, AID has a special Latin American Bureau that coordinates its operations with the policies of the Alliance for Progress. AID makes very flexible and cheap loans for projects that are not necessarily expected to be financially profitable. It seeks primarily to build self-sustaining institutions that will provide the basis for development. AID loans are eagerly sought by Latin American nations, but the agency's policy is to support only projects that cannot be financed either by private investors or by other public lending agencies. To implement this policy AID maintains close liaison with other United States government agencies and the various international banks. AID authorized $2,289 million, mostly in long-term development loans, from August 1961 through the end of December 1965, or about twice as much as the World Bank in the equivalent period.

# United States Problems

In spite of the variety of agencies that can provide public investment for Latin American development, the financing of the Alliance has aroused controversy and posed general policy problems for the United States. One has been how the Alliance should be administered and directed. Others related to the foreign aid program of the United States include the determination of the validity of that program, the ways in which it should be administered, and the purposes for which it should be employed. And again there are problems raised by Latin American interest in the economic integration and export promotion aspects of the Alliance.

A crucial question has been the administration and direction of the Alliance's all-important external public investment program. The delegates at Punta del Este created no new or elaborate international agency to implement the Alliance for Progress. Instead they placed its general supervision in the hands of the existing Inter-American Economic and Social Council which was given the duties of providing an annual progress report and of making appropriate recommendations to the OAS. The council was also to appoint the only new agency established by the Alliance—"a panel of nine high-level experts, exclusively on the basis of their experience, technical ability and competence in the various aspects of economic and social development"[6] from which three members would be selected to join with three other experts appointed by the Organization of American States to form ad hoc committees to evaluate the various national development programs submitted. A country whose plan had been approved by an ad hoc committee could then approach the Inter-American Development Bank which would proceed to arrange financing through either its own or outside resources. Failure to win an ad hoc committee's approval would not deprive a country of the right to take its plan directly to sources of public financing, but its chances of obtaining funds would obviously not be of the best. But the panel of nine experts, lacking in any real authority and weak as an executive agency in terms of structure, could not adequately coordinate and direct this immense investment program. As a result, the United States government—as the sole major lending power in the Alliance and because of its influence over international lending agencies—actually turned out to be making final loan decisions. Latin American leaders complained that progress was being delayed by the red tape involved in Washington's interminable interagency consultations, that decisions on loans and credits were being made on the basis of United States rather than Latin American interests, and that, in effect, the Alliance for Progress had promptly degenerated into

⁶ *Ibid.*, p. 273.

one more United States foreign aid program rather than fulfilling its supposed purpose as a collective effort to solve the development problems of Latin America. United States leaders countered with charges that the acceleration of the financing of the Alliance was being stalled by failure of Latin American governments to work out national plans and to undertake the reform measures specified in the charter.

## Inter-American Committee of the Alliance for Progress

As the Alliance came under mounting criticism, former Presidents Lleras of Colombia and Kubitschek of Brazil were asked by the OAS to study Alliance problems. In separate reports the two men recommended the creation of an inter-American committee to provide greater direction to the Alliance. As a result the Inter-American Economic and Social Council established the Inter-American Committee of the Alliance for Progress (ICAP) which began to function in the spring of 1964.

ICAP's composition was significant, for although the United States was to have a permanent place on the committee, there were to be six Latin American members representing specified groupings of nations, and it was stipulated that the president of the committee was to be "a distinguished Latin American." Carlos Sanz de Santamaría, an economist and former finance minister of Colombia, was chosen for that post.

This Latin American-dominated committee was to be the central agency, the executive committee, of the Alliance for Progress. This was indicated by the fact that heads of other agencies concerned with Latin American development, such as the Inter-American Development Bank, the Inter-American Economic and Social Council's panel of nine experts, and the United Nations Economic Commission for Latin America, were to act as advisors to ICAP. A major committee function was to recommend on the allocation of public funds for development purposes, but in this respect it was charged with taking into consideration both the opinion of the panel of nine experts and the efforts of the Latin American nations to undertake basic reforms. ICAP was not empowered to disburse funds, final authority for which remained in the hands of the lender, be it the United States government or an international lending agency. Nevertheless the recommendations of the prestigious ICAP would obviously carry great weight.

ICAP was established to give the Latin American nations both greater voice in the management of the Alliance and the responsibility for carrying out the reforms considered to be fundamentally prerequisite to development. From Washington's point of view such an arrangement was desirable not only because it would minimize charges of United States domination of the Alliance, but also because a committee controlled by Latin Americans would replace the United States government as the agent responsible for upholding the standards established in the charter. This, it was hoped, would not only make more politically feasible the pressuring of Latin American governments to institute reforms, but would also give Latin Americans a greater sense of responsibility for the success of the Alliance while in no way requiring the United States to relinquish control over the use of its foreign aid funds. From Latin America's point of view ICAP was desirable because it gave Latin Americans greater influence over both the Alliance's general direction and the allocation of development funds. In this latter connection it was obvious that the recommendations of a committee representing six Latin American nations would have great influence over the United States government or, if Washington refused to approve any given loan, other sources of public funds.

So far during its brief life ICAP has lived up to expectations. It drew strong approval from Latin American representatives at the December 1964 meeting of the Inter-American Economic and Social Council at Lima and special praise from President Johnson in his January 1965 message to Congress on foreign assistance. ICAP has carried on country studies, coming up with reports pinpointing major problems in development and recommending solutions. Confidence in its efficacy was shown by the Inter-American Economic and Social Council when it took two steps to give ICAP greater influence. In the first place the panel of nine experts was reduced to five and then incorporated into ICAP in a clearly subordinate position. Moreover, the council at its April 1966 meeting adopted a twenty-three-point "immediate action program" containing many of ICAP's recommendations and at the same time increased ICAP's responsibilities as executive organ of the Alliance.

Although ICAP has given the Latin Americans greater influence in directing the Alliance, the basic problem of the predominant role of the United States remains unsolved. This was pointed up in April 1966 when the panel of experts resigned, partly because they had been made subordinate to ICAP, it is true, but also in protest against what they considered to be the dominance of the Alliance by the United States. The experts charged that there was too much reliance in development programming upon bilateral relations between the United States and individual Latin American nations at the expense of the original idea of the Alliance that called for multilateral cooperation.

## Validity of Foreign Aid

Although the creation of ICAP appears to have strengthened the international underpinnings of the Alliance for Progress, the United States government is still confronted by other vexing policy questions in relation to both the Alliance for Progress and foreign aid in general. The major question is whether the very concept of foreign aid retains validity in the mid-1960's. In the past, few politically sophisticated elements in the United States have opposed economic aid, either in practice or principle, but a growing number have recently been disillusioned by the failure of various aid programs to live up to their expectations. Instead of the peaceful, democratic regimes, friendly to Washington and to United States business interests, that many expected the recipients of foreign aid to become, a number of the underdeveloped recipient nations have been characterized by instability, authoritarianism, and hostility to the interests and the government of the United States. Latin America, even since the inauguration of the Alliance for Progress, has been no exception. As a result there is a growing feeling that funds appropriated for foreign aid should be both reduced in quantity and subjected to greater restriction and supervision.

On the other hand, it has been argued that the general disillusionment with foreign aid is unwarranted and that in reality the problem lies with the United States' excessively high and unrealistic goals for the underdeveloped nations. According to this position, these nations, because of long-existing basic structural defects, could not possibly have been expected to transform themselves overnight. Moreover, it is claimed that foreign aid must be given some credit for the fact that in recent years the communist bloc has failed to gain significant new adherents in the underdeveloped world—a world that seemed very ripe for such conquest in the years immediately following the Second World War. On the basis of these as well as humanitarian arguments, influential individuals and groups have sought not merely to continue but to increase foreign aid. For example, in 1963 labor leader George Meany, as a member of President Kennedy's Committee to Strengthen the Security of the Free World, issued a minority report recommending that "AID funds should be substantially increased and geared to the increasing ability of AID personnel to implement a stepped up program."[7] And the congressional platform of Americans for Democratic Action stated that "Administration efforts in foreign aid are inadequate to meet the needs of the developing nations and to provide all peoples of the world with the hope of a future free from the fear of hunger and privation. A foreign aid budget of 6.5 billion dollars . . . is a necessity in 1965."[8]

At the same time that it must reconsider the validity of foreign aid, the United States government must face the probability that the amount of aid requested by its Latin American allies to fulfill their development needs will vastly exceed the yearly $2 billion stipulated in the Charter of the Alliance for Progress. ICAP's estimate of requirements for 1965 was $3.1 billion, and as the hitherto unimagined immensity of the Latin American development task becomes clear, the amount required could multiply. The United States government must therefore decide whether or not it will or can commit additional public funds to the development of Latin America.

### Arguments Against Increased Aid

The wisdom of markedly increasing the amount of external public aid to the Latin American nations must be judged partly on the basis of its probable impact upon their long-range development. For instance, how much external public assistance can they absorb? It is obvious that lack of certain technical skills or of adequate administrative machinery

[7] Committee to Strengthen the Security of the Free World, General Lucius D. Clay, Chairman, *The Scope and Distribution of United States Military and Economic Assistance Programs* (U.S. Department of State, 1963), pp. 24-25.

[8] Americans for Democratic Action, *Program for 1965*, leaflet.

could prevent effective use of additional capital that might therefore simply be wasted. Moreover, an excessive influx of public foreign capital might cause the economy to develop in such a lopsided fashion that existing values and institutions would collapse rather than change, producing anarchic conditions welcome neither to the recipient nation nor to the political interests of the United States. Too large an influx of external public capital might also discourage utilization of available domestic capital thus inhibiting establishment of the self-interest necessary to a viable free and independent state.

While consideration must be given to practical limitations on the amount of aid the United States can provide, such a relatively small percentage of the United States gross national product is actually devoted to foreign assistance for development purposes that the United States is financially able to increase easily the amount of its aid to Latin American nations if it so desires. Although the claims of other areas of the world upon funds are important, the main internal barrier to substantial augmentation of such assistance is psychological and political rather than economic. Psychological resistance results from many factors, among them (a) the failure of the underdeveloped nations to fulfill the expectations of United States citizens, (b) a disinclination among United States citizens to invest without tangible, visible return, and (c) a belief that development is to a large degree a matter for private enterprise and self-help. Such resistance might be counteracted by an extensive educational campaign within the United States, or by an obvious improvement in the condition of the nations being assisted, but psychological resistance presently does exist and translates itself into political terms that make it unlikely that the total amount of United states public financial assistance will be increased and even make it possible that there will be growing demands for its reduction.

## Alternatives to Additional Aid

But if Latin America needs and can utilize substantial additional capital for development, and if that capital is not forthcoming from the United States, or if the United States reduces its economic aid, whence will capital be obtained? Obvious sources include the governments of the other developed nations, and private investors rather than public.

ORGANIZATION FOR ECONOMIC COOPERATION AND DEVELOPMENT. Members of the Organization for Economic Cooperation and Development (OECD), which includes Japan and most of the Western European nations (as well as the United States and Canada), have both indirectly and directly provided official capital to the Latin American nations. Capital has been made indirectly available in the form of credits that enable export suppliers in a developed country to receive prompt payment from their government which later collects from the recipient developing country. About $200 million annually in export credits is presently being granted to Latin American countries by OECD nations. A problem inherent in such credits, however, is their relatively short-term nature, which often requires that the debt on a project be repaid before the project has begun to function and therefore before repayment can be made from the project's own income and thus without excessive strain on other sectors of the developing economy. In addition to export credits there have been direct grants and loans of official capital from OECD members to Latin American governments. In 1960 and 1961 these amounted to only about $25 million, but by 1964 they had risen to between $80 million and $100 million—less than 6 percent, however, of the total official capital sent by the European nations and Japan to all the developing countries of the world.

The percentage of European official capital finding its way to Latin America is trifling because the capital designated for underdeveloped areas has tended to go to Africa and the Far East where the European nations and Great Britain have continuing political commitments; Latin America on the other hand, has been considered to be in the sphere of influence of and therefore the responsibility of the United States. However, the Kennedy Administration initiated a policy of encouraging the European countries and Japan to increase financial assistance to Latin America on the grounds that because they had attained postwar economic recovery with United States assistance, they should now be willing to assume a larger share of the burden of assisting all underdeveloped nations, including those of Latin America. Latin Americans, anxious both to acquire more external capital and to reduce their dependence upon the United States, have courted European official capital. Reflecting the interest of both the United States and the Latin American nations, the chairman of ICAP, together with the president of the Inter-American Development Bank, assisted by the Assistant Secretary for Economic and Social Affairs of the OAS, began discussions in September 1964 with the Development Assistance Committee of OECD in the hope of bringing about greater European participation in the development of Latin America.

IMPLICATIONS OF EUROPEAN AID. Encouragement of the participation of European official capital raises a policy question that now seems remote but may have future significance—the question of the political repercussions in the Western Hemisphere of large-scale European investment in Latin America. Cuba has been able to defy the United States partly because of economic assistance from the Soviet Union. The Cuban situation provides an example of what might happen if one or several of the nations now being encouraged to invest in Latin America should participate in a third position movement in Europe. General de Gaulle, who has already moved France considerably in that direction, travelled through Latin America in the fall of 1964 attempting to wean its countries away from the United States with the reminder of common Latinity and vague promises of financial cooperation. If the General had been operating upon a base of considerable existing French investment, or if he had been able to offer concrete proposals, his hosts—wishing as they do to be rid of their almost total dependence upon the United States—would certainly have responded to his blandishments far more warmly than they did. The United States must foresee this possibility and have ready an appropriate policy.

MULTINATIONAL FINANCING. Another problem connected with the foreign aid program of the United States is the way in which it should be administered. One possible alternative to the present system is to rely more on multinational financing. In fact, United States policy is now ". . . to put more aid on a multinational basis."[9] There is a question, however, of whether it is in the interests of the United States to turn over the administration of more of its aid funds to one or several international agencies or consortia, or whether it should administer more of the funds on a bilateral basis. The answer to this question depends partly upon the choice of agency. In terms of the objectives both of United States foreign policy and the Alliance for Progress, those genu-

[9] *New York Times*, Jan. 15, 1965.

inely international agencies in which the nations of the Soviet bloc are participants would seem less appropriate than those agencies in which they are not, chiefly because of the differences that would arise over the methods and ideological aims of development. This does not imply that the United States should not wholeheartedly support United Nations development activities; merely that greater reliance should not be placed upon them for administering aid funds allotted to Latin America. For this purpose the World Bank and the Inter-American Development Bank seem particularly useful, because the objectives of their members harmonize philosophically with those of the United States.

There are both technical and political advantages to United States support of multinational aid. International bodies can provide a broader range of technical skills and more knowledge specifically relevant to the problems of Latin America than can the United States acting alone. Multinational agencies can demand conditions from loan recipients that the United States might be altogether unable to obtain or able to only at the risk of alienating the recipient. This political advantage would derive from both the recipient nation's membership in the multinational agency and its participation in decision making. Moreover, conditions imposed by a faceless, purely technical supranational agency are assuredly more palatable than those imposed by a single strong nation whom one fears to displease but fears even more to obey. Thus, by delegating the administration of aid funds to multinational bodies, the United States can work for the desired development of the Latin American nations more effectively and with fewer political problems than by administering its funds directly. Finally, by giving support to multinational aid entities, the United States is contributing to the building of an infrastructure for a peaceful world of free and independent nations.

Nevertheless, there are certain potential political difficulties in United States reliance upon multinational aid administration. In the first place, by its very nature a multinational body will not work specifically to advance the political and ideological objectives of United States foreign policy. In the second place, the very turning over of its financial assistance funds to a multinational agency deprives the United States of those funds as an instrument of immediate policy and reduces its operational flexibility in dealing with sudden political crises. Moreover, the government in power at the moment in the United

States risks the opposition's accusation of failure to husband United States funds and even of contributing to the strengthening of the "enemy" of the moment. A compromise solution to this problem, and one that enables the United States to retain control over its funds while giving great leeway in decision making to others, is of course that provided by ICAP.

ADMINISTRATION OF UNILATERAL FUNDS. If the United States continues its present program of a combination of multinational and unilateral assistance, it will be necessary to decide what is the most effective way of using the latter in order to advance the objectives of United States policy. What political strings, if any, should be attached to grants and loans? For example, should Washington refuse to aid nations that fail to support its cold war policies? A positive answer would require a highly inappropriate act—discontinuance of aid to Mexico, which alone among the Latin American nations has failed to abide by the decision of the OAS foreign ministers to cut off economic and diplomatic relations with Cuba.

It has already been pointed out that financial assistance from the United States has domestic Latin American political repercussions whether or not Washington so wishes. The question is therefore not *whether* but *how* United States influence should be exerted. Should the United States, for example, impartially aid all de facto governments, regardless of their nature, on the basis of their need and their acceptance of the economic and social standards of the Alliance for Progress? That policy could be justified on the grounds that the United States is not entitled to determine another nation's type of government, and that economic aid—by relieving suffering—could eventually create conditions favorable to representative, nonauthoritarian civilian political systems. Or, should assistance be utilized to promote political systems acceptable to United States standards? Such a policy might be implemented by directly supporting approved political parties, social or economic groupings, and government regimes, while withholding or limiting aid to all others.

Open financial support of domestic political groups would have very serious disadvantages, however, for not only would the reaction against such intervention be so violent as to neutralize any possible benefit, but it would destroy any confidence that might have developed in the

United States' claimed desire to establish a community of free and independent nations.

The efficacy of strengthening a particular social or economic group in the hope of gaining its sympathies for United States policies is highly problematical, if only because it would be so difficult to decide which group or groups should be the object of United States support. In the opinion of former United States Foreign Service Officer John Paton Davies, the hope for carrying out Latin American modernization lies with the wealthy, privileged minority of people educated abroad " . . . who would seem best equipped to make a workable synthesis of the three worlds which they know: the traditional Latin America, the computerized, socially tranquilized Yankee, and the uncomputed, untranquil Latin America now a-borning."[10] Mexican economist Edmundo Flores, however, believes it unrealistic to think that groups now in power will initiate and carry through tax and land reforms that, although necessary for development, will deprive them of their present position. In Flores' view, only revolution can effect the redistribution of wealth required for development and this revolution he wants the United States to accept, rather than continuing to support what he calls "quasi-feudal and militaristic governments."[11] Another specialist, John J. Johnson, has suggested that the middle groups in Latin American society have values most like those of the people of the United States and therefore cooperation with them for the modernization of Latin America would be reasonable. According to still another view, however, the basic weakness of United States policy with respect to the Alliance for Progress is its incorrect assumption that urban middle class elements will support Alliance reforms. Chilean economist Claudio Véliz has succinctly stated this point of view:

The fundamental error in the United States approach . . . has to do with its definition of the middle class. United States scholars, politicians and journalists have gleefully discovered a Latin American middle class, and without pausing to find out what kind of a middle class it really is they have proceeded to credit it with all sorts of qualities it does not possess. . . . There are groups which have superficial characteristics of the middle class; they even talk, write and think of themselves as being middle class, but

[10] *Ibid.*, Aug. 31, 1963.

[11] Laura Randall, *Economic Development: Evolution or Revolution?* (Heath, 1964), p. 54.

objectively they are not, and it is very hard to see how they can ever bridge the distance which separates their intrinsic conservatism, their respect for hierarchical values, their admiration for their national aristocracies, their overwhelming desire to rise and be accepted by those they regard as their betters, from the dynamic reformism which is usually associated with middle class idiosyncracy.[12]

The notion of supporting particularly promising regimes as "showcases" of the United States in carrying out the Alliance for Progress has been tried on several occasions in recent years and has not generally produced the desired results. Frondizi's Argentina, Alessandri's Chile, Bosch's Dominican Republic, Colombia, and Venezuela have variously been given special attention as showcases of development within a democratic framework, but with the exception of Venezuela none has equalled the hopes of the United States. The failures resulted partly because some of them were chosen in desperation—not because the chances of success were good, but because they were better than those of other nations. The failures do not necessarily mean that the policy will not work, but rather that more knowledge may be needed to make it viable.

Several other policy questions would arise in connection with the use of foreign aid to advance the specific objectives of United States Latin American policy. One is whether loans and grants should be employed to protect the economic interests of United States citizens. Another is whether aid should be used to promote concessions for American enterprise in areas generally reserved in Latin America to nationals or the government, such as oil in Brazil and Argentina.

Or, should the United States instead, denying itself any possible immediate self-advantage, assist development programs on the basis of purely nonpolitical, technical considerations? This might preclude the hostile reactions that have resulted from attempts to attach conditions to financial aid and might at the same time contribute to the establishment of free, independent, and friendly states in Latin America that would be able to sustain their growth and protect their own interests in world politics. There is, however, a major obstacle to the implementation of such a policy—the fact that technical specialists do not agree among themselves on the most effective ways of accelerating develop-

[12] Claudio Véliz, "Obstacles to Reform in Latin America," *The World Today,* January 1963, pp. 18-28.

ment. Their disagreement throws into relief a whole range of technical questions that must be considered in deciding upon the ways in which United States financial assistance, either bilateral or multinational, should be employed. It should be noted that each solution suggested can become a political weapon for some group either in the United States or in Latin America.

## Technical Problems of Development Policy

An important example of conflicting technical viewpoints is the question of inflation. So-called monetarist economists regard inflation as an inhibiting factor in economic development and insist that it be controlled through (a) monetary and fiscal policies that will maintain the value of the currency and (b) regulations to prevent sharply rising wage and price levels. Such financial practices, in the monetarist view, will encourage private investment and facilitate the accumulation of the capital necessary for sound economic development.

But so-called structuralist economists believe that inflation is a natural consequence of rapid development and that a reasonable amount of it stimulates rather than depresses development. They claim that orthodox monetary and fiscal policies and the stabilization of prices and wages through government controls will not alter the basic structural defects that produce inflation. They therefore advocate basic structural reforms in order to achieve a more viable economy, even though deficit financing, borrowing, or other inflationary measures may be necessary to finance those reforms. In short, the structuralists believe that the way to halt inflation is through facilitating more rapid economic growth.

These opposing views represent in reality different concepts of the nature of economic development and force Washington to elect to support either one or the other or to find navigable middle courses. The United States government, supported by the economists of the International Monetary Fund and the World Bank, has generally been sympathetic to the monetarist position, while the main strength of the structuralists has been among the economists of the United Nations Economic Commission for Latin America, whose ideas have been popular with several governments of the more highly developed Latin American nations. Although the lines have not always been clearly drawn, there has tended to be a United States position versus a Latin American position, with the United States having to decide whether to insist upon the adoption by Latin American governments of unpalatable monetarist norms as a sine qua non for United States assistance.

During most of the 1950's Washington's policy required "sound" financial practices, inspiring Latin American charges that the United States not only failed to understand Latin American problems, but that it was seeking to impose upon Latin America the system of the United States. Washington still theoretically adheres to monetarist ideas, but its willingness to provide funds for soft loans through the Social Progress Fund and the international lending agencies as well as the aid it has given to rescue several nations that failed to adopt "sound" financial practices are indications of its willingness to meet the structuralists part way. On the other hand, the prestige in Latin America of the structuralist position has been tarnished by the distress that Brazil and Chile suffered simultaneously from galloping inflation and economic stagnation when structuralists were influential in formulating their policies. Although structuralist influence appears at the moment to be on the wane, its vigor should not be discounted.

Another technical question concerns the desirability of assistance to special sectors of the economy of developing nations, such as agriculture, manufacturing, or mining. The United States believes that "a strengthened agriculture is the key to the further development of industry and over-all national economy."[13] Thus it has advocated policies that seek to create national markets within the Latin American nations by narrowing the chasm between developed urban centers and backward rural regions. This can be accomplished, according to United States policy makers, by building roads, increasing agricultural productivity, improving marketing techniques, emphasizing industrial production of items useful to agricultural regions, and augmenting the purchasing power of the rural population.

Assuming that the United States should in fact assist in the stimulation of self-sustained Latin American economic growth, a further technical question arises as to how this can best be accomplished. There exist at least six possible general approaches: (1) concentration upon

[13] Alliance for Progress, *Weekly Newsletter,* Nov. 2, 1964.

economic *infrastructure* on the assumption that it is the essential basis for any self-generating economic activity, (2) support of *model, key industries* in the hope that they will provide examples that will stimulate local economic activities, (3) assistance on a *matching funds* basis only, in the hope of promoting Latin American participation in essential development projects, (4) assistance dependent upon fiscal and administrative *reforms* that will generate internal capital investment, (5) assistance primarily for the building of *institutions* to create the economic and social conditions suitable for self-sustained growth, and (6) funds directed primarily toward social development upon the assumption that only through *changes in attitudes, values, and social structure* can the motivating forces necessary for self-propelled economic growth be attained.

The United States has in fact employed all of these approaches, or various combinations of them, in the attempt to secure the modernization of Latin America. Since World War II the use of external assistance to build economic infrastructure has been consistently recognized as essential. Increasing funds have been made available for such purposes by the United States, and their distribution is now routinely handled by the administrative staffs of the international lending agencies. On the other hand, full United States support of key industries has been reduced to a minimum while the matching funds principle has been increasingly applied. In recent years, however, the United States has moved away from direct support of economic development projects and used greater amounts of money to promote the building of basic institutions. For example, formation of savings and loan associations has been encouraged in the belief that they will triply serve as an institutionalized means for accumulating and investing local capital, as a source of financing for desperately needed low-cost urban housing, and as a promoter of local industry. At the beginning of 1965 about $75 million in local funds had been accumulated for investment purposes in such associations throughout Latin America, of which Argentina alone accounted for almost $70 million. The United States has also supported local institutions concerned with development, such as the Central American Development Bank and agrarian reform or colonization institutes.

In addition to emphasizing institution building, in recent years

United States policy has become increasingly concerned with the solution of Latin America's social problems. To promote the modernization of skills and values, Washington not only continues to devote funds to technical assistance but also is giving increasing support to attempts to modernize educational systems. By 1964, for example, more than fifty United States universities had accepted AID contracts to work with similar institutions in Latin America to help increase their effectiveness. The effort to improve education raises another series of problems, such as whether effort should be concentrated upon children or adults, or upon the elimination of illiteracy, or upon increasing the available pool of skilled manpower—problems that are soluble only within the context of the individual local situation. Within the last two years also moves have been made to solve the socioeconomic problems of a population growth that is extremely rapid. The United States government has unobtrusively made available financial and technical assistance on birth control, and in spite of its supposedly controversial nature, several countries have taken advantage of Washington's offer and are quietly laying the groundwork for the popular practice of family planning within the existing economic and social milieu.

## Rate of Change

A major policy question related to the social and economic problems of Latin America concerns the rapidity with which the Latin American nations should be expected to undertake basic reforms, or should be forced to undertake them under threat of United States withdrawal or withholding of financial assistance for development projects. Those who consider tax and land reform to be essential preconditions for further development demand their prompt enactment and charge the Latin Americans with lack of good faith when they fail to move ahead rapidly on these matters. Others, however, suggest that caution be exercised, pointing out that too rapid a rate of reform may lead to the collapse of the stabilizing elements in society and to consequent chaos. They feel that the United States' own slow progress toward the granting of constitutional rights to the Negro, or tax reform, or better balanced state legislatures should make Washington aware of how difficult it is rapidly to effect reforms in an established social structure.

*Private Versus Public Investment*

An extremely controversial question of United States policy on financial participation in Latin American development has concerned the role of private versus official public investment. Relying heavily upon private funds to stimulate Latin American development, during most of the 1950's United States policy was to provide public funds only for economically sound projects that failed to interest private investors. Between 1950 and 1959 United States private investments increased over 80 percent, from $4,445 million to $8,218 million. More than 60 percent of this increase was in the politically explosive petroleum and mining industries, with petroleum alone accounting for nearly 47 percent of the increase. Thus Latin Americans assumed that United States private capital was primarily interested in the very profitable extractive industries, and not concerned with overall Latin American development. The United States government, in the effort to support its private investment policy, claimed that any investment, regardless of type, could contribute to the economic welfare of the recipient nation. An analysis of United States private investments as of 1955 was issued to demonstrate that of the total receipts from sales of all American enterprises in Latin America, 76 percent went into local payments in a variety of ways including wages, materials, interest, and dividends, and only 11 percent was returned to the United States in the form of profits or dividends. Nevertheless, under political pressures (deterioration of United States-Latin American relations and the threat of the extension of the Cuban revolution), the United States government began to expand the use of public funds for financing Latin American development. In the Charter of Punta del Este of 1961 it was agreed that two-thirds of the estimated external United States capital required to carry out the Alliance for Progress would be provided from public funds, the remainder of approximately $300 million annually to come from private sources.

There has been disagreement as to whether private investors have fulfilled their quota. The United States Department of Commerce reported that during 1962 more United States private capital was brought back to the United States from Latin America than had been invested there, but it was subsequently charged that Commerce's figures were misleading. In particular it was noted that no credit had been given for the reinvestments of United States enterprises operating in Latin America and that 1962 had been abnormal because United States oil interests had chosen that year to make normal shifts of large amounts of capital from Venezuela to operations in other areas. If these and other hidden factors were taken into account, it was claimed, it would be seen that United States private investors had more than lived up to the commitment made for them by their government. Nevertheless, it seems clear that, whatever its amount, United States private investment was less than had been anticipated by the Alliance's makers. In 1963 and 1964 net United States private investment improved, reaching $64 million and $113 million, respectively, but these figures were far from the $300 million goal and made clear that new United States private investors had failed to rally behind the banner adopted at Punta del Este.

Several reasons have been advanced for that failure, including the traditional one that potential investors fear the political and economic instability of several Latin American nations and distrust the heightened economic nationalism manifested in forms considered hostile to United States investment. The Alliance for Progress itself was even blamed for discouraging the very private investment it sought to encourage. John Moore, of W. R. Grace and Company, in a 1964 congressional hearing charged that ". . . there have been certain emphases emanating from institutions concerned with the philosophy of the Alliance for Progress which have not been particularly encouraging to private investment. Specifically, an example would be the United Nations Economic Commission for Latin America known as ECLA . . . which up until recently was under the management of its executive secretary, Mr. Raúl Prebisch. . . . He was a major architect of the Alliance and is a man of tremendous influence in the economic policies of Latin American governments. He has taken some very strong anti-private investment positions. . . ."[14]

In another connection David Rockefeller has claimed that the social revolutionary aspects of the Alliance are incompatible with the promotion of external private investment in Latin America. "The Alliance," he

[14] *Private Investment in Latin America*, Hearings, Joint Economic Committee, Subcommittee on Inter-American Relationships, 88 Cong. 2 sess. (Jan. 14-16, 1964), p. 25.

charged in 1963, "has tended to stress reform movements which cannot be carried out swiftly without great social unrest and political uncertainty. This completes the vicious circle, for these are precisely the conditions least likely to provide a hospitable climate for savings and investment."[15]

On the other hand, Peter Nehemkis, a lawyer with extensive business contacts in Latin America, discounts the importance of instability and uncertainty in impeding the expansion of United States private investments in Latin America, pointing out that during the period when United States capital was supposedly fleeing Latin America, European and Japanese businessmen were increasing their investments there in the belief that they would reap rewards. The fault, according to Nehemkis, lay with the inability of United States businessmen to adapt themselves to conditions that differed markedly from those in their own nation.

Whatever the reason, or reasons, during the early years of the Alliance for Progress private United States investment in Latin America fell short of the planners' hopes. During that period, consequently, the United States government found itself under pressure to use its aid program on behalf of United States private investors. Business interests were not unique in seeking to influence AID administrators, for numerous organizations such as the Cooperative League, labor unions, and educational interests sought to gain acceptance for their particular points of view. Nor was the pressure to use the aid program to help private investors merely the result of the businessman's desire to make a good deal, for many business leaders and economists were convinced that private investment was essential to Latin American growth and development. But whatever its motivation, pressure on behalf of private investors was reflected in suggestions both to protect existing United States business interests in Latin America and to create conditions more favorable to future investment. Among the former were demands that assistance be denied to any nations that expropriated such interests without adequate compensation provisions—demands that were enacted into law by Congress.

Among suggestions for creating conditions favorable to United States private investment were several that taken together constituted a de-

---

[15] Mildred Adams (ed.), *Latin America: Evolution or Explosion?* (Dodd, Mead, 1963), p. 13.

mand that the United States government use its foreign aid program as an instrument par excellence for the promotion in Latin America of the free enterprise system. These included recommendations that Alliance for Progress funds be provided only to those nations that fulfilled specific financial and administrative conditions. For example, in 1963 the majority of the important Committee to Strengthen the Free World, appointed by President Kennedy to evaluate the foreign aid program, and headed by General Lucius D. Clay, recommended in connection with the Alliance for Progress:

The United States should be increasingly more specific on the self help and the reforms it seeks and do so on a country-by-country basis. At the top of such a list are the goals of monetary stability, sound financial and social budgeting, reduction and eventual elimination of subsidies to government enterprises, tax systems and administration which contemplate raising local revenue levels, stimulating private local and foreign investment and distributing the tax burden more fairly, and measures for the better utilization of land designed to increase agricultural productivity and credit, expand and diversify agricultural exports, encourage rural development, and increase income in the lower levels of society. . . .[16]

These recommendations were intended to establish conditions that would provide a "sound" basis for the evolutionary development of Latin America rather than a prescription for promoting United States private investments, but there is no question that had the report not been left to gather dust, their implementation would have provided the conditions that potential United States investors would consider attractive.

More specific were Peter Grace's proposals on behalf of the Department of Commerce advisory group, known as the Commerce Committee for the Alliance for Progress. Grace, while admitting that there was a place for public external financing, claimed that " . . . private capital with its greater effectiveness and far larger potential is of the essence and is the basic long-term sustaining factor that can maintain a high rate of growth."[17] The Grace committee report dealt primarily with investment incentives and recommended that United States aid be employed to encourage private investment. Three of Mr. Grace's colleagues on the committee, however, issued a supplemental report. They

[16] *The Scope and Distribution of United States Military and Economic Assistance Programs,* p. 12.
[17] As quoted in the *New York Times,* April 8, 1963.

were David Rockefeller, Henry Wriston, and Emilio G. Collado who felt that the Grace report had paid insufficient attention to the political and economic realities of Latin America. However, their dissenting memorandum did agree that private investment, both Latin American and external, should provide "the main thrust of the Alliance for Progress."[18]

## The Free Enterprise Question

Suggestions have also been made that the Alliance for Progress be used to strengthen the free enterprise system in Latin America in a way that would be advantageous to United States private investment. For example, numerous recommendations have sought to halt the trend toward state control of economic activity by prohibiting United States aid to any Latin American government-owned enterprise that would compete with private operations. In an even stronger suggestion, the chairman of International Bond and Share, Incorporated, speaking at a congressional hearing in 1964, advocated going beyond the mere refusal to support statism:

> Latin American governments should first take a clear stand against further entry into the enterprise field, whether by condemnation or otherwise. Then, to reverse course, they should sell the equity stock of these state-owned enterprises to the local people, including the employees concerned.... If our future aid did nothing more than to help finance these popular divestments and bring from United States industry the temporary management technology to put them on their feet, while also assisting our own industries there to take in local partners, so to speak, we would have made a great contribution to Latin American development.[19]

Few Latin American moderates have shared the enthusiasm of United States businessmen for promoting foreign private investment and the free enterprise system in Latin America through the Alliance for Progress. An advisory group to both ECLA and the OAS reported several years ago that except in the case of Venezuela the majority of politically articulate Latin Americans "is rather against than in favor of foreign capital."[20] An eminent Mexican intellectual, Daniel Cosio Ville-

---

[18] *Ibid.*

[19] *Private Investment in Latin America,* Hearings, p. 19.

[20] As quoted in Victor L. Urquidi, *The Challenge of Development in Latin America* (Praeger, 1962), p. 56.

gas, points out that foreign capital and technical skills must be given most of the credit for the development of Latin America in the nineteenth and early twentieth centuries and that although "it would be logical to suppose that the Latin American countries . . . should wish to seek more foreign capital and technology . . . this is not so; rationally they desire and seek these, but emotionally and irrationally they fear and resist them."[21]

Latin American moderates have made clear their attitude toward United States-style free enterprise in their reactions to both the Grace report and the dissenting memorandum of its critics. The insistence of both that the main thrust of the Alliance for Progress should be private investment was seen as an attempt to subvert the Alliance into an instrument for the promotion of United States business interests. This conviction produced unfavorable reactions from such quarters as the anticommunist *El Tiempo* of Bogotá and moderate leaders like former President Lleras of Colombia and Costa Rica's Gonzalo Facio who was president of the Council of the OAS.

Latin Americans do not share the enthusiasm of some United States business leaders for foreign capital and the free enterprise system in part because they believe that the foreign investors' desire for profit seldom coincides with the genuine national needs of their nations and that foreign investment has often been followed by political penetration that has in turn caused international complications and decreased the independence of the nation. Moreover, it is believed by some that the free enterprise system, with its emphasis on reliance upon free market mechanisms, is inherently advantageous to the more highly developed nations and must therefore be countered in Latin America by government intervention. Former President Quadros of Brazil has clearly expressed this view in stating that "we are not in a position to allow the free play of economic forces in our territory, simply because those forces, controlled from outside, play their own game and not that of our country."[22]

THE MEANING OF FREE ENTERPRISE. But the single most important reason for Latin America's distrust of the United States economic system is a misunderstanding of the meaning of the term "free enterprise." It is

[21] Adams, *Latin America: Evolution or Explosion?* p. 120.
[22] As quoted in Irving Louis Horowitz, *Revolution in Brazil* (Dutton, 1964), p. 104.

unfortunate that the most strident United States advocates of the implantation of "free enterprise" in the underdeveloped countries advertise it as a system based upon enlightened managerial and capitalistic classes imbued with social consciences and recognizing their obligations to society in general and to labor in particular, and sincerely concerned with increasing productivity for the benefit of society as a whole as well as, incidentally, for their own profit. Those who indulge in such talk seem to overlook, perhaps in honest ignorance, the historical fact that the existing United States system evolved painfully and slowly and is the product of a long and bitter struggle in which the free enterprisers of the nineteenth century were socialized and tamed as a result of an outraged public's reaction against their flagrant excesses. As one phase of this conflict, United States management and capital were most reluctantly forced to accept labor's right to organize itself for the advancement of its own interests. And not even the fiercest struggles of capital and management succeeded in preventing the establishment of a broad range of governmental regulation of their activities— regulation that compelled United States free enterprise to pursue its quest for profits in more enlightened terms.

Not only do the advocates of free enterprise for Latin America fail to point up this evolutionary process, knowledge of which might well encourage acceptance of free enterprise among those who see the transparent impossibility of the advertised product, but they also fail to admit that the system that they hold up as a model is in reality a very mixed bag, containing not only government regulation for the purpose of protecting United States citizens against the ruthless exploitation of yore but also active official participation in economic life by means of government-sponsored research, protective tariffs, services useful to business in many different ways, as well as sophisticated methods of government financial manipulation and intervention to maintain employment, to increase productivity, and to augment the welfare of the business community. Nor do the advocates of a simon-pure free enterprise system for Latin America take the trouble to point out the role that cooperatives, municipally owned utilities, the Tennessee Valley Authority, etc., play in the total economic functioning of the United States, leaving it to be understood that untrammeled and unmixed free enterpise has brought the United States to its present high material level. It should not be surprising therefore that the advocates of free enterprise for Latin America see nothing incongruous in their insistence that the financial aid of the United States government under the Alliance for Progress be used primarily for the promotion of free enterprise.

The Latin American concept of a free enterprise system is, in contrast, based upon the image of the still untamed Latin American capitalist who seeks large and fast profits and is totally unconcerned with the social implications of his activities. Whether this image reflects the real Latin American businessman or not is a matter of some disagreement even among very experienced observers. "To put it bluntly," writes Nehemkis, "the trouble with the Latin American capitalist is that by and large he is a hundred years behind the times. Speaking generally, the Latin American capitalist represents the stereotype whom Karl Marx and Friedrich Engels denounced. . . ."[23] On the other hand, John Moore told a congressional committee:

> We have to get to know the Latin American businessman better. I do feel . . . that throughout the last two or three years that there has been a lot of inexact thinking with regard to the role of the local Latin American businessman. Your committee has made trips around those countries and you have seen great new cities and industrial centers, and those were not built by foreigners. They were built by local men, most of whom came from humble origins and built up their businesses and investments in the pattern with which we are familiar in this country. And [by] this criticizing them generally as oligarchs and undesirable persons, which is all too common, I think we are discouraging the very creative responsible element of Latin America that can make the wheels turn down there.
>
> Naturally, they have their undesirables . . . but as a business community . . . they are a progressive and patriotic, basically constructive element.[24]

It is instructive to note that in spite of their differences, both Moore and Nehemkis accept the existence of an unfavorable image. And that image is associated in the Latin American mind with the free enterprise system.

The unfavorable Latin American image of the free enterpriser is intensified by the distorted view that United States businessmen give of their free enterprise system. Their failure to provide an exact description of the economic system of the United States and of its background makes it impossible for United States and Latin American citizens to

[23] Peter Nehemkis, *Latin America: Myth and Reality* (Knopf, 1964), p. 246.
[24] *Private Investment in Latin America,* Hearings, pp. 8-9.

discuss "free enterprise" with each other, for they are simply not talking about the same thing. And so, United States government attempts to promote free enterprise in Latin America are not viewed as the sincere efforts they are to encourage enlightened and progressive capitalism, but rather as self-serving devices to inculcate an exploitative system that many Latin Americans who favor modernization consider to be highly reactionary.

This point of view was implicit in a speech by the chairman of ICAP in which he was at the same time trying to make it clear that the Alliance for Progress was not an instrument for the promotion of government-controlled economics. In his March 1964 speech he said:

> The Alliance for Progress is not meant to supplant the free enterprise system. It fully recognizes the important role private initiative should play in the task of development. But make no mistake about it: the private enterprise system conceived of in the Charter of Punta del Este is not that of the nineteenth century.
>
> Today, a system of mixed economy, involving both government and free enterprise, governs to a greater or lesser extent in all industrialized countries. It is accepted as desirable and necessary. In trying to stimulate development in Latin America, it would be illogical for us not to apply the historical experience of Western Capitalism. We cannot declare ourselves advocates of untrammeled free enterprise to suit minority groups within or without our countries.[25]

UNITED STATES PROMOTION OF FREE ENTERPRISE. While the United States government has by no means become an advocate of "untrammeled" free enterprise, it has responded to domestic political pressures by using its own resources and its influence in international agencies to encourage "responsible" free enterprise and political and economic systems in which it may thrive. Continuous efforts are made to encourage financial and administrative stability in the Latin American countries and to stop inflationary tendencies. Investments by United States citizens in Latin America have been encouraged through a variety of techniques including a program under which AID has negotiated investment guarantee agreements with at least a dozen Latin American nations to protect investors from losses resulting from expropriation, war, revolution, and insurrection. Along similar lines the United States strongly supported a World Bank proposal of a con-

---

[25] As quoted in Nehemkis, *Latin America: Myth and Reality,* pp. 271-72.

vention on settlement of questions arising from the expropriation of foreign properties under which the Bank would act as arbiter or conciliator if both the government and the investor agreed to use its services. Under such an agreement, it was assumed, the signatory nations would promise investors to make use of the Bank's services. However, the proposal encountered decisive Latin American opposition within the Bank's Board of Governors. Speaking for Latin America, following a caucus, the Chilean representative castigated the proposed convention as both unnecessary and unfair—unnecessary because protection for private investments was already provided by all Latin American countries and unfair because it would give foreign investors a special advantage not enjoyed by nationals.

Another United States government approach to the promotion of private investment in Latin America is the provision of information to United States citizens on opportunities for such investments. AID has established a "one stop" information center in Washington, for example, to provide interested businessmen with information about its program. AID has also assigned an officer on the staff of each of its overseas offices the sole responsibility of dealing with private investment matters. Moreover, AID funds have been made available to encourage businessmen to make surveys of specific potential private investment opportunities in Latin America.

High government officials have cooperated with businessmen in an attempt to encourage private investment. Under the sponsorship of Senators Javits and Humphrey a group of business leaders from the United States and Europe began in January 1964 to organize the Atlantic Community Development Group for Latin America (ADELA). From this group there emerged the ADELA Investment Company which was established to provide, at a profit for the investors and in collaboration with Latin American businessmen, financing for new medium-sized private business operations and for the expansion of old ones. By October 1964 the fifty-four European, Japanese, and North American companies involved in ADELA had raised $17 million of the $40 million of planned investment and had made their first investment—in a steel forging plant in Colombia.

The United States government has also encouraged nonofficial agencies and private citizens to participate in carrying out the objectives of the Alliance for Progress so that private initiative, an essential part of the free enterprise system, would become part of the Alliance, minimizing the influence of various governments. Thus at the suggestion of the OAS the Pan American Development Foundation was able to raise funds in the United States to support projects in Latin America. The foundation was given a tax exempt status by the United States Internal Revenue Service. Branches of the foundation in each Latin American country raise funds from local sources to match those provided by individuals and corporations in the United States.

AID also cooperated in the establishment of a United States Executive Corps, suggested in 1963 by David Rockefeller as a private-enterprise counterpart to the Peace Corps. Members of the Executive Corps are businessmen on leave with full pay from their companies who, upon invitation from a Latin American nation, devote two or three years to the organization and development of specific projects in that nation.

Attempting to institutionalize the promotion of private participation in the Alliance, the Office of the United States Coordinator of the Alliance for Progress has created a division known as the Partners of the Alliance which, working with state governments and private groups, seeks to bring businessmen and civic and educational leaders throughout the United States into contact with their counterparts in Latin America to carry out specific projects. By the end of 1964 seventeen states had established relations with Latin American nations or communities and a number of private groups, such as the Texas Good Neighbor Commission, the Cooperative League of the United States, the United States Junior Chamber of Commerce, and Tools for Freedom, had undertaken specific projects related to the objectives of the Alliance for Progress. Nevertheless, the main thrust of the Alliance for Progress is not yet private enterprise, for it still depends primarily upon public external capital for financing.

The total supply of external capital, public and private, available to the Latin American countries has increased markedly since the commencement of the Alliance for Progress. Development problems are now less those of obtaining funds than of obtaining suitable modernization projects. An additional problem in some of the Latin American nations is a lack of local currency to supply the matching funds called for in many public external loans. Moreover, an oppressive burden of short-term debts and credits absorbs existing revenues and threatens the financial situation in a number of Latin American nations.

The latter problems have led many Latin Americans to seek alternatives to external financing—alternatives that will provide their countries with increasing income and reduce their dependence upon the United States and other developed nations. They have become increasingly interested in the economic integration of Latin America and improving the condition of their export trade—both matters which at the insistence of Latin American leaders were included as special chapters in the Charter of Punta del Este.

## Latin American Export Trade

Latin American export trade is crucial to the supplying of the $80 billion of savings for development investment estimated as Latin America's minimum contribution under the Alliance for Progress. In their export trade Latin Americans seek (a) to maintain prices at satisfactory levels and (b) to expand their present markets. To achieve those objectives Latin American nations have tended increasingly to work together. They have cooperated in ECLA to collect data and prepare proposals for the solution of the export trade problem and have collaborated to put those proposals into effect. In inter-American meetings, they began in the 1950's to seek acceptance of their proposed solutions and finally succeeded in incorporating their ideas into the Alliance for Progress, within whose framework a Special Committee for Latin American Coordination was established in November 1963 to seek a unified Latin American trade policy. Under the new committee's auspices, Latin American representatives met at Alta Gracia, Argentina, in March 1964 to discuss common policies that could be supported at the forthcoming United Nations Conference on Trade and Development (UNCTAD). That meeting resulted in the Charter of Alta Gracia, which contained specific proposals that were then supported by Latin American delegations to the United Nations conference. An outstanding feature of that United Nations conference in the spring of 1964 was the cooperation of the Latin American delegates with those of fifty-six other less developed nations to form an effective bloc for pressing the developed nations to accept what was fundamentally the Latin American position on world trade. Then at an OAS commission meeting in Panama in March 1966, where preparations for a proposed revision of the OAS Charter were being made, the nineteen Latin American delegations joined forces to demand that specific measures for implementing their position be incorporated in the OAS Charter.

### Stabilization of Export Prices

The fundamental position of the Latin American nations is that their economic problems originate in the inequitable world trading system that favors developed nations at the expense of the less developed. Latin Americans therefore believe that the developed nations have a responsibility to revamp the existing system to improve the position of the less developed. On the basis of this assumption the Latin American nations, at international conferences and in bilateral negotiations, have proposed a variety of measures for alleviating their trade problems. Important among them have been suggestions for assuring stable prices and a fair return for basic primary exports. Such assurances could be obtained, it has been proposed, either through commodity price agreements or by means of compensatory financing. The commodity price agreement, signed by the major producers and consumers of a given primary product, provides for the maintenance of minimum prices by means of production and consumption quotas and through the establishment of a mechanism for active participation in the market to stabilize prices. Compensatory financing involves the principle that if the return for a given export or exports falls below an established level due to circumstances beyond the control of the exporting nation, then that nation will be given balance-of-payments compensation. Both methods are similar in purpose to United States farm price support programs in that they attempt to provide stable base income levels for producers of products whose prices are determined in an otherwise highly unstable market.

Two commodity price agreements have been drawn up in which Latin American nations participate. Bolivia is a signatory to the International Tin Agreement, along with five other producing and sixteen consuming nations. Of importance to fourteen Latin American nations is the International Coffee Agreement which took effect in 1963 and is based upon established export quotas that seek to maintain prices by restricting production. In addition to these two existing agreements, studies are underway on the desirability and feasibility of similar pacts on cocoa, wool, lead, and zinc, all of which are important to one or more Latin American countries.

No compensatory financing agreements are yet in effect although there is under study by the United Nations the possibility of establishing an international fund to which importers and exporters of a number of products would contribute so that when prices decline producers can draw on the fund to offset their losses. That fund would be worldwide; however, at the third annual review conference of the Alliance for Progress, in December 1964, Brazil's minister of planning suggested a similar organization within the more limited framework of the Alliance. His suggestion was turned over to a committee for consideration.

*Expansion of Export Markets*

The problem of insufficient Latin American export earnings might also be solved through an increase in the volume of exports. Toward that end three types of measures were advocated by Latin Americans at Alta Gracia and at the United Nations Conference on Trade and Development. One was a demand that developed nations halt such practices as import restrictions and special taxes that prevent increased sales in their domestic markets of Latin America's primary products. Further, the industrial nations of the world were asked to grant preferential tariff treatment to the industrial products of the underdeveloped nations so that those nations might improve their production efficiency through large-scale industrial operations made possible by expanded foreign trade. A third measure favored by the Latin Americans was abolition of the General Agreement on Tariffs and Trade (GATT) and its replacement by a new agreement with provisions more favorable to underdeveloped nations.

The Latin American nations, in cooperation with other developing countries, have had some success in implementing their demands. Although GATT has not been abolished, UNCTAD has become a permanent organ of the United Nations and other United Nations administrative machinery has been created to study further and make recommendations upon the proposals discussed at the 1964 meeting of UNCTAD. On the other hand, little progress has been made toward reducing restrictions against Latin American exports or in obtaining preferential tariff treatment for Latin America's industrial products.

Although during most of the 1950's the United States government opposed commodity price agreements and advocated permitting the free play of international market forces to determine the prices of primary commodities, it ultimately modified its position and accepted many Latin American positions on trade in the Charter of Punta del Este. Moreover, Washington has made serious efforts to implement some of these ideas. In several international organizations it has taken the lead in promoting the study of primary commodity pricing based on the policy that raw-material-consuming nations and raw-material-exporting nations are equally responsible for working out trading arrangements; examination of the problem should be conducted on a commodity-by-commodity basis rather than an all-inclusive one; and solutions should be on a global basis.

The International Coffee Agreement was negotiated under United States auspices. Moreover, although Washington opposed abandonment of GATT in favor of a new world trade organization and was cool to the granting of preferential tariff treatment to Latin American industrial products, it did support modification of the GATT agreement to make it into an instrument more useful to less developed nations.

In spite of Washington's acceptance of important Latin American trade positions, during recent years disagreement over trade questions has marred relations between the United States and Latin American nations and has prompted the latter to consider further joint political action to obtain their economic goals. A major reason for this disagreement is that, largely as a result of domestic political pressures, the United States government has been unable to implement policies that it had publicly accepted. In the case of the International Coffee Agreement, for example, in spite of its acceptance by the Administration in 1962, Congress refused to pass implementing legislation when first requested to do so by the President. The main objection was the failure of the agreement to protect coffee consumers in the United States against rising prices. Only when provision for such protection was included in the implementing legislation did Congress approve in May 1965.

*Repercussions of United States Restrictions*

Domestic pressures for protection against certain competitive Latin American imports also led to the intensification of old tensions. In the late 1950's restrictions were placed on imports of lead, zinc, meat, copper, sugar, and petroleum. Strong protests promptly followed, including a Peruvian charge of United States economic aggression in connection with the establishment of quotas for lead and zinc. While not concurring in this and similar accusations against the United States, a 1960 report of the National Planning Association's Inter-American Research Committee (composed of United States and Latin American business, labor, agricultural, and professional leaders) pointed up the seriously unfavorable impact of the United States' restrictive import policy upon the export earnings of the Latin American nations. The report estimated that United States removal of import restrictions on some twenty-nine items would increase Latin American exports to the United States by between $850 million and $1,678 million. The report stated that "there can be no doubt that United States import policy can exert a powerful influence for or against the growth of Latin American exports to the United States in the 1960's. This may make the difference between achieving or failing to achieve a rate of growth that will keep the Latin American countries in a tolerable balance-of-payments equilibrium and thus make possible an adequate rate of economic growth."[26] The following year Washington seemed to be moving toward a change in its import policy when it accepted the Charter of Punta del Este which stated that "importing member countries should reduce and if possible eliminate, as soon as feasible, all restrictions and discriminatory practices affecting the consumption and importation of primary products . . . except when those restrictions are imposed temporarily . . . to establish basic national reserves."[27] Nevertheless no action was taken on United States import restrictions until the summer of 1964 when the United States Congress enlarged and extended them.

In August 1964 Congress approved legislation reducing meat imports 15 percent below what they had been in the previous year—a restriction

[26] Louis O. Delwart, *The Future of Latin American Exports to the United States: 1965 and 1970* (National Planning Association, 1960), p. 97.
[27] Schmitt and Burks, *Evolution or Chaos*, pp. 265-75.

chiefly affecting Argentina and Uruguay. For Argentina the emotional consequences were more serious than the economic, for United States restrictions on Argentine beef had in the minds of the Argentinians long been a symbol of United States hostility to their nation. But for Uruguay the newly imposed restrictions were likely to have serious economic results. The United States Congress also shocked the eleven Latin American countries whose major export is sugar by bowing to the pressure of United States sugar producers and failing to renew the Sugar Act which had provided quotas for the importation of sugar. These severely restrictive acts, coinciding with the refusal of the House of Representatives to implement the International Coffee Agreement, which affected fourteen coffee-producing nations, aroused not only Latin American protests but also their deep fears that the United States government was either unable or unwilling to live up to its commitments to help the Latin American nations to increase their exports.

The Argentine senate unanimously passed a protest against the United States meat restrictions and the measure was also criticized in Uruguay. The chairman of ICAP condemned United States congressional action in a public statement. "I can't believe," he said, "that this action is final. It would be a complete denial of the principle of 'trade not aid' long advocated by both political parties in the United States in their relations with the developing world. It also shows me there is not a clear picture of how seriously these measures can harm the goals of the alliance. . . ."[28] ICAP's chairman was later reported to have told President Johnson directly that these actions of Congress had amounted to pulling the rug out from under the economies of the Latin American nations. Several months later, at the December 1964 review of the Alliance for Progress held in Lima, Peru, all of the Latin American delegates approved a report of a committee on foreign trade that gave the Coordinator of the Alliance specific instructions for action against trade restrictions (the United States voted against the report). Moreover, the objections to United States policy were so numerous that Assistant Secretary of State Thomas C. Mann felt it necessary to beg the Latin American delegates to be reasonable in their attitudes toward the United States. But apparently that request, and Mann's assurances that the Johnson Administration would press Congress to pass the enabling legislation for the International Coffee Agreement, fell on deaf ears. To

[28] As quoted in the *New York Times*, Aug. 24, 1964.

protect their menaced vital export trade interests the nineteen Latin American nations represented at Lima joined together to create a permanent Special Coordinating Committee for Latin America and charged the committee with improving the terms of trade between the Latin American nations and the more highly developed countries of the world. While the Alliance review was still in progress, a Latin American parliamentary conference, also meeting in Lima, established a permanent organization of congressional delegates from the various Latin American nations to work for the advancement of the common economic interests of their nations. During its proceedings the parliamentary group found time to approve resolutions condemning United States restrictions on Latin American imports.

But Latin American protests seemed to have little effect. For example, in 1965 a Venezuelan mission sent to the United States to negotiate for the removal of restrictions on the importation of Venezuelan oil had no substantial success, and in March 1966 the United States and nineteen Latin American nations clashed openly at the Panama meeting that was preparing preliminary proposals for the revision of the Charter of the OAS. At that meeting the Latin Americans succeeded in winning acceptance for twenty-one suggested new articles to be added to the charter including specific provisions for the reduction by importing countries of barriers to trade such as tariffs and restrictions against primary products and the granting of special trade concessions to underdeveloped nations. Although the United States representative had voiced objections to some of the proposals during discussion, the twenty-one articles were approved by the meeting without objection. Bitter feelings among the Latin Americans were produced when the State Department notified the meeting that the United States could not accept the suggested revisions and offered a more general compromise proposal.

## Economic Integration of Latin America

Latin America's failure to secure its objectives in trade with the United States and other industrialized nations has strongly stimulated its movement toward integration of its national economies. One objective of integration is to increase trade among the Latin American nations by removing such obstacles as artificial trade barriers and inadequate communications. The hope is eventually to create a free trade area that will provide a larger market for Latin American industries by pooling potential consumers and thus make feasible the investment of the huge amounts of capital necessary to develop efficient, large-scale industry like that in such countries as Japan, Germany, and the United States. A companion objective of economic integration is the cooperative establishment of particularly elaborate and costly key industries that would supply all of the Latin American member nations with products now obtainable only at high prices from the world's most industrialized nations. Those favoring integration seek ultimately the complete transformation of the economies of the Latin American nations from essentially primary-materials producers to essentially elaborated-goods manufacturers. Selling their manufactures in the large market created by integration, the Latin American nations could overcome the problem created by deterioration in terms of trade and would become less dependent upon the outside world. A final objective of economic integration is to provide the basis for political unity that will enable the Latin Americans to deal more effectively with the United States and other greater powers.

Many articulate and economically sophisticated Latin Americans desire economic integration; there are, however, major obstacles to its achievement, chief among them the vested interests in each nation—interests that might be endangered by the competition engendered by a broad free market. Another barrier is the strident nationalism characteristic of contemporary Latin America that manifests itself both in reluctance to cooperate with traditional rivals and in the desire of each nation to possess all the trappings and symbols of modernization.

*The Central American Common Market*

The goal of the integration movement is the welding of Latin America into a viable economic bloc, step by step, beginning with limited groups of nations but ultimately including all. Activities to date have centered in two separate integrated economic units, the Central American Common Market and the Latin American Free Trade Association (LAFTA). The former has its roots in the early nineteenth century when five of the present Central American nations briefly comprised a single country. In 1950 studies of the possibilities of their economic integration were initiated and this work culminated a decade later in the signing of the General Treaty on Central American Economic Integration (GETI) and an agreement establishing the Central American Bank for Economic Integration (CABEI).

These general agreements, and others more specific in nature that preceded them, provided for the creation of a Central American Common Market in which duties and restrictions on trade among the members were eliminated except for a list of specified items. On the latter, annual negotiations were to take place for ten years until they too were on the free list. In addition, members of the common market were to work toward the adoption of uniform tariffs with respect to non-Central American nations and to coordinate their industrial development through adoption of similar legislation in the field. Financing of regional development was to be carried out under CABEI, and policy for the common market was to be determined by an economic council composed of the ministers of economy of the member nations, with agreements being administered by a permanent secretariat headed by a secretary general.

Since its creation the Central American Common Market has steadily moved forward. At first only El Salvador, Guatemala, Nicaragua, and Honduras ratified the 1960 agreements; but in 1963 Costa Rica joined; Panama may soon swell the number of members to six. Member nations have adhered so closely to the schedules established for reducing trade restrictions among themselves that in 1966 there were no restrictions on 95 percent of the items involved. They have also moved rapidly toward adoption of a common tariff schedule with respect to non-Central American nations. Moreover, funds obtained from the United States, the Inter-American Development Bank, and local sources have been employed by CABEI for planning technical and economic studies, for undertaking a regional program of roads, for the promotion of regional higher education, and for housing construction. By the close of 1965 CABEI had made 112 loans totalling $45 million for such purposes. In the process, intra-Central American trade increased significantly from $33 million in 1960 to an estimated $138 million in 1965.

## The Latin American Free Trade Association

The Latin American Free Trade Association (LAFTA), established in 1960 in Montevideo, has not developed as far as its Central American counterpart. This is partly because the Central Americans started first and had less complex problems and partly because the Central American countries have a population of less than twelve million and relatively simple agricultural economies while the ten members of LAFTA (Argentina, Brazil, Chile, Colombia, Ecuador, Mexico, Paraguay, Peru, Venezuela, and Uruguay) possess rapidly expanding populations already totalling 173 million in 1963 and include the four Latin American nations that have taken the most significant steps toward industrialization.

The objectives of LAFTA are similar to those of the Central American Common Market—to establish a free trade area among the signatories, to work out common trade policies with respect to nonmembers, and to bring into closer conformity the industrialization, agrarian, and development financing policies of the members. Schedules adopted provide for an average minimum annual reduction in intra-LAFTA customs duties of 8 percent. A secretariat has been established in Montevideo.

Since its founding LAFTA has made slow progress. Tariffs have been reduced on more than eight thousand items constituting about 30 percent of the trade among LAFTA's members; trade among members rose by 44 percent from 1961 through 1963, increasing from 6 percent to 8.4 percent of those nations' total foreign trade. Members of LAFTA have also begun to consult with each other on industrial development, and at the organization's 1964 meeting, steps were taken toward establishment of common tariff barriers against the products of non-LAFTA countries. But by 1965, strains were beginning to show. The differences between the more and less industrially advanced members were so marked that Brazil suggested that Argentina, Chile, and Mexico join with it to expand trade among themselves without reference to the states whose development lagged behind.

Its difficulties notwithstanding, the concept of Latin American economic integration retains powerful supporters. In 1965, responding to a suggestion by President Frei of Chile, four of the most respected leaders in the field of Latin American development—Raúl Prebisch of ECLA, Carlos Sanz of ICAP, Felipe Herrera of the Inter-American Development Bank, and José Antonio Mayobre of ECLA—issued a document on the acceleration of integration. Emphasizing the great need for economic integration, they insisted upon the necessity for a single

Latin American common market as opposed to two or more regional associations. Pointing out that political action would be required to bring about a common market, they made many specific recommendations for the institutional foundations upon which such a market would have to rest. In 1965 also a meeting of the Latin American foreign ministers gave strong support to the integration movement.

Then the United States, previously reluctant to support a Latin American common market, altered its position. President Johnson, speaking in April 1966 in Mexico, stated that one of the "basic convictions" upon which the United States' faith in the future rests is "that the drawing together of the economies of Latin America is critical to this hemisphere's future. Only in this way can the hemisphere develop truly efficient industry, expanded foreign exchange earnings and a sound foundation for a full Latin-American partnership in building a peaceful world community."[29]

## Status of the Alliance

The situation of the integration movement is typical of the total program of the Alliance for Progress: the first steps have been taken at various points along the line of proposed advance, but their significance and their degree of genuine forward movement are still unclear. On the positive side, after two years of failing to reach the established goal of 2.5 percent annual increase in gross per capita national product, the Latin American nations as a whole surpassed it slightly in 1964 and equalled it in 1965. While that rise was due partly to price increases of certain exports rather than exclusively to a rise in productivity, it was encouraging. There were also signs of progress toward the fundamental changes envisaged in the Charter of Punta del Este. Meaningful and functioning national and international institutions have been established to plan and carry out Latin American development, such as ICAP, eighteen national planning agencies, development banks, agrarian institutes, and loan associations. Particularly noteworthy has been the formulation of comprehensive programs of economic and social reforms by most of the Latin American nations. Moreover, attempts have been made to translate those plans into legislation, nineteen nations

[29] As quoted in the *New York Times,* April 16, 1966, p. 6.

now having land and tax reform laws of some type. Finally, some observers believe that the pressure of the Alliance has led many Latin American leaders to accept both the necessity for and the inevitability of reform.

There is, however, a darker side of the Alliance for Progress picture, for except in the area of tax collection (where receipts increased 26 percent between 1960 and 1964), little planning and legislation in the area of social and economic reform has actually been implemented. Moreover, regression seems to have taken place in certain areas. Per capita food production has actually declined in the face of population expansion. Housing, public health facilities, and drinking water supplies have also lagged behind the goals of the Alliance for Progress.

## Alliance's Assumptions Questioned

Among various doubts that have been expressed concerning the fundamental assumptions upon which the United States' Alliance policy rests is the question of whether a peaceful social and economic revolution such as that envisioned in the Charter of Punta del Este is in fact possible. It has been suggested that the concept of a "peaceful revolution" is inherently contradictory. Moreover, revolutionary rather than gradual social changes would produce dislocations, it is argued, that would have unfavorable repercussions upon the economic progress necessary to sustain reform. For example, investment capital may be channeled into basic reforms rather than into more immediately productive economic activity; or such great instability may result from basic reforms as to discourage both foreign and domestic capital; or the Latin American elites who must necessarily take the lead in any peaceful revolution may be alienated by the Alliance's emphasis upon reform. Is it not, moreover, altogether unrealistic to expect elite groups voluntarily to effect reforms that will ultimately deprive them of wealth and power. Even middle classes in Latin America might be expected to resist reforms, for they tend to emulate the aristocracy and have not relinquished the hope of somehow reaching the top of the existing pyramidal social structure. If such were the case, it has been argued, only revolution could destroy the grip of the elites and middle classes and bring about the conditions in which basic reforms might take place.

Doubt has also been raised concerning the United States' obvious conviction that the social and economic revolution envisaged in the Charter of Punta del Este is largely a technical problem responsive to the application of appropriate tools, techniques, and capital. Tad Szulc points this up in writing that ". . . the dollars and cents of the Alliance are not enough. . . . Revolutions deal primarily with ideas, and in the final analysis, the battle for Latin America must be fought in the field of ideas."[30] In fact, as this study has repeatedly pointed out, the controversies engendered in the course of attempting to foment Latin American development have been political par excellence, and the differences between aspiration and reality have been clearly reflected in domestic politics. For example, in the United States internal political pressures from oil, lead, zinc, sugar, and livestock producers have thwarted the United States' fulfillment of its Latin American export trade commitments; and many Latin American governments have been prevented by vested interests from abiding by their agreements to carry out specified reforms.

International politics has played a major role even in apparently purely technical approaches to development. Agile United States development specialists, for example, have adapted their technical recommendations to the economic doctrines most in harmony with the international political needs of the moment, but nevertheless have more or less consistently emphasized the need for stability, efficiency, and private enterprise—all of which would (incidentally?) greatly facilitate the extension of the economic and political influence of the highly organized and competitive United States. On the other hand Latin Americans, while far from despising stability, efficiency, and their own brand of free enterprise, tend to emphasize "technical" approaches that assure the independence of their own countries and prevent them from becoming mere ancillary units of the vast economic complex centered in the United States.

The differences in approach to economic development between Latin Americans and spokesmen for the United States reflect differing images of Latin America. Citizens of the United States consider the Latin American states to be within their country's sphere of influence. They regard the development of the Latin American countries as a kind

[30] *The Winds of Revolution: Latin America Today and Tomorrow* (Praeger, 1963), p. 301.

of civilizing "burden"—a concept that is not without certain overtones of Anglo-Saxon superiority. And they seek to make the Latin Americans over in their own image—the image of the United States. Latin Americans, on the other hand, consider their nations to be free and independent and within no nation's sphere of influence, least of all that of the United States. They prize highly their unique cultural heritage and deeply resent the United States' long-prevailing attitude of condescension toward them.

Latin Americans are indeed desperately seeking to modernize and develop their nations. They are doing so, however, not to become like the United States but to rid themselves of dependence upon the United States.

# IX

# Conclusion

As the foregoing survey has attempted to indicate, the problems confronting United States Latin American policy are extremely diverse, highly complex, and inextricably entangled with interests that appear superficially to be unrelated to those problems. Thus the reluctance of certain important Latin American nations to second Washington's policy of excluding the Castro regime from the Organization of American States involved not only inter-American relations but also the global position of the United States and domestic politics in every nation concerned. Because Cuba had suddenly become a crucial stake in the cold war, the way in which the United States would deal with it would have measurable world repercussions. But the United States government was also under purely domestic political pressures from both genuinely terrified citizens and an opposition that would not fail to exploit fully both popular fears and government mistakes or vacillation. Those who demanded a "hard line" charged that nations reluctant to support Washington's Cuban policy were pro-Castro if not procommunist, and hostile to the United States. Yet, in fact, the hesitancy of those nations was the result of their individual domestic political situations that later coalesced in a collective international position; and those domestic political considerations were in turn the product of tensions created by social and economic distress and dislocation and of unique visions of national self-interest. Thus, the failure of important countries to support the sanctions the United States urged against Cuba represented not one problem but a chain of problems no single one of which could realistically be dealt with in isolation.

Increasing the complexity of the problems in United States-Latin American relations are the various meanings they hold for different individuals and groups. For example, the problem of foreign investment in Latin American development is for the United States investor one of security and profitability, while for the Latin American nationalist it is a matter of husbanding natural resources and preventing foreign economic-political domination. Washington, on the other hand, is concerned with providing sufficient capital, in the "correct" proportions of public and private, to speed the modernization of Latin America while satisfying the Latin American nations and keeping United States private investors happy. Individual Latin American governments, in their turn, want enough investment, on reasonable terms, to get the modernization job accomplished without risk of loss of office or of political instability. If the number of links in each problem chain is multiplied by the number of viewpoints that must be considered as a prelude to correct decision making, the complexity of the problems in Latin American-United States relations begins to become apparent.

Largely because of their complexity, the problems in United States-Latin American relations assume an essentially political character and require an essentially political solution. As each problem is probed, however delicately, there occurs in either the international or domestic power hierarchies, or both, an adjustment in power relationships that fans out to embrace and affect many sectors whose relationship to the original problem may have been but dimly perceived if at all. An obvious example is the question of land reform which in certain instances may weaken the power of large landholders and improve the relative position of their political opponents. And in the United States removal of import restrictions on oil, meat, and metals may cost political and financial support to the party in power even as it improves the economic and social picture in certain Latin American countries. To foresee, evaluate, and control such shifts in power position, and to reconcile the various clashing interests of each of the many sectors involved, is a political task.

The fact that there is no distinct line separating the domestic and international implications of such political problems cannot be overemphasized. For example, restrictions on the United States' use of its power—restrictions imposed by the nonintervention doctrine accepted by the Organization of American States—prevented Washington's use of certain drastic actions against Cuba and therefore exposed the Administration to violent denunciation by certain elements of the domestic political opposition. On the other hand, modification of the nonintervention doctrine to permit greater use of United States power would have had serious domestic repercussions in most of the nations of Latin America, endangering the tenure of approving governments. In another instance, increased restrictions upon Latin American goods imported into the United States will arouse opposition from the governments of producing nations not only because of the directly damaging effects upon their domestic economies, but also because the resulting loss of revenue may make it impossible for them to cope with domestic social problems whose solutions appear important to political stability. And again, the expropriation of the property of United States citizens in any given Latin American country may not only slow the inflow of needed private capital but also result in retaliation by Washington.

Thus it is that every serious problem in Latin American-United States relations has political repercussions of at least four dimensions, affecting (1) the domestic politics of the decision-making nation, (2) that nation's relations with the nation affected by the decision, (3) the domestic politics of the affected nation, and (4) the relations of the decision-making nation and the affected nation with other nations of the world. In dealing with the nations of Latin America the United States must operate in an extremely complex milieu, within a system whose components are amorphous, constantly shifting, and ambivalent in their relationships, and whose boundaries are increasingly vague in an age when nuclear warfare and the ideological struggle to gain the favor of political blocs throws the validity of the "Western Hemisphere idea" into greater and greater doubt.

Possible approaches to the United States' management of its Latin American relations range from the undisguised and unbridled use of military power and economic coercion to attain its objectives to the peaceful, orderly reconciliation of the interests and objectives of the Latin American nations with those of the United States as a basis for their cooperation in global politics. Under the chaotic circumstances of contemporary international life, any "practical" approach will inevitably embrace elements from each extreme. It is nevertheless vitally important to restrict to a minimum the use of force and to expand to a maximum the method of reconciliation. In the remaining third of the twentieth century, investment in naked power will bring increasingly diminishing returns. Not only are there real limitations upon the power of the United States, but use of a significant amount of that power to maintain prepotence in the Western Hemisphere would weaken its position vis-à-vis genuine adversaries. A policy of brute force would greatly strengthen elements in Latin America who already distrust the United States and who would appeal for help from European, African, and Asiatic lands where antagonists of the United States could not long remain deaf to their pleas without losing significant status in the eyes of their constituents. Such a policy would repel the still uncommitted nations of the world. Such a policy would run counter to deeply ingrained ideals held in the United States concerning the right of self-determination of peoples and would arouse the opposition of articulate academic, business, intellectual, journalistic, labor, and religious elements who would condemn it on ethical grounds. Such a policy is unrealistic in an age of nuclear warfare when promise of total disaster makes it necessary to avoid any move that might constitute the first step toward a world holocaust. For all these reasons it is necessary to minimize the use of force and to win the support of weaker nations by reconciling their interests with those of the United States. Effectively to protect and advance the interests of the United States, which are its primary concern, Washington must curtail its present role of a condescending paterfamilias who amusedly tolerates dissent on the part of obstreperous children but always reserves the right to make important final decisions. Washington must substitute for that unproductive and unattractive role that of the tireless, ubiquitous, practical politician, achieving his purposes not through bribery, threats, or demagoguery, but rather by painstaking arrangements, discussions, and compromises that simultaneously reconcile and promote the interests of his many constituents.

The role of skillful politician is infinitely more difficult than that of paterfamilias, but one of the prices the United States government and people must pay for mutually productive relations with Latin America is its mastery, the first indispensable step toward which must be a radical reorientation toward reality. Senator Fulbright addressed himself to this vital matter in "Foreign Policy—Old Myths and New Realities," calling upon the citizens of the United States to question some cherished but anachronistic beliefs concerning foreign relations. In dealing with Latin America specifically, I would take the liberty of substituting the term "illusion" for the term "myth." For "myth" is associated with the largely imaginary while "illusion" is "a perception which fails to give the true character of the object perceived" and well describes the belief that prevailed between 1948 and 1958. During that decade the view of Latin America as it had existed at the end of World War II persisted, in spite of the fact that the many different nations of Latin America had undergone and were undergoing fundamental and dramatic alterations. The United States government, because it was conducting its relations on the basis of an illusion, encountered mounting difficulties that climaxed in the hostile reactions to the Nixon tour and the Sino-Soviet penetration of Cuba.

About 1958, however, some illumination did lighten the darkness that covered the image of Latin America in the minds of United States citizens. Politically sophisticated and articulate individuals and groups commenced to investigate the Latin America of the moment and to interpret their findings to a larger public. In the process several significant layers of illusion were stripped away. Among the first to be modified, if incompletely, was the one that ascribed all Latin American social and economic discontent to the machinations of an international communist conspiracy, failing to recognize the part that misery, starvation, political oppression, and hopelessness can play in arousing discontent. It became apparent that much more than augmented private investment, coupled with a restricted amount of public capital and technical assistance, would be required to solve Latin America's problems in time to avert political disaster, and it became dimly realized that measures once useful in promoting the growth of the world's highly developed capitalistic nations were not necessarily appropriate to solving the problems of the Latin American nations. Finally it became clear that the Alliance for Progress, which was developed in response to these perceptions, was merely a starting point and that its program would have to be modified in response to continually emerging problems uncovered by those who were delving deeper and deeper into the Latin American reality.

But if certain illusions have been stripped away, others remain that must be recognized if Washington is to deal effectively with its constituents both at home and in Latin America. The image of each individual Latin American country must be made increasingly distinct so that the people of the United States may become aware that those states are not mere instruments for the advancement of United States interests but are real nations with legitimate interests of their own—interests that their citizens must defend and that must be given serious consideration by United States policy makers. The illusion that there are any simple solutions to Latin America's intricate problems—solutions such as more free enterprise or free elections or education—must be abandoned, along with the prevalent illusion that Latin Americans are politically inept. For while Latin Americans have not chosen to do things "the American way," the political elites in many Latin American nations have demonstrated remarkable capacity to maintain their power and privileges while simultaneously securing outside assistance in the solution of critical problems.

Latin America too has illusions that the United States must understand in order to operate effectively. One of many is the crippling assumption that committing a plan or program to paper is equivalent to putting it into effect. Another is the self-defeating idea that forces outside Latin America—imperialism, foreign investment, the international monetary or trading systems, etc., etc.—rather than domestic conditions are responsible for their difficulties.

But the United States government, as politician, must be concerned with more than dispelling illusions. It must as a basis for cooperation develop a substantial mutuality of real interests with the Latin American nations. Such mutuality of interests can be best developed in an environment wherein the United States maintains sufficient military strength to deter hostile action against any American state from a non-hemispheric force at the same time that Latin American nations establish a community of free and independent democratic states sufficiently strong to resist subversion—states whose style would therefore be more compatible with that of the United States. The requisite United States deterrent power already exists, but the Latin American nations, because large numbers of them are in important respects underdeveloped, do not yet constitute a community of free and independent democratic states. In achieving its policy objectives, therefore, the United States confronts three interrelated challenges: maintaining hemispheric security pending maturation of an independent and self-sufficient Latin America; helping Latin America to build free, strong, and democratic nations; establishing, meanwhile, satisfactory relations with the countries of Latin America.

Satisfactory relations can be achieved if the United States assumes the role of politician and dispels the existing illusions, thus adopting a more realistic and productive policy toward which Latin American nations will respond positively upon sensing that the United States is genuinely convinced of their intrinsic value. But cordial relations will not come about until the other two challenges have been decidedly and successfully confronted. Basic causes of Latin American ill-feeling toward the United States will until then continue to be, first, the fear and envy of the strong and rich that have always characterized the weak and poor, and second, the conviction that the United States would not hesitate, if it thought its security threatened, to use its power to subordinate the interests of the Latin American nations to its own.

Two problems connected with the security of the United States require special attention—military assistance programs and military intervention. Suspension of military assistance to the Latin American nations is not going to end militarism and produce an immediate flowering of democracy. A program of military assistance can have value for the Latin American nations if it contributes to strengthening orderly governmental processes while depoliticizing the military, and does so without placing additional impediments in the way of social, economic, and political modernization or strengthening repressive government. If these conditions are to be imposed, as they should be, they must be based upon an intimate knowledge of each individual nation and must accord with overall development policy for each.

The Organization of American States (OAS) as presently constituted is not capable of dealing with the problem of internal subversion to the satisfaction of the United States, and it appears improbable that the Latin American nations will accept either a collective peacekeeping force or legalization of unilateral United States intervention. The United States government has announced that it will, in violation of treaty commitments, intervene if the "circumstances warrant."

The occasion for intervention may not arise again. In the more highly developed countries such as Argentina, Chile, and Mexico there would seem to be little possibility of conditions arising that would make it necessary. Moreover, United States action in the Dominican Republic may discourage the development of a similar situation in other countries. Whatever the likelihood, however, the United States cannot relinquish the right to intervene if there arises a clear and present danger to its security. Its policy on this matter must therefore consist of the unremitting attempt to build collective security institutions; if unilateral intervention appears necessary before such institutions are established, the United States should take extreme care to intervene only in a manner consonant with the ideals of a community of free and independent democratic nations. There must exist a clear and present danger that can be handled in no other way; other members of the OAS must be consulted or at the very least notified that action is to be taken; and it must be understood that the whole matter will be immediately turned over to the OAS for its judgment as to whether the intervention was justified and for any action it may choose to take.

The possibility of intervention should decrease as the Latin American nations advance and it is in this connection that the United States must act as an effective practical politician, simultaneously reconciling and promoting the interests of both its domestic and its Latin American clients. The practical politician will have to deal with strong United States views on free enterprise, the United States' assurance that its way of life is superior, and the illusions of United States citizens concerning Latin America. On the other hand, the practical politician must decisively dispel unfounded Latin American illusions concerning the United States and cope intelligently with constant intensification of nationalism in Latin America.

There are three prerequisites to an effective United States contribution toward the establishment of a Latin American community of free and independent democratic states. One prerequisite is a sophisticated model of such a community, indicating how it would differ from what exists now and what it should be like in twenty years. Planning under the Alliance for Progress is a step in this direction, but intelligible studies, in depth, of Latin American societies are indispensable to the establishing of useful and realistic guidelines. A second prerequisite is recognition of the need to answer certain crucial questions concerning the development process: it has yet to be satisfactorily explained in specific terms why the Latin American nations are not already modernized or why some nations are democratic and others not—questions upon whose correct answers depend correct techniques for accelerating modernization. A (third) prerequisite is a statement, based on existing knowledge, of approaches to solutions of the problem of development that seem most valid from the point of view of the United States' objectives. Such a statement might include the following: (1) Inasmuch as the retardation of development in Latin America is related to its value systems, effort should be directed toward transformation of those values that act as impediments into values that would be useful in promoting modernization. (2) Because values are transmitted through educational institutions of various types, and because the developmental process is carried out through governmental and private institutions, emphasis should be placed upon institution-building. (3) Inasmuch as nationalism is one of the most potent forces in contemporary Latin America, its positive aspects should be exploited; directed away from xenophobia and toward securing national development as a basis for independence, it could become a powerful tool in the service of modernization. (4) Because it would be desirable from the point of view of harmonious inter-American relations for the Latin Americans to be less dependent upon the United States, independence should be encouraged through: (a) stimulation of measures tending to provide the Latin American nations with greater wealth and productive capacity, such as the movements for Latin American economic integration and improvement of export trade, and (b) reduction of direct United States contact with the modernization process through progressively greater mutilateralization of economic and technical aid. (5) Inasmuch as the Latin American nations are in a stage of transition, their political systems may go in the direction of either authoritarianism or democracy; the United States should employ all its resources to persuade those nations to move toward democracy, emphasizing particularly political education for both United States citizens and Latin Americans.

Several useful instruments are available to the United States in pursuing its objectives. One of these is the Alliance for Progress, which is important not merely because of its role in strengthening the Latin American nations, but also because it acts, in spite of itself, as a major educational device for accomplishing needed adjustments to reality. By focussing upon a set of goals and constantly analyzing reasons for failure or success in its operations, the Alliance has already revealed the fact that the American nations have undertaken a long-term project to find solutions for their problems. The search for those elusive solutions will prove enlightening to all cooperating in the Alliance and may lead to the modification of values and attitudes presently beclouding international relations in the Western Hemisphere. The Alliance for Progress should therefore receive strong continued support. At the same time the United States should encourage greater Latin American leadership in the Alliance in recognition of the legitimate nationalistic sensibilities of Latin Americans and of the obvious advantage Latin American leaders have in urging upon their countries what is possible within existing frameworks.

Along with the Alliance for Progress, the Organization of American States offers to the new United States practical politician a vehicle of great value in seeking to create a community of free and independent states in the Western Hemisphere. The OAS must be maintained and made more effective. Meanwhile, pending its transformation and perfection, the OAS should be put to an entirely new and productive use as a formulator of policy. In other words, instead of presenting to the OAS unilaterally designed policies that are faits accomplis, and demanding its rubber stamp of approval, the United States should encourage anticipatory policy formulation by the OAS and give weight to its findings on matters that are of equal concern to all of the nations of the Western Hemisphere. It goes without saying that the United States practical politician will in that process of OAS policy formulation be put to the most severe tests, but it is precisely in such a milieu and in such a manner that the United States must operate if it wishes to achieve genuinely satisfactory relations with the nations of the Western Hemisphere. Placing emphasis on the OAS does not mean playing down the importance of the United Nations and particularly its Economic Commission for Latin America (ECLA) and its Conference on Trade and Development (UNCTAD), both of which can play vital roles in the development of Latin America.

One further instrument, in addition to the Alliance for Progress and the Organization of American States, that can well serve the new United States practical politician in his task of creating a new community of free and independent states in the Western Hemisphere is the nongovernmental sector including the educational and research establishment, business interests, and the communications media. Various institutions in that sector concerned with Latin American relations should be given financial support to dispel the illusions within the United States concerning the nations of Latin America, so that the people of the United States may come to understand that the Western Hemisphere nations are not cardboard caricatures. Latin America must be recognized as part of, and be brought into the mainstream of, Western civilization by including study of its history and culture in courses on Western civilization and also by offering multidimensional studies of individual Latin American nations. Moreover, United States citizens must be encouraged to probe more deeply the nature of their own self-image as contrasted with their reality, on both the individual and the group level. Such programs would illustrate that nationalism, political struggles for power, reversals of policy, and failure to abide by commitments have been a part of United States history as well as of the history of the nations of Latin America. Such studies would also seek the establishment of desirable general goals for the United States, making clear the fact that United States interest is best served by the existence in the Western Hemisphere of a community of strong, independent nations that feel free to determine their own destinies as long as they do not trample the rights of others.

In the process of effecting the transformation of the lands of the Western Hemisphere into a community of strong, free, and independent states, there will emerge many differences of opinion between various Latin American nations and the United States. And if the United States is true to its higher interests, it will attempt neither to suppress those differences by force nor to ignore them in the hope that they will simply disappear. In other words, the United States will be subjected to a trial by fire of its good intentions and its genuine motives. In this trial the most effective advocate will be the practical politician, supported by an informed United States public able and willing to ride out the rough waters that will become calm only when the nations of Latin America are secure in their freedom from fear of the "colossus of the north."

# Bibliography

ADAMS, MILDRED. *Latin America: Evolution or Explosion.* New York: Dodd, Mead, 1963.

ALBA, VICTOR. *Alliance without Allies.* New York: Praeger, 1965.

ALEXANDER ROBERT JACKSON. *Today's Latin America.* New York: Doubleday, 1962.

————. "Trade Policies in Latin America," *Current History,* Vol. 17, Aug. 1962. pp. 77-81.

ALLIANCE FOR PROGRESS. *Weekly Newsletter,* Washington, D.C.

ALMOND, GABRIEL A. *The American People and Foreign Policy.* New York: Praeger, 1960.

ASHER, ROBERT E., ed. *Development of the Emerging Countries.* Washington: Brookings Institution, 1962.

ASHER, ROBERT E. "The Economics of United States Foreign Policy," *Bulletin,* Department of State, July 6, 1953.

BEMIS, SAMUEL FLAGG. *The Latin American Policy of the United States, an Historical Interpretation.* New York: Harcourt, Brace, 1943.

BERLE, ADOLF A. *Latin America, Diplomacy and Reality.* New York and Evanston: Harper & Row, for the Council on Foreign Relations, 1962.

BERNSTEIN, HARRY. *Venezuela & Colombia.* Englewood Cliffs, N.J.: Prentice-Hall, 1964.

BLACK, JOSEPH E., and KENNETH W. THOMPSON, eds. *Foreign Policies in a World of Change.* New York: Harper & Row, 1963.

BLANKSTEN, GEORGE. "Political Groups in Latin America," *Foreign Affairs,* Vol. 53, No. 1, March 1959. pp. 106-27.

BLUM, ROBERT, ed. *Cultural Affairs and Foreign Relations.* New York: Prentice-Hall, for the American Assembly, 1963.

BRANDENBURG, FRANK. "A Contribution to the Theory of Entrepreneurship and Economic Development: The Case of Mexico," *Inter-American Economic Affairs,* Vol. 16, Winter 1962. pp. 3-24.

BURR, ROBERT N. *By Reason or Force: Chile and the Balancing of Power in South America, 1830–1905.* Berkeley and Los Angeles: University of California Press.

239

BURR, ROBERT N., ed. "Latin America's Nationalistic Revolutions," special issue of *The Annals of the American Academy of Political and Social Science*, Vol. 334, March 1961.

BURR, ROBERT N., and ROLAND D. HUSSEY, eds. *Documents on Inter-American Cooperation.* 2 vols. Philadelphia: University of Pennsylvania Press, 1955.

CASTAÑEDA, JORGE. *México y del orden internacional.* México, D.F.: El Colegio de México, 1956.

CLAUDE, IRIS L., JR. "The OAS, the UN and the United States," *International Conciliation*, No. 547, March 1964.

CLINE, HOWARD F. *Mexico: Revolution to Evolution. 1940-1960.* London: Oxford University Press, 1962.

———. *The United States and Mexico.* Rev. ed., enlarged. New York: Atheneum, 1963.

COMMITTEE FOR ECONOMIC DEVELOPMENT, Research and Policy Committee. *Economic Development of Central America.* New York, 1964.

COMMITTEE TO STRENGTHEN THE SECURITY OF THE FREE WORLD, General Lucius D. Clay, Chairman. *The Scope and Distribution of United States Military and Economic Assistance Programs*, Washington: U.S. Department of State, March 20, 1963.

CROW, JOHN A. *The Epic of Latin America.* Garden City: Doubleday, 1946.

DAVIDS, JULES. *The United States in World Affairs, 1964.* New York: Harper & Row, for the Council on Foreign Relations, 1965.

DECE, *al Servicio de la Democracia Christiana de América Latina.* Santiago de Chile, Ano I, No. 1, June 1964.

DELWART, LOUIS O. *The Future of Latin American Exports to the United States: 1965 and 1970.* Washington: National Planning Association, Interamerican Research Committee, 1960.

DOZER, DONALD M. *Are We Good Neighbors.* Gainesville: University of Florida Press, 1959.

DRAPER, THEODORE. *Castro's Revolution, Myths and Realities.* New York: Praeger, 1962.

DRAPER, THOMAS J. "The Alliance for Progress: Failures and Opportunities," *Yale Review*, Vol. 55, No. 2, Dec. 1965. pp. 182-90.

DREIER, JOHN C. *The Organization of American States and the Hemisphere Crisis.* New York: Harper & Row, for the Council on Foreign Relations, 1962.

DREIER, JOHN C., ed. *The Alliance for Progress: Problems and Perspectives.* Baltimore: Johns Hopkins Press, 1962.

DUGGAN, LAWRENCE. *The Americas, the Search for Hemisphere Security.* New York: Henry Holt, 1949.

ETZIONI, AMITAI. "No Short Cut to Progress," *Saturday Review*, July 18, 1964. pp. 18-19.

FEIS, HERBERT. *Foreign Aid and Foreign Policy.* New York: St. Martin's Press, 1964.

FRANCIS, MICHAEL J. "Military Aid to Latin America in the United States Congress," *Journal of Inter-American Studies,* Vol. 6, No. 3, July 1964. pp. 389-404.

FLORES DE LA PENA, H. "La Alianza para el progreso y la economia Mexicana," *Trimestre Economico,* July-Sept. 1962. pp. 385-90.

GIL, FEDERICO G. *The Political System of Chile.* Boston: Houghton Mifflin, 1966.

GILLIN, JOHN. "Ethos Components in Modern Latin American Culture," *American Anthropologist,* Vol. 57, No. 3, Pt. 1, June 1955. pp. 488-500.

GLADE, WILLIAM P., and CHARLES W. ANDERSON. *The Political Economy of Mexico.* Madison: University of Wisconsin Press, 1963.

GOMEZ-QUINONES, J., ed. and compiler. *Statistical Abstract of Latin America, 1964.* Los Angeles: University of California, Latin American Center.

GORDON, LINCOLN. *A New Deal for Latin America. The Alliance for Progress.* Cambridge: Harvard University Press, 1963.

GORDON, WENDELL. "The Motivation Underlying Foreign Investment," *Inter-American Economic Affairs,* Vol. 13, Winter 1959.

HASSON, JOSEPH A. "Latin American Development: The Role of the Inter-American Committee for the Alliance for Progress," *Orbis,* Vol. 9, No. 4, Winter 1966. pp. 1042-66.

HANSON, SIMON G. "The Alliance for Progress: The Third Year," *Inter-American Economic Affairs,* Vol. 19, No. 4, Spring 1965. pp. 3-102.

HEILBRONER, ROBERT L. *The Great Ascent.* New York: Harper & Row, 1963.

HIRSCHMAN, ALBERT O. *Journeys Toward Progress: Studies of Economic Policy-making in Latin America.* New York: Twentieth Century Fund, 1963.

HIRSCHMAN, ALBERT O., ed. *Latin American Issues.* New York: Twentieth Century Fund, 1961.

*Hispanic American Report.* Stanford: Bolívar House, Stanford University.

HUELIN, DAVID. "Conflicting Forces in Argentina," *The World Today,* Vol. 18, April 1962. pp. 142-51.

HUMPHREY, JOHN P. *The Inter-American System, A Canadian View.* Toronto: Macmillan, 1942.

INTER-AMERICAN DEVELOPMENT BANK. *Proposiciones para la Creación del Mercado Común Latinoamericano.* Washington, 1965.

JOHNSON, HAYNES. *The Bay of Pigs.* New York: Norton, 1964.

JOHNSON, JOHN J., ed. *Continuity and Change in Latin America.* Stanford: Stanford University Press, 1964.

JOHNSON, JOHN J. *The Military and Society in Latin America.* Stanford: Stanford University Press, 1964.

————. *Political Change in Latin America: The Emergence of the Middle Sectors.* Stanford: Stanford University Press, 1958.

————. "Politics and Economics in Brazil," *Current History,* Vol. 42, Feb. 1962. pp. 89-95.

KANTOR, HARRY. "The Development of Accion Democratica de Venezuela," *Journal of Inter-American Studies,* Vol. 1, No. 2, April 1959. pp. 237-51.

LEAGUE OF NATIONS. *Ten Years of World Cooperation.* Geneva, 1930.

LEONI, RAÚL. "View from Caracas," *Foreign Affairs,* Vol. 43, No. 4, July 1965. pp. 639-46.

LIEUWEN, EDWIN. *Arms and Politics in Latin America.* Rev. ed. New York: Praeger, 1961.

————. *Generals vs Presidents: Neo-Militarism in Latin America.* New York: Praeger, 1964.

————. "Neo-Militarism in Latin America: The Kennedy Administration's Inadequate Response," *Inter-American Economic Affairs,* Vol. 16, No. 4, Spring 1963. p. 11.

————. *U. S. Policy in Latin America.* New York: Praeger, 1965.

MATTHEWS, HERBERT L., ed. *The United States and Latin America.* New York: The American Assembly, Columbia University, December 1959.

MCGANN, THOMAS F. *Argentina, the United States and the Inter-American System, 1880-1914.* Cambridge: Harvard University Press, 1957.

MECHAM, J. LLOYD. *The United States and Inter-American Security, 1889-1950.* Austin: University of Texas Press, for the Institute of Latin American Studies, 1961.

MURCIA, LUIS MARÍA. *La armonía boliviana; exposición y desarrollo de la "doctrina Suárez."* Bogotá: Editorial Minerva, 1925.

NEHEMKIS, PETER. *Latin America: Myth and Reality.* New York: Knopf, 1964.

*New York Times.*

OSGOOD, ROBERT ENDICOTT. *Ideals and Self-Interest in America's Foreign Relations.* Chicago: University of Chicago Press, 1953.

PADILLA NERVO, LUIS. "Presencia de México en las Naciones Unidas. El Caso de Cuba," *Cuadernos Americanos,* Vol. 116, May-June 1961. pp. 72-83.

PALMER, THOMAS W., JR. *Search for a Latin American Policy.* Gainesville: University of Florida Press, 1957.

PERKINS, DEXTER. *Foreign Policy and the American Spirit.* Ithaca: Cornell University Press, 1957.

————. *Hands off: A History of the Monroe Doctrine.* Boston: Little, Brown, 1945.

————. *The United States and Latin America.* Baton Rouge: Louisiana State University Press, 1961.

PIKE, FREDERICK B. *Freedom or Reform in Latin America.* An Occasional Paper based upon an address of May 16, 1963. Nashville, Tennessee: Vanderbilt University, Graduate Center for South American Studies.

————. "Guatemala, the United States, and Communism," *The Review of Politics,* Vol. 17, April 1955. pp. 232-61.

PLAZA, GALO. "For a Regional Market in Latin America," *Foreign Affairs,* Vol. 37, No. 4, July 1959. pp. 607-17.

POPPINO, ROLLIE E. "Imbalance in Brazil," *Current History,* Vol. 44, Feb. 1963. pp. 100-105.

PRATT, JULIUS W. *A History of United States Foreign Policy.* New York: Prentice-Hall, 1955.

PREBISCH, RAÚL. "Joint Responsibilities for Latin American Progress," *Foreign Affairs,* Vol. 39, No. 4, July 1961. pp. 622-33.

————. *Towards a Dynamic Development Policy for Latin America.* United Nations Economic and Social Council, Economic Commission for Latin America, E/CN. 12/680, April 14, 1963.

RANDALL, LAURA. *Economic Development: Evolution or Revolution?* Boston: D. C. Heath, 1964.

RODRIGUES, JOSÉ HONORIO. "The Influence of Africa on Brazil and of Brazil on Africa," *Journal of African History,* Vol. 3, No. 1, 1962.

RONDERO, JAVIER. "México en Punta del Este," *Cuadernos Americanos,* Vol. 121, March-April 1962. pp. 91-114.

RONNING, C. NEALE. *Law and Politics in Inter-American Diplomacy.* New York: John Wiley & Sons, 1963.

————. *Punta del Este: The Limits of Collective Security in a Troubled Hemisphere.* New York: Carnegie Endowment for International Peace, 1963.

RUSCOE, GORDON C. *Inter-American Education Relations: Proceedings of the Fourth Western Regional Conference on Comparative Education, 8-10 October, 1962.* Los Angeles: University of California, School of Education, 1965.

SCHMITT, KARL M., and DAVID D. BURKS. *Evolution or Chaos.* New York: Praeger, 1963.

SCHNEIDER, RONALD M. *Communism in Guatemala 1944-1952.* New York: Praeger, 1959.

SCOBIE, JAMES R. *Argentina: A City and a Nation.* New York: Oxford University Press, 1964.

SCOTT, ROBERT E. "Nation-Building in Latin America," *Nation-Building.* New York: Atherton, 1963. pp. 78-83.

————. "Political Culture and Modernization in Mexico," *Political Culture and Political Development,* eds. Sidney Verba and Lucien Pye. Princeton: Princeton University Press, 1965.

SILVERT, KALMAN H. *The Conflict Society: Reaction and Revolution in Latin America.* New Orleans: Hauser Press, 1961.

SMITH, ROBERT F. *The United States and Cuba.* New York: Bookman Associates, 1960.

STARK, HARRY. *Social and Economic Frontiers in Latin America.* Dubuque, Iowa: Wm. C. Brown Company, 1961.

STEBBINS, RICHARD P. *The United States in World Affairs 1961.* New York: Harper and Brothers, for the Council on Foreign Relations, 1962.

SZULC, TAD. *The Winds of Revolution: Latin America Today—and Tomorrow.* New York: Praeger, 1963.

TANNENBAUM, FRANK. *Ten Keys to Latin America.* New York: Knopf, 1962.

———. "The Political Dilemma in Latin America," *Foreign Affairs,* Vol. 38, No. 3, April 1960. pp. 497-516.

TAYLOR, PHILIP B. "The Guatemalan Affair: A Critique of United States Foreign Policy," *The American Political Science Review,* Sept. 1956. pp. 787-806.

TOURTELLOT, ARTHUR BERNON, ed. *Toward the Well-Being of Mankind: Fifty Years of the Rockefeller Foundation.* Garden City, N.Y.: Doubleday, 1964.

UNITED NATIONS. *Statistical Yearbook.* New York, 1961-64.

U.S. CONGRESS. *Congressional Record,* Vol. 108, Pt. 4, 87 Cong. 2 sess. (March 24, 1962); Vol. 110, No. 56, 88 Cong. 2 sess. (March 25, 1964).

———.House. Committee on Foreign Affairs, Subcommittee on Inter-American Affairs. *Hearing on Castro-Communist Subversion in the Western Hemisphere.* 88 Cong. 1 sess. (Feb. 18, 20, 21, 26-28, March 4-6, 1963).

———. Joint Economic Committee, Subcommittee on Inter-American Economic Relationships. *Private Investment in Latin America.* Hearings, 88 Cong. 2 sess. (Jan. 14-16, 1964).

———. Senate. Committee on Appropriations. *Foreign Assistance and Related Agencies Appropriations for 1963.* S. Rept. 13175, 87 Cong. 2 sess. (1962).

U.S. DEPARTMENT OF COMMERCE. *Foreign Grants by the United States Government, Calendar Year 1964.* Washington, 1965.

U.S. DEPARTMENT OF DEFENSE. Statement of Robert S. McNamara, Secretary of Defense before the Senate Foreign Relations Committee in support of the FY 1966 Military Assistance Program. March 24, 1965.

U.S. DEPARTMENT OF LABOR. *The Racial Problems Involved in Immigration from Latin America and the West Indies to the United States.* Washington: Government Printing Office, 1925.

U.S. DEPARTMENT OF STATE. *Bulletin.*

U.S. DEPARTMENT OF STATE, Bureau of Intelligence and Research. *World Strength of the Communist Party Organization.* 17th Annual Report. Washington, Jan. 1965.

U.S. TARIFF COMMISSION. *The Latin American Free Trade Association.* Publication 60. Washington, July 1962.

URQUIDI, VICTOR L. *The Challenge of Development in Latin America.* New York: Praeger, 1962.

VÉLIZ, CLAUDIO. "Obstacles to Reform in Latin America," *The World Today,* Vol. 19, No. 1, Jan. 1963. pp. 18-29.

VERNON, RAYMOND. *The Dilemma of Mexico's Development.* Cambridge: Harvard University Press, 1963.

VIDAL, E. CARLOS. "Radioscopia de un Enfermo. Las Contradicciones de la Alianza para el Progreso," *Panorama Económica,* No. 238, Santiago de Chile, 1963. pp. 124-31.

WAGLEY, CHARLES, ed. *Social Science Research on Latin America.* New York: Columbia University Press, 1964.

WARD, BARBARA. "Foreign Aid *Has* Succeeded," *The New York Times Magazine,* July 12, 1964. pp. 9, 18-19.

WASHINGTON, S. WALTER. "Student Politics in Latin America: The Venezuelan Example," *Foreign Affairs,* Vol. 37, April 1959. pp. 463-73.

WEINTRAUB, SIDNEY. "After the UN Trade Conference: Lessons and Portents," *Foreign Affairs,* Vol. 43, Oct. 1964. pp. 37-50.

WHITAKER, ARTHUR P. *Argentina.* Englewood Cliffs, N.J.: Prentice-Hall, 1964.

――――. "Guatemala, OAS and U.S.," *Foreign Policy Bulletin,* September 1, 1954. pp. 4-7.

WHITAKER, ARTHUR P., ed. *Inter-American Affairs, 1941.* New York: Columbia University Press, 1942.

WHITAKER, ARTHUR P. *Nationalism in Latin America.* Gainesville, Florida: University of Florida Press, 1962.

――――. *The Western Hemisphere Idea: Its Rise and Decline.* Ithaca: Cornell University Press, 1954.

WHITEFORD, ANDREW HUNTER. *Two Cities of Latin America.* Garden City, N.Y.: Doubleday, 1964.

WOOD, BRYCE, and M. MINERVA MORALES. "Latin America and the United Nations," *International Organization,* Vol. 19, No. 3, 1965. pp. 714-27.

WOOD, BRYCE. *The Making of the Good Neighbor Policy.* New York: Columbia University Press, 1961.

YDIGORAS FUENTES, MIGUEL. *My War with Communism.* Englewood Cliffs, N.J.: Prentice-Hall, 1963.

# Index

247